THESE WERE
THE GREEKS

H. D. Amos and A. G. P. Lang

HULTON EDUCATIONAL PUBLICATIONS

Preface

Interest in the classical world is, and should be, as great as ever, and it is reflected in schools by the growing number of courses dealing with Greek and Roman civilization. Yet there have been available few introductions to these subjects appropriate for students in the years approaching, or just after, their O Level (or C.S.E.) examinations. This book, a companion volume to *These Were the Romans*, by G. I. F. Tingay and J. Badcock, also published by Hulton Educational Publications, is intended to be of use for Greek, Ancient History, General Classics and 'Classical Civilization' courses at those levels. It may also provide a basis for a General Studies course in the Sixth Form, or form part of an outline course in Ancient or European history.

We have attempted to describe Greek society from about 1500 B.C. down to Roman times, and to show something of the changes that took place during that long period. We have included more history than perhaps is now fashionable, because of our belief in the importance of historical perspective. In dealing with a very substantial subject we are conscious of many omissions. We have tried to include what seems to be most relevant and interesting to the modern student, at the expense of what may be less so.

We have quoted frequently from ancient sources, both to show the nature of a great deal of our evidence for the Greeks, and in the hope that at least some impression of the style and quality of Greek literature will be given. Translations, except as acknowledged, are our own, and it has been found necessary in some cases to make slight alterations or abbreviations. Many of the works quoted are widely available in paperback translations, which would provide further course-material.

The illustrations, too, have been chosen in an attempt not only to show the physical world of the Greeks and the kind of non-literary evidence about them which is available, but also to represent their high attainments in the visual arts.

Greek names and words in the text have been transliterated as closely as possible from their original Greek form, except where there is an established spelling in English which the student is more likely to meet in other reading. Thus 'paidagogos', but 'Thucydides' rather than 'Thoukydides'. Inevitably some inconsistencies result. A sign has been placed on the final 'e' of Greek words to shows that it is to be pronounced. Single dates after a name indicate the peak time of his career.

© 1979
H. D. Amos and A. G. P. Lang
ISBN 0 7175 0789 0

First published 1979
Hulton Educational Publications Ltd.,
Raans Road, Amersham, Bucks.
Filmset and printed in Great Britain by
BAS Printers Limited, Over Wallop, Hampshire

Contents

Acknowledgements

The authors wish to express their thanks to Dr. J. T. Killen of Jesus College, Cambridge, who read the manuscript, and to Lorraine Phillips who drew the maps.

Photographs are reproduced by kind permission of the Greek National Tourist Office; the British Museum; John Topham; J. Allen Cash Ltd.; the Mansell Collection and Giraudon; the Ashmolean Museum; the Rev. J. C. Allen; the Bodleian Library; the American School of Classical Studies at Athens; the Rev. Professor R. V. Schoder, S.J.; Alison Frantz.

The illustration of Doric and Ionic columns is from *A Handbook of Greek Art* by G. M. A. Richter, published by Phaidon Press Ltd., Oxford. The plan of a Greek theatre is taken from *An Introduction to the Greek Theatre* by Peter D. Arnott and is reproduced by permission of Macmillan, London and Basingstoke. The map of Miletus was first published in *Cities of Ancient Greece and Rome* by Ward-Perkins and is reproduced by permission of Sidgwick & Jackson. The diagram of the front section of the Parthenon is reproduced from *Greek and Roman Art in the British Museum* by B. F. Cook, published by British Museum Publications Ltd.

Thanks are also due to the following for allowing the use of copyright material: Oxford University Press for an extract from *Aristophanes: Plays I*, translated by Patric Dickinson (1970), and also for 'The Poet's Shield' by Archilochos translated by Sir William Marris from *The Oxford Book of Greek Verse in Translation* edited by T. F. Higham and C. M. Bowra (1938), which was revised by Sir William Marris from *Translations from the Greek Anthology* (privately printed at the Bharat Bandhu Press, Aligarh, U.P., India, 1919). Reprinted by permission of Penguin Books Ltd.—an extract from *The Histories* by Herodotus (p. 71), translated by Aubrey de Sélincourt, revised by A. R. Burn (Penguin Classics, Revised edition, 1972) pp. 536–7, © the Estate of Aubrey de Sélincourt, 1954, © A. R. Burn, 1972 and also 8 lines from *Pythian VIII 5* from *The Odes of Pindar* (p. 87), translated by C. M. Bowra (Penguin Classics, 1969) p. 236 © C. M. Bowra, 1969. The extract from *Before and After Socrates*, by F. M. Cornford, is reproduced by permission of Cambridge University Press. The extracts from *The Olympic Games* by M. I. Finley and H. W. Pleket, and the quoted portion of text and two diagrams from *Engineering in the Ancient World* by J. G. Landels appear by permission of Chatto and Windus Ltd.

CHAPTER ONE

People and Land

The Hellenes

It is important to realize, when we talk of 'the Greeks of classical times' and 'classical Greece', that there was never a Greek nation in the sense that we speak today of, say, the French nation. During most of the period covered by this book, approximately from 1500 to 300 B.C., there was no central government, and Greece contained many separate states, each centring on one city. Such a unit is often referred to as a 'city-state', for which the Greek word was *polis*, giving us such words as 'politics'. Of course all the Greeks had a great deal in common, most obviously in their language and their religion, but it took a great crisis, such as the invasion by the king of Persia in 480 B.C., or an exceptional man, such as Alexander the Great in the fourth century B.C., to create any sort of national unity. These occasions were rare, and any harmony was short-lived.

The name 'Greeks' was not one which they themselves used. It is the Latin name for them, originally that of a small Greek tribe, with whom the people of Italy had early contact. The Greeks of classical times called themselves 'Hellenes' and their country 'Hellas' (as they still do today). The first Hellenes, too, were an obscure Greek tribe, whose name, by accidents of history, came to be applied to the whole race. This book is mainly concerned with the Hellenic people, although we shall first be looking at their predecessors, the Minoans and the Mycenaeans.

In classical times the Greeks inhabited an area extending far beyond the Greek peninsula. The Greek islands, though many are nearer Asia than mainland Greece, have always been inhabited by Greeks from very early times. After passing through the hands of various conquerors over the centuries, they are again under Greek rule. Yet, for reasons which will emerge in later chapters, the Greeks settled over a wider area still. The coast of Asia Minor became full of Greek cities, so making the Aegean Sea, as this part of the Mediterranean is called, almost entirely a Greek sea. Later on the Greeks were spread throughout the Mediterranean and Black Sea regions.

Citizens of one Greek state tended to be fiercely proud of it, and often scornful of others. The people of Boiotia, for instance, were something of a laughing stock to other Greeks, being proverbial for their gluttony and lack of brains. On a broader scale, Greeks regarded other races as distinctly inferior—they called them barbarians (*barbaroi*), because their languages seemed merely a succession of 'bar-bar' noises. In a play by Euripides appear the words, 'It is proper that Hellenes should rule over barbarians,' and the philosopher Aristotle took the view that 'barbarians are by nature more slave-like than Hellenes.'

Mountain and Plain

A study of the relief map of Greece (fig 1.1) will show that one of the reasons for the Greeks' lack of unity lies in the very nature of their country. A large proportion of it is mountainous, and the plains, on which the cities and their surrounding villages were situated, are often separated from each other by a barrier of mountains. Although communication between the various plains was by no means impossible, it was not easy, so that the inhabitants of different plains tended to organize their affairs independently. This was also likely to occur, of course, in the many islands inhabited by the Greeks. Yet alliances might be formed for military purposes, and sometimes one city became the subject of another as the result of war.

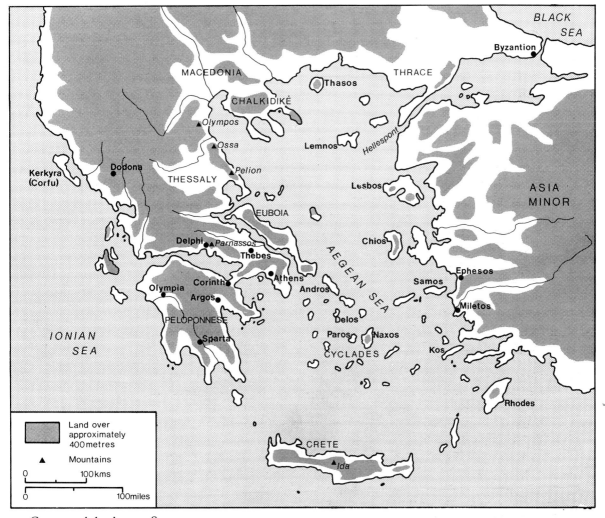

1.1 Greece and the Aegean Sea.

The plains themselves were quite fertile but generally not large. A few, however, like the plain of Thessaly, were big enough to hold more than one city. Today only about a fifth of Greece is cultivated, and the area cannot have been much different in ancient times. Farms were small and they grew mainly grain, although conditions were not ideal for it, vines, and most important of all, olives. Olive-oil was one of the very few things which Greece could produce in quantity. In addition to cooking, it was used for bathing purposes and as fuel for lamps. There was not enough pasture-land to keep many horses and cattle, but oxen were essential for ploughing, and mules and donkeys much used for transport.

Higher ground was used for keeping sheep, goats—which provided milk and cheese—and pigs. There was a good deal of bee-keeping as well. To grow anything in these areas it was necessary to cut terraces on the slopes, a back-breaking task on rocky ground. The mountains were originally more wooded than they are now, with cedar, cypress and pine to supply timber for buildings and ships, but wood for these also had to be imported. In the fourth century B.C. the Athenian philosopher Plato wrote of his country:

> '. . . what now remains, just as on small islands, compared with what there used to be, is like the bony body of a sick man, with all the rich and fertile earth fallen away and only the scraggy skeleton of the land left.'

(Critias 111B)

1.2 Mountain and plain at Olympia in the Peloponnese.

The picture is exaggerated, perhaps, but it shows that already by Plato's time mountains had been stripped of trees and soil had been eroded from them. This process has been helped over the years by the appetite of goats for young trees.

The limestone mountains are cut by many ravines and narrow valleys, in which rivers and streams often flow only in winter, or after storms, leaving at other times dried-up beds. Greece simply does not possess major rivers, or indeed very many that flow all year. The mountains are not very high, the biggest being Mount Olympos at about 2900 metres. Many are high enough, however, to have snow on their peaks for most of the year.

The Sea

As the shores all round the Aegean Sea, and its numerous islands, were inhabited by Greeks, the Aegean became in effect the focal point of the Greek-speaking world. A further look at the map will show that some of the islands continue, to the east and south, the lines of the mountain ranges of the mainland. They are in fact what remains of a submerged mountain system and are like stepping stones across the sea in the directions of Asia and Egypt. This was of great significance in Greek history.

1.3 The harvesting of olives: a vase-painting of the sixth century B.C.

1.4 An olive-grove today.

In early times Greece was strongly influenced by the more advanced civilizations in those areas, and later on spread her own culture in the opposite direction. In all there are more than two thousand islands in the Aegean, and it is unusual for a boat to be out of sight of land in good weather. Other Greek islands lie to the west of the main peninsula, but not in the same quantity.

The coastline of the mainland itself, with its many deep bays and especially the Gulf of Corinth, is very long. Few mainland Greeks can have lived more than about seventy kilometres from the sea. The many mountains and hills, and the scarcity of roads good enough for wheeled vehicles, meant that it was often easier to get from one place to another by sea.

When Greeks wished to trade, to make military expeditions, or simply to communicate with other Greeks, they as often as not would do so by sea. It was also, of course, a source of food. So, in one way or another, the sea was a most important element in the history of the Greek race and in the lives of many individual Greeks. It is not surprising that two of the most famous of all Greek stories, the return from Troy of the hero Odysseus and the voyage of Jason and the Argonauts, are very much sea-adventures. Even in a poem called *Works and Days*, which was intended as instructions for the year's work of a farmer, the early Greek poet Hesiod included a section on sea-travel. This is not to say that every single Greek was directly involved with the sea or that, if he were, he much liked sailing. Hesiod certainly looked on it as an unpleasant, risky, but sometimes necessary activity

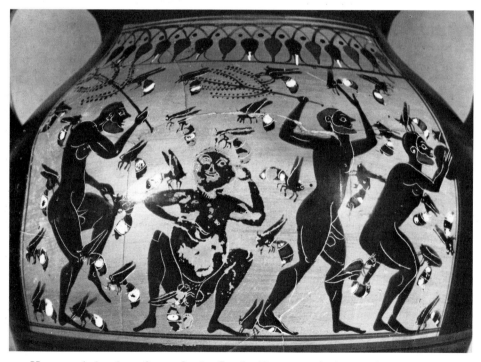

1.5 Honey took the place of sugar for the Greeks. Here men who have stolen some honey are painfully attacked by the bees. *Reproduced by Courtesy of the Trustees of the British Museum.*

8

One further point remains to be noted from the map. The sea, in the form of the Gulf of Corinth, very nearly cuts the Greek peninsula in two. In fact the name of the region to the south, the Peloponnese, literally means 'the island of Pelops'. (Pelops was a legendary king.) As a result, the people who lived there often felt that their interests were not the same as those of the Greeks to the north. The very narrow strip of land which does connect the Peloponnese with the north is called the Isthmus of Corinth. It was of great military importance in classical times, as it was easy to defend against an enemy invading by land.

Although the Corinthians built a paved roadway across the Isthmus, with grooves for wheels on which ships could be transported, it was usually necessary for travellers to and from the west side of Greece to make the long voyage round the Peloponnese. This was one of the reasons why those who lived in the solidly mountainous area of north-west Greece were, at least in early times, rather cut off from other, more advanced regions. Nowadays there is a spectacular canal cut through the rock of the Isthmus.

The City

Few of the Greek cities were situated on the coast itself. The Athenian historian Thucydides, writing in the fifth century B.C., gave a reason for that:

'The ancient cities were established rather away from the sea, because of the large amount of piracy which went on. This applied to cities both on the mainland and on the islands, and to this day they are still situated inland. The pirates used to plunder each other, and any people who were not seafarers but lived by the sea.'

(I, 7)

It was also for reasons of defence that the city-states centred on a hill. The requirements for this were that it should have steep sides and a flat top, and be on or by a fertile plain. The nature of the Greek landscape fortunately provided such places. A hill of this type was called an *akropolis* ('upper-city'), the best known being that at Athens. Here in times of war or pirate raids the population could gather, to undergo a siege if necessary. Sometimes there was secret access to a water supply (see fig 2.16), as at Mycenae and Athens. The most important religious buildings were also on the *akropolis*, since they were the vital parts of the city to defend.

The sharp difference which we know today between life in the country and life in the city was not nearly so strong. Industry was on a far smaller scale, and an ancient Greek city was more like a country town than a modern industrial and commercial centre.

Many city-states had a combination of coast, plain, hill-pasture and mountain within their boundaries. Here was another reason for independence from neighbours, for such states did not rely on each other for essentials which they could not produce themselves. For some things, however, such as corn, timber and metals, they had to look beyond Greece to supply their needs. Greece was not rich in minerals, but there were some gold and silver mines.

The Climate

The weather of Greece is very fine by most standards. Annual rainfall is moderate in quantity (there is more in the west), but when rain does fall, it tends to do so heavily. The winters are relatively mild, though the weather in the mountains is more severe. There is a good deal of wind—in particular the north-west wind which blows across the Aegean in the summer, so regularly that the classical Greeks called it the Etesian, that is 'annual', wind. The winds from the sea make the climate more agreeable on the coast than the plains inland which are hemmed in by mountains and can be unpleasantly hot. Violent storms are not unusual, and the winds can make the sea very rough, even in summer. Yet, after a storm, it is not usually long before the sun shines, as it does most of the time throughout the summer. After all, the southern parts of Greece are on the same latitude as regions of north-west Africa.

The worse side of the climate is gloomily described by Hesiod. His father had come from Asia Minor to settle in Boiotia:

'He settled near Mount Helikon,' says Hesiod, 'in a wretched village called Askra, bad in winter, oppressive in summer, good at no time.'

(Works and Days 639f.)

The bad winter is vividly described:

'Beware the month of Lenaion'—equivalent to our late January and early February—'terrible days, all enough to skin an ox, and beware the frosts, which are bitter while the north wind blasts across the land. It blows across horse-breeding Thrace on to the broad sea and stirs it up, and the earth and the woods

1.6 The *akropolis* at Lindos on the island of Rhodes. The town still clusters around the fortified rock.

roar. In the mountain glens it descends on the oaks with their lofty branches and the stout pines, bringing them down to the nourishing earth; then the whole forest roars, and the animals shiver and put their tails between their legs, even those with hides covered by fur . . . it makes an old man bent like a wheel.'

(504ff.)

The summer, of course, is too hot for him:

'When the artichoke flowers,'—this would be in June—'and the chirping cicada sits in a tree and incessantly pours down the song from its wings, at the time of exhausting heat, then goats are at their fattest and the wine is at its best, women are at their friskiest, but men are most feeble, because the sun burns their head and knees, and their skin is parched by the heat.'

(582ff.)

Yet, for all that Hesiod says, the climate was healthy enough for active old age to be reached by a fair number of the Greeks about whom we know. There was, for example, the playwright Sophocles, who wrote one of his finest plays, *Oedipus at Kolonos*, when he was ninety, and there was Agesilaos, king of Sparta, who was still fighting battles at eighty. Many similar instances could be quoted.

The general kindness of the weather meant that it was possible for even a poor man to lead a fairly comfortable life, despite the fact that Greece did not supply an excess of food. His house did not need to be big or elaborate, nor, unless he lived in the mountains, did he need heavy clothing. Much of his life was lived in the open air. Not only eating and drinking, but public meetings, law-cases, theatrical performances and other activities, which in many other parts of the world would have to take place indoors, were outdoor matters for the Greeks.

Much of what is regarded as typical of the Greeks derived from this. Since they spent a lot of time in each other's company, out of doors, their minds were constantly being exercised in the cut and thrust of conversation and debate. They took a lively interest in the affairs of their city-state, and anybody with a new political, philosophical or scientific theory had a ready-made audience.

The opportunities for taking part in politics, or at least knowing what was going on, were great, since public business was conducted so much more within the hearing and view of the ordinary citizen than it generally is nowadays. This was especially true, naturally, in a state where the government had come into the hands of the people—in Greek, a *demokratia*. Relationships with the fellow-citizens with whom they spent so much time were not always friendly, so the law-courts, a perpetual source of interest, were kept busy. The Greeks, like the Romans, reserved some of their greatest admiration for the good orator, whether in the public assembly or in the law-court. The open-air theatres were well attended, with the result that an unusually large proportion of the population, in Athens at any rate, was familiar with the plays, some of which have rarely been equalled to this day.

In the following chapters, the effect on the Greeks of their natural surroundings—the mountains, the plains, the sun, the sea—should be kept in mind. That factors like these help to shape the history of any race is obvious. Those of us who live in rather different climates and places need especially to remind ourselves of the setting in which the Greeks, by any standards a remarkable race, lived out their lives.

CHAPTER TWO

Minoans and Mycenaeans
Part I

King Minos

In Greek legends and literature there occurred many references to a King Minos of Crete who had in very early times ruled over a great kingdom from his palace at Knossos. In the best-known legend, Minos, after defeating the Athenians in a war, had ordered them to send annually seven youths and seven girls as food for the Minotaur. The Minotaur had the head of a bull, but a human body. Poseidon, god of the sea, had sent up a bull from the waves in answer to Minos' prayer for a sign proving that the gods had given him his throne. When Minos failed to fulfil his promise to sacrifice the bull, Poseidon punished him by making Pasiphaé, wife of Minos, fall in love with it: so she gave birth to the Minotaur. The monster was imprisoned in the labyrinth—a maze so complicated that none who entered it could ever find the way out again. This was an example of the wonderful skill of the architect and craftsman Daidalos, an Athenian in the service of Minos.

One day Theseus, son of the king of Athens, came as part of the annual offering to the Minotaur. Ariadné, Minos' daughter fell in love with him and saved him by giving him a thread, which he tied to the door of the labyrinth and trailed after him as he went in. He then killed the Minotaur and found his way safely back by means of the thread.

Less incredible were traditions about Minos as a law-giver and as controller of the first known naval power. In the fifth-century B.C. the historian Thucydides wrote:

'For Minos was the first person we hear of to acquire a fleet: he had over-riding control of the Aegean Sea, governed the Cycladic islands and was the first to colonize most of them . . . he also eliminated piracy as far as possible, so that more revenue should come to him.'

(I, 4)

Nevertheless, in terms of detailed factual knowledge of Minos and his kingdom, the ancient Greeks were largely ignorant.

Knossos

In A.D. 1900 the British archaeologist, Arthur Evans, began to excavate on the site of Knossos, near the modern town of Heraklion in the north of Crete. Over a period of many years, he brought to light an entire civilization, centred on Knossos, which was previously unknown to us, apart from the legends and other vague references in ancient authors. These discoveries have confirmed the traditions of a great king with a large navy, ruling in Crete; they also hint at some of the facts which may have developed into the legends.

This Bronze Age civilization, named Minoan by Evans after the legendary king, lasted well over a thousand years, reaching its peak in the later stages, between about 1650 and 1450 B.C. The palace at Knossos was begun some time after 2000 B.C., and was enlarged and rebuilt over the years, particularly after damage by earthquakes.

Among the rulers in the various Minoan places in Crete—that at Phaistos is best known after Knossos—the king at Knossos seems to have been supreme. The poet Homer speaks of a Minos who 'was on familiar terms with great Zeus'. This, taken with other evidence, suggests that he was a priest-king, whose main function may have been to administer the religious affairs of his kingdom.

On the western side of the palace at Knossos, which has now been reconstructed as far as possible, stood the official quarters, including a throne-room and capacious store-rooms. Here royal ceremonies took place and the administrative offices were situated. To the east, beyond a large courtyard, was the domestic area. The whole palace was built with remarkable skill, rising to several storeys in places. Among its notable features were the use of light-wells and an elaborate water and drainage system, with a type of flushing lavatory.

The paintings decorating the interior walls—called 'frescoes'—were particularly important and exciting discoveries by Evans. Their artistic quality is outstanding, especially in vividly coloured scenes of nature, and they also provide us with important glimpses of Minoan life. Some show crowds watching dancing or sports, including what appears to be the extremely dangerous activity of bull-leaping, in which youths and girls caught hold of the horns of a charging bull and somersaulted along its back. Such displays were possibly part of religious celebrations.

The crowds contain a high proportion of women, and their status in society appears to have been high. In appearance the ladies of the court were very sophisticated. One such figure, depicted on a surviving fragment of fresco, was christened 'La Parisienne', so closely did she resemble the smart Parisian women of the time of her discovery. Their hairstyles were elaborate, and so were their 'topless' dresses, with flounced skirts, narrow waists and puffed sleeves.

In the store-rooms huge jars were found, for keeping olive-oil, wine and, probably, grain. Perhaps these were the form in which the king was paid taxes. They may have been among the chief exports to Egypt, with which Crete had close contact—Egyptian paintings show Minoan objects and also foreign ambassadors who look very like Minoans. The strong fleet also helped a flourishing trade to develop with the coast of Asia and the Greek mainland. This trade was helped by the establishment of Minoan settlements at places like Miletos in Asia Minor, the islands of Rhodes, Melos and Thera, and the coast of Greece itself. The influence of Minoan craftsmen and artists spread even further.

Sunk in the floor of the store-rooms were lead-lined chests, long since looted, where traces of gold foil were found. They were the safe-deposits for the royal wealth, more proof of which is given by the precious metals and stones used in jewellery and ornaments also found.

However, the life of the peasants varied little from that of their counterparts in

2.1 The north entrance, partly reconstructed, of the palace at Knossos.

2.2 The throne-room at Knossos, with what is said to be the oldest throne in Europe. The fresco is a reconstruction.

2.3 Store-rooms at Knossos. Stones in the foreground are blackened by smoke from fires accompanying the destruction of the palace (see page 17).

many societies, although theirs was a society more peaceful than many. Wildlife was plentiful in the mountainous island, and the sea offered a wide variety of fish. Marine life is a common subject in paintings on walls and pottery. The peasants liked company and lived in villages rather than isolated homes, and, both here and in the towns, the house or palace of the most important man was the focal point around which the other congregated.

The 'Town Mosaic' found at Knossos shows some Minoan houses (fig 2.4). They are tall and rectangular, with what looks like an attic on the top. Windows are more frequent in the upper parts, and oiled parchment may have been used as a substitute for glass. The houses of the rich contained many of the features of a palace, such as frescoes, store-rooms and an efficient drainage system.

Other Minoan towns and their central palaces or large villas closely resembled Knossos, the capital. A network of roads linked towns, the most important of which was the road through the mountains between Knossos and Phaistos, protected by police posts at regular intervals. An impressive viaduct carried this road across the gully just south of the palace at Knossos, and it has been said that the road to the north, linking Knossos with its port of Amnisos, is the oldest road in Europe.

Many religious objects have been found, but our exact knowledge of Minoan religion is incomplete. The leading deity was a sort of Mother Goddess, especially associated with snakes. Double-bladed axes were clearly of religious significance, as were the symbols in the shape of bull's horns which appear frequently at Knossos. The latter and the bull-leaping frescoes suggest that bulls were sacred, probably to the deity of the underworld. The noise of an earthquake is said to resemble the bellowing of a bull underground.

2.4 The 'Town Mosaic' from Knossos gives an idea of the appearance of Minoan houses.

The Fall of the Palaces

The details and causes of the end of the brilliant Minoan civilization are still far from being definitely established. In about 1450 B.C. the majority of the palaces in Crete were destroyed, either from natural causes or by human violence. It is very tempting to link this destruction with the enormous volcanic eruption on the island of Thera (modern Santorini), about 128 kilometres north of Crete. The calculated date of the eruption, however, is too early for it to be connected with the destruction of the palaces.

Knossos itself, in fact, survived the other palaces for another fifty years or so, and then in its turn was destroyed, again for uncertain reasons. During this last phase it seems very likely that Greek speakers from Mycenae in the Peloponnese had control at Knossos. The evidence for this comes mainly from one of the two types of writing found there. These are known as Linear Scripts A and B, and are of a type known as syllabic, since signs represent syllables of words rather than single letters. They have been discovered mostly engraved on clay tablets used for such purposes as listing the contents of store-rooms and recording the payment of dues. The tablets which survive have done so after being baked hard when buildings caught fire. There is no Minoan literature known to us.

2.5 A statuette of the Minoan 'Mother Goddess', holding sacred snakes.

2.6 Minoan double-bladed axes.

16

Linear A has not yet been deciphered; Linear B was eventually decoded by an Englishman, Michael Ventris, and unexpectedly was found to be a form of Greek, not 'Minoan'. Since it replaced the earlier script only in the last phase of the palace at Knossos and is found there only in Crete—though it occurs at several places elsewhere in Greece—this fits well with a theory of Mycenaean domination of Knossos during its last years. For long Mycenae, in the Peloponnese, had been developing as mainland Greece's most powerful rival to Knossos. Previously Knossos had exerted great influence on Mycenae in its art and had dominated trade between the two, as well as in the rest of the Mediterranean; but now the situation was reversed.

A reasonable interpretation of the inadequate evidence at present available would be to suppose that around 1450 B.C. Mycenaean Greeks, growing steadily more powerful, took over Knossos and eliminated rival palaces in a Crete seriously weakened by damage from the Thera eruption. About fifty years later, they either abandoned Knossos itself after an earthquake, or deliberately destroyed it for unknown reasons. In any event, the excavations show that the palace finally collapsed in flames. One can still see the marks made on stones by blazing wood and black smoke. These clearly show that on that day the wind was from the south, the prevailing direction of the wind in spring in Crete.

How far have the ancient stories been found true? That there were great kings at Knossos, with a strong fleet, is beyond doubt, yet we know nothing further about an individual 'Minos'. Stories of Daidalos, a craftsman and architect of fantastic skill,

2.7 Linear B tablets from Knossos: a sign representing chariot wheels can be clearly distinguished.

may have stemmed from admiration of the advanced skills shown in all kinds of workmanship in the palace. This palace, large and complicated in layout, with many stairways, long corridors and countless rooms, may itself have been the labyrinth. *Labrys* was the word used for an axe in Karia in Asia Minor, and 'labyrinth' probably meant 'the place of the double-axe', acquiring the meaning of a maze from the complex plan of the palace. The origins of the Minotaur story—the name simply means 'bull of Minos'—are possibly to be detected in the religious importance of bulls.

These examples show that Evans had some justification for writing, 'The work of the spade has now brought out the underlying truth of the old traditions that made Knossos—the home of Minos and Daidalos—the most ancient centre of civilized life in Greece and with it, of our whole Continent.'

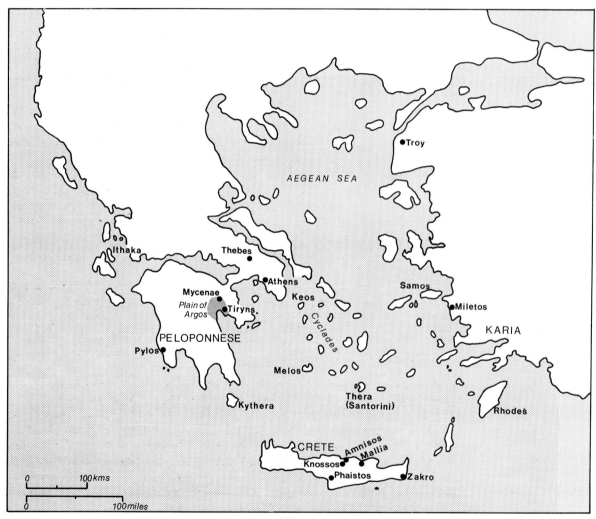

2.8 The Minoan and Mycenaean world.

Part II

The Mycenaeans

The Mycenaeans were of different racial origins from the Minoans. They were not the first inhabitants of Greece, but exactly where they came from, and when, remains a mystery. They seem to have arrived in Greece around 2000 B.C.

The newcomers spoke an early form of Greek, yet they absorbed into their language a number of words used by the people they found and conquered in Greece. These were particularly place-names ending in -nthos, -sos, -ttos, e.g. *Korinthos* (Corinth), and the mountains of *Hymettos* and *Parnassos*. There are also names of plants, and the Greek words for the sea (*thalassa*) and an island (*nesos*) fall into the same category. The common link between such words is that they stood for things probably unfamiliar to the new arrivals, so that they borrowed the names. Some of the words, like 'hyacinth' and 'narcissus', survive in English.

It is probable that these people first brought the domesticated horse into Greece. This was above all a military asset, mainly used at that time for drawing war-chariots. The Mycenaeans were more warlike than the Minoans, and military strength was the foundation of their later power.

By the sixteenth century B.C. the Mycenaeans, through trade and piracy, were becoming steadily more wealthy and powerful, and the Mycenaean Age had begun. The name Mycenaean is used to describe the whole civilization of which the city of Mycenae was the centre. On the face of it this was the world depicted by the Greek poet Homer in the *Iliad* and the *Odyssey*, but as we shall see later in Chapter 3, only part of what he says there can be treated as historical evidence for the Mycenaean Age.

The main area of the civilization was in the Peloponnese, where the most important towns were Mycenae itself, Pylos and Tiryns, and in central Greece, where Athens and Thebes were prominent.

Royal Burials

Like Knossos, Mycenae is closely linked with the name of a famous archaeologist. In this case it was a German, Heinrich Schliemann. A wealthy merchant, he devoted his fortune to proving that his great passion, the poetry of Homer, was historical fact, contrary to the scholarly opinion of the time. His excavation at Mycenae in 1876 produced sensational results, for he discovered royal tombs containing unbelievable treasure, including a large amount of gold. One of the bodies had a face remarkably well preserved beneath its gold funeral mask. After seeing it Schliemann sent a telegram to the King of Greece, saying that he 'had gazed upon the face of Agamemnon'. Agamemnon was the supreme commander of the Greek expedition to Troy, described in Homer's poem, the *Iliad*. Subsequently, however, it has been proved that these tombs must be dated some three hundred years before the probable date of the Trojan War.

The burials were in what are known as shaft graves, being sunk vertically into rocky ground. They were grouped inside a circular wall at the edge of the citadel at Mycenae, and several graves were used more than once. By the bodies was the treasure, objects of gold, silver, bronze, ivory and pottery. Among them, besides the gold masks, were diadems of gold, bronze daggers inlaid with gold, and jewellery of great richness. Homer had some reason for always describing Mycenae as 'rich in gold'.

During the period of the shaft graves, the sixteenth century B.C., it is clear from the artistic style and subject matter of the discoveries that Mycenae was deeply influenced by the Minoans. At the beginning of the fifteenth century B.C., however, the situation began to change. A new type of royal tomb was used: the '*tholos*' tombs, also called 'beehive tombs' because of their shape. They were often built into the side of a hill and approached by a corridor cut into the slope. The construction of the entrance itself was a major feat: in one case the single stone block forming the top of the door weighs a hundred tonnes or more.

Presumably the change in the method of burial reflects a change of the ruling household. Certainly Mycenaean civilization was now reaching its peak. They established some sort of control at Knossos and from now on they were the major power of the Mediterranean area.

2.9 Death-mask of finely beaten gold, wrongly thought by Schliemann to have been that of Agamemnon.

20

Palace Societies

Mycenae itself stood on an easily-defended hill on the edge of the Plain of Argos, one of the largest and most fertile plains in Greece. It was well placed for controlling the best land route through the Peloponnese, and for trading and military operations by sea.

Mycenae and the other centres were not so much cities as fortresses, the greater parts of which were occupied by the royal palaces. Pylos was an exception in being undefended. Most of the population lived in villages in the surrounding countryside. Any knowledge of the society must be pieced together from the evidence of Linear B tablets (mainly from Pylos and Knossos), other archaeological remains and Homer. In the various palaces were a number of kings, of whom the king at Mycenae itself

2.10 A stone circle enclosing royal 'shaft graves' at Mycenae.

2.11 The entrance to a 'beehive tomb' near the palace at Mycenae.

was the most important. That is the position held by Agamemnon, 'lord of men', in the *Iliad*. When the mighty Achilles quarrels with Agamemnon in that story, even he is advised to give way, for

'although you are powerful and the mother who bore you is a goddess, yet Agamemnon is superior and he rules over more men.'

(I, 280f.)

The tablets, especially those from Pylos, which was scarcely inferior in wealth to Mycenae, show that the kingdoms were very highly organized and kept careful records of taxes, palace stores, slaves and animals owned, land-holdings, offerings to gods, military equipment and so on. In addition to the obvious elements of royalty, nobility, peasants and slaves, the society apparently included a considerable number of officials with special responsibilities, such as the headmen of villages; we know, too, of priests and a surprising variety of specialist craftsmen, such as chariot-builders and wheelwrights, in the service of the palaces; of course the scribes, who alone had the skill of writing and therefore kept these royal records, must have been especially important.

Among the more important agricultural products were wheat, barley, olive-oil and wool. There were not many cattle, but some are referred to in the tablets by pet names, like 'Dapple', 'Darkie' and 'Whitefoot'.

The palaces themselves were on a smaller scale than the Minoan ones, but still impressive. The core of the building was the central hall or *megaron*, entered from the courtyard by a pillared porch. The main feature of the *megaron* was the large circular hearth in the centre; around this were four pillars supporting the roof, with a hole to allow the smoke to escape.

To the rear and sides of the *megaron* stood the domestic quarters, as well as the guardrooms and stores, chariot-sheds, and the many workshops. Almost every requirement was made on the spot, whether it was building materials, nails, cooking utensils or clothing. Naturally enough in this Bronze Age society, pride of place went to the bronze-smiths, whose work was vital in the manfacture of weapons and armour. They even appear from the Linear B tablets to have enjoyed special tax benefits.

The palaces and richer private houses were elaborately decorated inside and out.

2.12 The *megaron* (central hall) of the palace at Pylos, showing clearly the position of the pillars around the circular hearth.

There were many frescoes, which varied little in style from those of the Minoans, from whom the Mycenaeans learnt the art. However the Mycenaeans were fonder of scenes of hunting and war.

Mycenaean religion shared with the Minoan the Mother Goddess and other elements. Yet the Mycenaeans brought with them into Greece their own religion, in which the more important deities were male. Old and new beliefs merged, and the Mycenaean religion formed the basis of that of the later Greeks. Names of gods and goddesses like Zeus, Poseidon, Hera and Artemis appear on Linear B tablets.

The wealth revealed at Mycenaean sites in mainland Greece was principally acquired by the energy and skill of Mycenaean traders, especially after they had taken over many of the Minoan trading posts in the Mediterranean. The main need was for copper and tin to make bronze. This would be one of the chief reasons for their interest in Cyprus, which was rich in copper. Cyprus and other settlements in the Mediterranean, such as that at Rhodes, were in good positions for trade with Asia Minor, Palestine, Egypt and Syria. There was also contact to the west with islands off the west coast of Italy and with southern Italy and Sicily. By trading over a wide area, Mycenaeans were able to import precious metals and stones, ivory, and perhaps spices.

Without great natural resources, Mycenaeans partly acted as distributors of other people's products and partly must have relied on their own special skills to create desirable goods from imported raw materials. So bronze could have been re-exported in the shape of weapons made by Mycenaean craftsmen, and a great deal of jewellery was produced. Olive-oil may have gone abroad, often with spices added, for use as body lotions. Wine and wool were other likely exports. The palaces themselves were the most important trading centres. The 2853 stemmed drinking cups found in a single store-room at Pylos were probably not all for use in the palace, but were awaiting sale either abroad or elsewhere in Greece.

General Unrest

In the poems of Homer, 'Sacker of cities' is a frequent and complimentary description of a hero, and plundering raids are clearly regarded as normal. During the campaign at Troy, Achilles boasts:

> 'I have sacked twelve cities from the sea, and by land eleven in the fertile region of Troy. From all these I took much plunder, and brought it all back and gave it to Agamemnon, son of Atreus.'
>
> (*Iliad* IX, 238f.)

It seems that here Homer is reflecting the realities of the Mycenaean world. There is no doubt that the Mycenaeans had always added to their wealth not just by peaceful trading, but also by the use of brute force in wars and piratical raids. They were not alone in this, and by the end of the thirteenth century B.C. increasingly warlike activities on the part of the Mycenaeans and others had helped to create a seriously disturbed situation at the eastern end of the Mediterranean. This also appears to have involved whole-scale migrations of peoples, but the exact pattern of events and the underlying causes are simply not known to us, at least as yet.

2.13 This vase, dated to about 1200 B.C., gives important evidence of the equipment of Mycenaean soldiers.

2.14 A Mycenaean gold cup of outstanding craftsmanship: the scene is the capture of a wild bull.

2.15 The Lion Gate at Mycenae.

2.16 Stairs at Mycenae leading down to the secret water-supply, vital in times of siege.

It cannot be coincidence that Mycenae herself in the second half of the thirteenth century B.C. extended her defensive walls and secured an ingenious secret water-supply. Three flights of steps were built underground through the walls to a cistern fed from a nearby spring. All over the Mycenaean world fortifications were being constructed or strengthened.

Asia Minor during the Mycenaean period had been dominated by the Hittite empire. Hittite records almost certainly referring to the Mycenaeans point to quite friendly relations between the two powers. Around 1200 B.C., however, the Hittite kingdom fell, victim of the general unrest. Further south at the same time Egyptian records refer to 'Peoples of the Sea' threatening the Nile Delta, and some scholars identify the Mycenaeans among those taking part. Egypt held out with difficulty. Whoever the sea raiders were, some were migrating, either because of famine or because they themselves were being driven out by others from their homelands.

The date of the Trojan War, made famous by Homer, must also be placed during this unsettled time. According to the poet, the reason for the Greek expedition to Troy was the stealing of Helen from her husband Menelaos, king of Sparta, by the Trojan prince, Paris. If true at all, that can only have been an excuse for a raid to plunder a city which had recently been weakened by an earthquake. The Trojans apparently resisted nobly.

The Mycenaeans themselves did not long survive the fall of Troy. During the twelfth century B.C. the Mycenaean world collapsed dramatically, as the various fortresses were destroyed by violence and settlements were abandoned. Traditionally this was said to be the work of the Dorians, a people who seem to have arrived in Greece from the north in the centuries following the Mycenaean collapse. They brought with them their own 'Dorian' dialect of Greek and settled in large areas of mainland Greece, particularly in the Peloponnese. However, the archaeological evidence does not support the view that the Dorians were actually the conquerors of the Mycenaeans, rather that they came a considerable time later. The Mycenaeans may, it is thought, even have destroyed themselves by bitter civil wars.

Whatever the reason, all the Mycenaean centres fell, except Athens, where the secret water-supply in the Acropolis may have been her salvation. After one severe attack the fortress at Mycenae was briefly reoccupied, but with nothing like its former glory. By 1100 B.C. at latest it was in ruins, together with what little had remained of its civilization.

2.17 Part of dagger blade decorated in bronze, gold and silver—Mycenae c. 1500 B.C.

CHAPTER THREE

Homer

Dark Ages and Migrations

The collapse of the Mycenaean world was followed by the Dark Ages of Greek history. The Dorians were less sophisticated than the Mycenaeans and did not leave behind evidence of themselves on nearly the same scale. For one thing, the art of writing was lost. Its principal use had been for keeping royal records, and when the Mycenaean palaces went, so did the writing. It reappeared centuries later, but with a new alphabet.

Furthermore, the Dorians were farmers rather than traders: so there are not the widespread clues of the type left behind by Mycenaean traders. Nor did they have large stone buildings and the range of arts and crafts encouraged by luxurious palace life, survivals of which tell us so much about the Minoans and Mycenaeans.

A major development of the Dark Ages about which we do know, however, was a further series of migrations, which may have taken many years to complete. In a chain reaction to the Dorians' arrival in Greece, the west coast of Asia Minor and most of the islands near to it were inhabited by migrating Greeks.

The northern section of this coast and the island of Lesbos were inhabited by people from north and central Greece. They spoke the Aiolic dialect of Greek, and the area became known as Aiolis. To the south of this was the region of Ionia, inhabited by people both from central Greece and the Peloponnese. The Ionian migration traditionally originated from Athens, which survived the Dorian attacks and was a refuge from them for others. Their dialect was called Ionic.

These Ionians established fine cities, with good harbours, on the mainland and the neighbouring islands. They were well placed for trade. Chios and Samos could control the sea-route along the coast from north to south, and Ephesos and Miletos lay at the end of important trade routes coming from the interior down the valleys of the rivers Kaystros and Maiandros. Therefore it is not surprising that Ionia was to become for some time the most prosperous and civilized part of the Greek world.

Further south, some of the Dorians themselves moved on from mainland Greece to islands such as Crete, Rhodes and Kos, and settlements on the coast of Asia like Knidos and Halikarnassos. At these points the Dorian movements came to a halt.

Oral Poetry

In the Ionian area the first works of Greek literature were created. The epic poems of Homer, the *Iliad* and the *Odyssey*, belong to the end of the Dark Ages. They are generally agreed to be the final version of songs which had been passed on orally for some centuries previously. The Greeks who had migrated in the face of the Dorians kept alive the traditional songs about the heroes of the Mycenaean age, which they naturally regarded as the good old days. These would be recited, to the accompaniment of the lyre (see fig 15.1), by minstrels or 'bards'. The occasion might be a feast or a religious festival—there are descriptions in Homer of such recitals, where guests are entertained at the end of a feast. The bards relied entirely on

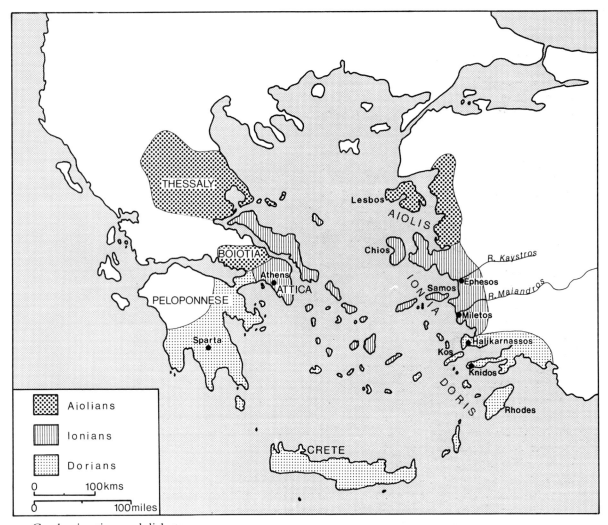

3.1 Greek migrations and dialects.

memory, as, of course, they had to, when writing did not exist. Similar examples of 'oral' poetry, passed on only by word of mouth, have been recorded in modern times, for instance in Yugoslavia. The audience would usually have heard the stories many times, but familiarity only added to their pleasure.

Such songs Homer moulded into single masterpieces, which retain much of their original nature. Most obvious in this respect is the constant repetition of stock phrases, in descriptions of people, things, places and events which naturally recur many times in the long stories. For instance, a new day is again and again introduced by the line, 'And when early-born rose-fingered Dawn appeared . . .', Odysseus is usually 'the cunning Odysseus', the king of the gods is 'Zeus the cloud-gatherer', and so on. In 28 000 lines of poetry there are, it has been calculated, 25 000 repeated phrases, and they are among the things which strike a reader coming to the poems for the first time. They greatly eased the task of the bard—the *Iliad* would take perhaps five evenings to recite—freeing him from the need to think about each individual word and allowing him to concentrate on what was to come next.

Of Homer himself scarcely anything is known. Indeed some have thought that the *Iliad* and the *Odyssey* are the work of different poets. Although many cities later claimed that Homer was theirs, the strongest claim came from the island of Chios. There was a tradition that he was blind. The poems as we have them were probably composed in the eighth century B.C.

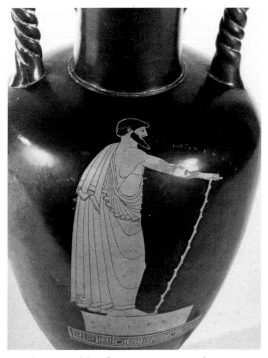

3.2 A man reciting from memory an epic poem: an Athenian vase-painting of the fifth century B.C.

3.3 A later version of Homer's portrait.

The Iliad

Epics are poems about heroes, and the main figures of the *Iliad* and the *Odyssey* are heroes on the grand scale. They are all aristocrats, and many are kings and princes. Above all, they are fighting men, capable of incredible feats in battle. The thing they prize most is their honour, for which they are fully prepared to die.

The *Iliad* revolves around this question of honour. The Greeks, called Achaians by Homer, are led by Agamemnon, king of Mycenae, and his brother, Menelaos. They have come to Troy to avenge the stealing of Menelaos' beautiful wife, Helen, by Paris, who is the son of King Priam of Troy. Agamemnon has roughly refused to allow the ransom of a captured girl, who is part of his share of the spoils after a raid. The girl's father is a priest of Apollo, and so Apollo has sent a plague on the Greeks. Eventually, under pressure from the others, especially Achilles, Agamemnon agrees to give the girl back, but insists on taking Briseis, a captured girl awarded to Achilles, to replace her. Achilles is only restrained from physical resistance by the goddess Athena. He retreats to his tent, where he angrily sulks, refusing to fight. This is the famous 'wrath of Achilles', spoken of by Homer as he calls on the Goddess of Poetry to inspire him in his opening lines:

'Sing, Goddess, of the fateful wrath of Achilles, son of Peleus, which brought countless troubles on the Achaians and sent the spirits of many mighty heroes to the Underworld and left their bodies as prey for all the dogs and birds.'

(*Iliad* I, 1ff.)

The point is that Agamemnon has taken away from Achilles the prize given to him as a symbol of his *honour*. As Achilles complains:

'The great king, Agamemnon, son of Atreus, dishonoured me. For he has robbed me of my prize of honour and taken it for himself.'

(*Iliad* I, 355f.)

Nothing will now induce Achilles to fight, however badly the Achaians fare at the hands of Hector and the other Trojans, until his beloved comrade, Patroklos, is killed. Then, in a fury, he joins battle, kills Hector and maltreats his corpse. The *Iliad* ends with great funeral games held in honour of Patroklos, and a truce when Achilles finally allows Priam to take back the body of Hector for burial. The capture of Troy is not described—the poem is about one crucial episode in the war.

A large proportion of the *Iliad* is taken up by descriptions of fighting, in which the limelight is firmly fixed on the deeds of the central heroes. Here in a typical passage is the death of Patroklos:

'Patroklos charged, intending terrible things against the Trojans. Three times he charged with a dreadful roar, like the swift God of War, and three times he killed nine men. But when he charged like a demon the fourth time, then, Patroklos, your end was in sight. For in the heat of the fight the dread Apollo came to meet him. Patroklos did not see him coming through the fray, for he came against him clothed in a great mist: he stood behind him and hit his back and broad shoulders with the flat of his hand, so that Patroklos' eyes spun round. And Apollo hurled the helmet from his head and the plumed helmet rolled and clattered beneath the hooves of the horses, and its crest was dirtied by blood and dust . . . His huge spear too was completely shattered in his hand, his great, sturdy, bronze-tipped spear; his fringed shield, as well, and its strap, fell from his shoulders to the ground, and Apollo, son of Zeus, made his breastplate come loose. Patroklos was bewildered and his limbs were weak and he stood in astonishment. Then a Trojan, Euphorbos, struck him at close range from behind, on his back between the shoulders . . . Patroklos, overcome by the god's blow and the spear, shrank back among his comrades to avoid death. But when Hector saw brave Patroklos shrinking back, wounded by the sharp bronze, he came near him through the ranks and pierced him with his spear in the bottom of his stomach and drove the bronze right through. He fell with a thud and caused great grief to the Achaian army. Just as when a lion beats a strong boar in a struggle, when the two fight fiercely on the mountain-top over a small spring, when they both want to drink, and the lion overwhelms his panting enemy by brute force, so Hector, son of Priam, killed the mighty Patroklos, who had himself killed many men, with his spear from close range.'

(*Iliad* XVI, 783ff.)

3.4 On this plate, from Rhodes, Hector and Menelaos fight over the body of Euphorbos.

Here again a god interferes in human affairs. The gods in Homer often do this and many are quite openly on one side or the other in the war. Zeus, the father of the gods, is for the most part neutral, although he is on the side of Achilles against Agamemnon. The gods are not judges of morality. They are often shown to be just as immoral as humans. Men fear and respect their supernatural powers. The gods become annoyed and use their powers against humans if they are insulted or dishonoured, for instance by a failure to carry out a promised sacrifice.

In their dwelling-place, at the top of Mount Olympos in Thessaly, the gods banquet, have love affairs, plot, quarrel, mock and deceive each other, just like human beings.

Homer is quite happy to invite his audience to smile at the gods, as in the case of the lame Hephaistos—the supreme craftsman of the gods, but also their main source of amusement, both because he is lame and because he is rather slow on the uptake. In this passage he patches up a quarrel between Zeus and his wife Hera:

'Hephaistos, the great craftsman, addressed them, wanting to help his mother, white-armed Hera. "This will be a terrible and intolerable situation, if these two fight and cause a brawl among the gods. And we won't enjoy our good dinner, because of this bad business. I advise my mother, though she is sensible enough herself, to make it up with my dear father Zeus so that he doesn't tell her off again and spoil our dinner. Olympian Zeus, God of Lightning, can blast us from our seats if he wants to, for he is by far the strongest. You calm him with sweet words, then he will soon be kind to us." So he spoke and jumping up put a two-handled goblet in his mother's hand, and said, "Be patient, mother, and put up with it, although you are upset, so that I don't see you getting a beating before my very eyes. If that happened, I wouldn't be able to help you at all, because Zeus is a terrible one to take on. Once before when I was trying to defend you, he grabbed me by the foot and hurled me from the threshold of heaven. I flew all day and fell on the island of Lemnos at sunset, and there wasn't much spirit left in me . . ." At his words the white-armed goddess Hera smiled and smiling took the cup from her son. Then he went from left to right round all the other gods and poured out sweet nectar for them, drawing it from the bowl. Uncontrollable laughter arose among the blessed gods, as they saw Hephaistos bustling around the hall.'

(*Iliad* I, 571ff.)

3.5 Mount Olympos: 'the home of the gods'.

31

This lighter side makes a welcome contrast to all the bloody battles. Homer is capable also of showing the sadder side of the heroic way of life, as when Hector says goodbye to his wife, Andromaché and their son, Astyanax, before setting out to battle. To her pleas not to risk his life his answer is that he must, rather than be thought a coward, although he knows that Troy will be destroyed in the end. The thought of his wife's enslavement by the Greeks when that happens causes him more grief than anything else . . .

'"I hope that heaped-up earth will cover my body before I hear your cries and your capture." With these words glorious Hector reached out for his son, but the child cringed crying into the arms of his nurse, terrified by the sight of his father and afraid of the bronze armour and the horsehair crest, seeing it swaying frighteningly from the top of his helmet. His mother and father laughed aloud, and immediately glorious Hector took his helmet from his head and laid it gleaming on the ground. And when he had kissed his son and played with him in his arms, then he prayed to Zeus and the other gods: "Zeus and the other gods, grant that this son of mine may also become distinguished among the Trojans, like me, and be great in strength and rule by might in Troy. Then someone may say, 'He's much better than his father,' as he returns from war. May he kill his enemy and bring back blood-stained armour to delight his mother."'

(*Iliad* VI, 464ff.)

3.6 A vase-painting of the Greek heroes Achilles and Ajax relaxing from battle with a game of dice or draughts.

The Odyssey

The *Odyssey* relates the return of one Greek hero, the cunning Odysseus, to his native island of Ithaka after the fall of Troy. On his journey, which takes ten years, he has many adventures, most of them unpleasant, including encounters with the fearsome Cyclops (the one-eyed giant, who eats alive some of Odysseus' companions) and Kirké, who turns all his companions into pigs, a trip to the Underworld and several terrible storms. This home-coming gives ample opportunity for exciting stories and vividly imaginative descriptions, at which Homer excels. One of the more alarming episodes involves sailing between the rocks of Skylla and Charybdis, of whom Odysseus is warned in advance by Kirké:

'There lives Skylla, with her terrible barking. Her voice is as loud as a new-born puppy, but she herself is an evil monster. Nobody would be glad to see her, not even a god if he met her. She has twelve feet, all of which dangle down, and six very long necks on each of which is a monstrous head with three rows of teeth, lots of them, all close to each other, full of black death. Her middle is inside the hollow cave, but she holds her heads outside the fearful chasm and fishes there, keeping a watch round the rock for dolphins and sharks and any larger monster she can catch, which the roaring sea feeds in great numbers. The day has not come when sailors can boast that they have sailed past there unharmed. She snatches a man from the dark-prowed ship with each of her heads and carries them off.

Then you will see the other rock, Odysseus, which is not so high—they are near each other and you could shoot an arrow across. On this one there is a great fig-tree in full leaf. Beneath it the fantastic Charybdis gulps down the dark water. Three times a day she belches it out and three times a day she gulps it back in dreadful fashion. Don't you be there when she is gulping the water down, for not even Poseidon could save you. Keep your ship close to Skylla's rock and row through quickly, since it is better to mourn six comrades from your ship than the whole lot at once.'

(Odyssey XII, 85ff.)

3.7 Achilles fights Hector outside the walls of Troy: on vase-paintings the victor was shown on the left.

33

The warning was accurate, but in true heroic style and with his immense cunning, Odysseus survives all to reach Ithaka.

In Ithaka his house is full of the suitors of his wife, Penelopé. They believe that Odysseus is dead and, while waiting for Penelopé to choose one of them as her husband, they are eating and drinking Odysseus out of house and home. Penelopé and Odysseus' son, Telemachos, are powerless to do anything except play for time in the increasingly forlorn hope of Odysseus' return. Penelopé's most effective method of putting off the suitors had been to ask them to wait until she had finished the burial sheet which she was making for her father-in-law, Laertes. Each night in secret she undid what she had woven during the day. It apparently took more than three years for her trick to be discovered.

It is fortunate for Odysseus that he arrives back in Ithaka before his authority and wealth are completely gone. He enters his palace disguised as a beggar—only Telemachos and a faithful swineherd, Eumaios, know who he really is—manages to kill all the suitors and is re-established as king in Ithaka. There is a touching moment when he first enters the palace in his disguise:

> 'A dog lying there lifted its head and pricked its ears: Argos, belonging to brave Odysseus, whom once he himself had trained, but never got the benefit of, for he went off to sacred Troy before that happened. In earlier days the young men used to take him after wild goats and gazelles and hares. But now he lay abandoned, in his master's absence, in a great pile of dung, which was heaped up from the mules and cattle in front of the gates . . . There lay the dog, Argos, covered in vermin. Then, when he recognized Odysseus nearby, he wagged his tail and lowered his ears, but he no longer had the strength to come nearer his master. Odysseus looked away and wiped away a tear . . . And the fate of black death straightway overtook the dog when he saw Odysseus again after nineteen years.'
>
> (*Odyssey* XVII, 291ff.)

3.8 Odysseus escaping from the Cyclops' cave by clinging to the underside of a ram.

Since much of it is set in Greece itself, the *Odyssey* gives a much clearer picture than the *Iliad* of life there in the age of heroes. Although apparently about the Mycenaean Age, in that it is about people and places of that era, the poem shows a society and a way of life less sophisticated, without the elaborately organized government revealed by the Linear B tablets. There are other inconsistencies, too, such as the fact that in Homer the dead are cremated, whereas we know from the archaeological evidence that burial was the rule in Mycenaean times. The world described by Homer contains many elements ranging in date from the time of Mycenae's supremacy to that of the final composition of the poems.

Although the emphasis is so strongly on the central, aristocratic heroes, we do find in the *Odyssey* some glimpses of the others. There are the women servants in the palace of Odysseus. One of these is Eurykleia, the old nurse, who sees through Odysseus' disguise when she recognizes an old scar. Then there is Eumaios, who has remained loyal to Odysseus and continued to look after his pigs in the countryside, living a life by no means easy, as Odysseus himself came to realize when he sheltered with him on his return to Ithaka.

'Yet the swineherd was not content to sleep in the hut, away from the pigs, but got himself ready to go out, and Odysseus was delighted that he looked carefully after

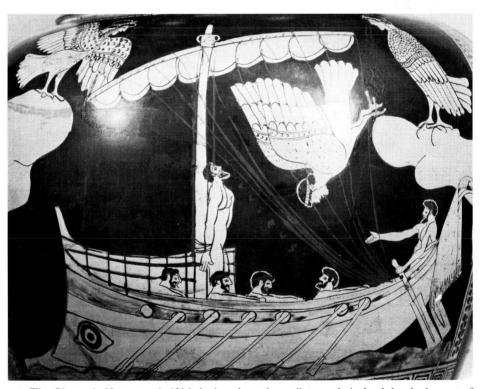

3.9 The Sirens, half women, half birds, lured passing sailors to their death by the beauty of their song. Odysseus escaped by blocking his crew's ears and having himself tied to the mast of his ship.

his property in his absence. First he slung a sharp sword over his broad shoulders, then a very thick cloak to keep off the wind, and he took the fleece of a fine large goat, and he took a sharp javelin to keep off dogs and men. He went off to lie down where the white-tusked pigs slept beneath a hollow rock, out of the north wind.'

(*Odyssey* XIV, 524ff.)

Besides these members of the royal household, Homer mentions bards, craftsmen, Phoenician merchants, hired labourers, whose lives are even less secure than those of the slaves, and the shadowy *demos* or people—the free peasants. Yet Homer is telling a story, not writing a history book, and the use of his poems as historical documents must therefore be cautious.

It has frequently been said that the poems of Homer were the Bible of the Greeks. For about a thousand years they played a central part in Greek education. Homer was quoted to settle moral questions. Greek artists and writers turned above all to Homer for their subjects and inspiration. Alexander the Great modelled himself on Achilles and kept a copy of the *Iliad* with him on all his campaigns.

The *Iliad* and the *Odyssey* are in effect the first literature of our western civilization. Many would claim that they are still the finest.

3.10 Telemachos and Penelopé, in front of her loom, await the return of Odysseus.

CHAPTER 4

City-States

The actual world, in which the *Iliad* and the *Odyssey* were composed, was very different from the world they portray. The kings and the chariots had disappeared; their broad realms had been broken up. In their place there had developed through the Dark Ages that most Greek of political institutions, the city-state. 'Man,' as the philosopher Aristotle said much later, 'is a political animal'; by which he meant that, just as birds live best in the air and fish in the sea, so human beings do in the *polis*. It was the smallness of these communities and the close-knit pattern of life in them that, allied to the Greek character, seems to have produced the vigour and brilliance of the Greek achievement. In Aristotle's view they had to be small: 'You can't have a state of ten citizens. But when you have 100 000, it is no longer a *polis*.' This was because it had to be big enough to be self-sufficient, but small enough for 'the citizens to know one another's characters. Where this is not the case, both elections and decisions at law are bound to suffer.'

And small these city-states were. As we saw in Chapter 1, the geographical character of the land helped this development: a mountainous country discouraged large political unions. But the Greek love of freedom and independence was as important as geography in determing the political map of Greece. The size of the city-states was, by our standards, laughable: Boiotia, an area somewhat smaller than Kent, had twelve independent states in it; in Amorgos, an island in the south Aegean, thirty-two kilometres long and eight kilometres wide, there were three; and in the north-east of the Peloponnese three states, Epidauros, Troizen, Methane, coexisted along a coast of thirty kilometres. Each of them had its own constitution, laws, parliament, generals, army and taxation; sometimes even their own systems of coins, weights and measures. Athens, with its hinterland of Attica and its many villages, an area of 2500 square kilometres or so, was unique, as was Sparta with her control of two-fifths of the Peloponnese. In the case of most Greek city-states, things were very small: Mycenae, for example, although reduced from her great days under Agamemnon, was still independent and therefore patriotically sent an army to help the Greeks against the Persians at the battle of Plataia: it was eighty strong. . . .

The emergence of these city-states was the greatest contribution of the Dark Ages to Greek history. Two other developments are noteworthy, too. Although pottery in the Minoan and Mycenaean style continued to be made after the arrival of the

37

Dorians, it gradually deteriorated. What took its place from about 900 B.C. onwards was abstract geometric design. At first this was simple, broad bands and concentric circles of dark colour contrasting with the pale clay of the plain areas. But it developed over two centuries, and the final products in the geometric style, the huge funeral jars found in Athens, are marvellously impressive pieces of work, with their formalized stick-people and complicated patterns.

The second important change during the Dark Ages was the substitution of iron for bronze as the most common metal. Iron in Homer is spoken of as a rare and therefore precious metal; but in the centuries after the Dorians arrived, new processes of smelting meant that the greater toughness of iron was made more widely available.

Aristocracies

Most city-states in 800 B.C. were ruled by aristocrats. The kings had gradually disappeared, peacefully, it seems, on the whole. Power was in the hands of a small number of wealthy families, who maintained and strengthened their position by ownership of the best land, by restricting membership of the council and the holding of magistracies to themselves, and by emphasizing their noble ancestry, tracing it back to heroes or even gods. Ordinary people were usually poor, often living on less fertile land further away from the town, forced sometimes into debt or even slavery.

4.1 Geometric pot (*pyxis*) of the 8th century B.C. Notice the stylized horses and the swastikas.

And so not surprisingly, 'there was,' in Aristotle's words, 'conflict between the nobles and the people for a long time' because 'the poor with their wives and children were enslaved to the rich and had no political rights.'

One man who suffered under this system was Hesiod. In his long poem *Works and Days*, already quoted (see p. 10), he also complains about the wickedness of greedy nobles. He was particularly angry about this, because his brother had seized the best part of their father's property by 'gratifying the bribe-devouring judges.' Although he lived probably at the same time as Homer, there are no heroes or glamorous wars for him. He talks of the countryside, of the drudgery and uncertainty of the small farmer's life:

'There will be no rest ever from toil and hardship during the day, nor from suffering at night; for the gods will give us pain and anxiety.'
Work is necessary 'so that Famine will keep away from you, and august Demeter (the corn-goddess) with her garlands will love you and fill your barn with crops. . . By work men become wealthy and their flocks increase, and they become much better liked by gods and men. It is the idle who are hated.'

(176–8, 299–301, 308–310)

He is full of advice:

'Don't let a woman fool you with her flattering chatter and a short skirt—she's after your barn.'
'Don't go for unfair gains; unfair gains are madness.'
'Look for a maidservant without a child: those with young children are a nuisance.'

(373–4, 602–3)

There are times, after the harvest, when you can take it easy:

'Give me then the shade of a rock and wine from Biblis, a curd cake and creamy goat's milk.'

(588–90)

Colonization

Since in every *polis* good farming land was in short supply and the population was increasing, unrest was bound to grow. One solution to it for the aristocratic governments was to encourage emigration. Just as the end of the Mycenaean Age had seen large numbers of Greeks moving across the Aegean (see p. 26), so the first great change in the Greek world after the Dark Ages was a huge geographical expansion. Their first venture was to Italy, where about 750 B.C., just north of Naples, a city, Cumae, was founded by settlers from Kymé in Aiolis and from two cities in Euboia, Chalkis and Eretria. This first colony, through which, incidentally, the alphabet reached the Romans, may have been established for trade: Etruscan metal was near and valuable. But it showed how people, too, could be exported. Thus the main reason for Greek colonies was land rather than trade. The word 'colony' is therefore misleading: to us it suggests the exploitation of primitive natives by selfish imperialists. Greek colonies were not this at all. They were independent city-states. They often indeed maintained religious and cultural links with their mother-cities. But they were self-governing and self-sufficient.

The century and a half between 750 and 600 B.C. saw this spread of Greek people, and therefore Greek ideas, all over the Mediterranean, first westwards and then to the east and north-east (see fig 4.3). North-west Greece, then Sicily and southern Italy, finally southern France and Spain, all received Greek settlements: Taras (Taranto), Syracuse, Massalia (Marseilles) were founded in this period, as well as many less famous cities. The influence of the Greeks was so enormous that southern Italy and Sicily became known as Magna Graecia or Greater Greece. The same process eastwards led first to many colonies in the northern Aegean and then to the Greek encirclement of the Black Sea, from Byzantion (Istanbul) on the Bosphorus to Trapezous (Trabzon) in the south-east corner.

All these cities were coastal settlements, and some had to struggle to survive against attacks by the tribes from the interior. But survive the vast majority did, so that by 600 B.C. there were perhaps 1500 Greek city-states round the Mediter- ranean. They survived as *poleis*, too, despite external threats, which might well have forced a closer political organisation. But their position did emphasize the Greekness they had in common, what Herodotus, the fifth century B.C. historian, called 'our being of the same stock and same speech, our shared temples of the gods and religious rituals, our similar customs'. They were Greeks, even if from different mother-cities (although many of the colonies were joint efforts by two or more cities), and the rest were *barbaroi*.

4.2 Marseilles, the Old Port: this was the port which attracted colonists from Phokaia in Ionia to settle here.

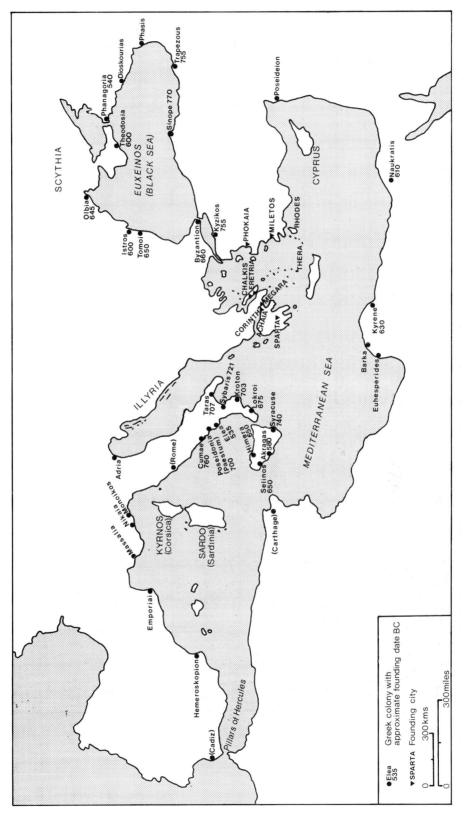

4.3 Greek Colonization 750–600 B.C. Only some of the very large number of colonies are shown.

Colonization had begun as an answer to land-hunger and political unrest. It did something to reduce the first of these problems, but, paradoxically, it increased the second. This was because the growth of Greek centres overseas led to an increase in trade and in the products, pottery, metalwork, cloth, wine, which supplied that trade. The old aristocratic families did not on the whole engage in trade—their wealth was on the land—and so a new middle class emerged of people whose wealth came from industry, on a small scale, and commerce. As their wealth grew, so did their wish to share political power.

Tyrannies

Their hopes were achieved in very many *poleis* under the leadership of a tyrant. This is another misleading word. To the Greeks it meant an unconstitutional ruler, not necessarily or even usually a harsh and brutal one. Tyrants came to power, generally with the support of this new class, and in many cases showed themselves vigorous, successful, even enlightened rulers. Pheidon of Argos in the Peloponnese is remembered for his establishment of weights and measures; Theagenes of Megara brought running water into the city by an aqueduct; Periandros of Corinth established that city's strong influence in north-west Greece and planned, unsuccessfully, a canal through the Isthmus. And Polykrates of Samos, an island just off the Ionian coast, made Samos powerful and rich, Herodotus says, by 'indiscriminate plundering. He used to say that a friend would be more grateful if he gave him back what he had taken than if he had never taken anything in the first

4.4 A hoplite and his armour: he is already wearing a breastplate over his *chiton*, and is fixing the second greave. His high-crested, vizored helmet, sword and scabbard, shield, and spears can also be seen.

42

place' (III, 39). He also dug a water channel, three metres square and four hundred metres long, through a hill; the digging started from both ends and met in the middle with only a very small error, a very considerable feat of sixth century B.C. surveying and engineering.

But, despite the benefits tyrants brought to their cities, they tended to become too authoritarian, and hardly any tyranny lasted for more than two generations. The period in which they flourished (650–500 B.C.), however, saw remarkable advances: the re-introduction of writing with the 'new' alphabet (see Appendix); the writing down of law-codes in many states; the rise of the oracle at Delphi (see Chapter 7) to an influential position in the whole Greek world; the establishment of that other pan-Hellenic activity, 'Games' of athletic, musical and dramatic contests (see Chapter 8); and the introduction of coinage, following its invention in Lydia at the end of the seventh century B.C.

One other change may have helped tyrants to take over power, the emergence of a new type of soldier, the heavy-armed hoplite. These were citizens who were wealthy enough to provide their own armour and weapons. The hoplite phalanx, whose success depended on solidity and co-operative effort, decided land battles for the next three hundred years. Thus the new middle class produced a new military strategy, too.

Poetry, Science and Philosophy

The eighth and seventh centuries B.C. were a period of enormous and exciting growth in Greek society in almost every sphere. Although this was true of the old mainland states, it was even more true of the new colonies, and of Ionia and Magna Graecia particularly. Ionia, as was said in Chapter 3, produced in Homer the

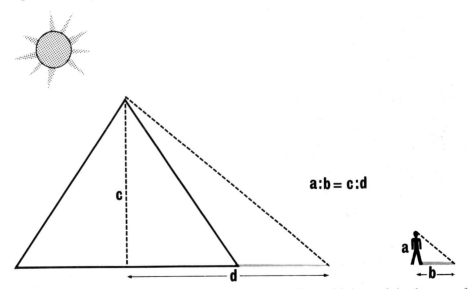

$$a:b = c:d$$

4.5 Thales' method of calculating the height of the Great Pyramid: he used the theorem of similar triangles, based on the relationship between a man's height and his shadow.

first and perhaps the greatest European poet. Epic poetry after Homer gradually declined; but instead there grew up a new poetry*, which was personal, non-heroic and contemporary. Not much of it has survived; but there is enough to see some of its genius. Archilochos from the island of Paros (*c.* 650 B.C.) shows the change in attitude:

> 'A perfect shield bedecks some Thracian now;
> I had no choice; I left it in a wood.
> Ah well, I saved my skin, so let it go!
> A new one's just as good.'
>
> (*Oxford Book of Greek Verse*, 104)

Not that Archilochos was a coward: he became a professional soldier and gives us his idea of a good captain, not 'Tall and loose-limbed, proud of his curly hair and carefully shaved, but a man who is small and bandy-legged, firm on his feet and full of guts.' And he was killed defending Paros against the neighbouring Naxians.

Lesbos, further north-east, just off the Ionian coast, had two great poets, Sappho and Alkaios. Sappho's fame as a poet was great in her lifetime (parents used to send their daughters to be taught by her) and greater after her death. The simplicity and sensitivity of her poems is lost in translation:

> 'The stars near the moon hide their gleaming shapes
> When she shines out full and beautiful
> Over the whole earth
> In silver.'
>
> (*Oxford Book of Greek Verse*, 142)

Here is another short poem that may be hers:

> 'The moon has set, and so have the Pleiades.
> It is midnight; time passes;
> and I sleep alone.'
>
> (*Oxford Book of Greek Verse*, 156)

Another side of the Ionian intellectual ferment is seen in the beginnings of science. Hesiod and the poets had given an elaborate mythological description of how the world was created; Thales and his successors now asked 'What is it made of?' His answer was water; and two of his successors suggested air and 'the Boundless'. Not right of course, although one of them at least is a useful attempt to define the general concept of matter. What is important is that they represent a search for a rational understanding of the universe. These Ionians knew of Babylonian mathematics and astronomy. But their use of it was remarkable: Thales is said to have measured the height of the Great Pyramid (see fig 4.5) and to have predicted an eclipse, in 582 B.C. Anaximandros believed that 'the earth floats in space, held up by nothing, steady because of its equal distance from all things'—a possible theory of gravity. And on geology, Xenophanes argued that 'in the past everything was covered with mud (that is, under the sea): the evidence is of the following kind: shells are found inland; the impressions of a fish and of seaweed have been discovered in the quarries at Syracuse; and in Paros there is the impression of a bay-leaf in the centre of a rock.'

The line between science and philosophy was not clearly drawn. Many of these thinkers did both. Herakleitos, for example, who came from Ephesos, believed that

*Called 'lyric' because it was sung with an accompaniment on the lyre.

44

the primary substance was fire. He went on to develop a whole theory of the universe: this is eternal, but inside it 'all things are in flux'. This lies behind his famous statement that 'you cannot step into the same river twice'. Harmony is the final aim, but it is the union of opposites. That is why he thought that 'war is the father of all things' and that 'justice is strife, and all things happen through strife and must do so.' Marx and Lenin followed the same line of thought to produce their 'dialectic', the belief that one idea (thesis) is opposed by another idea (antithesis) and the result of this conflict is an improved idea (synthesis).

Philosophy flourished also in Magna Graecia. The best known of the western philosophers was Pythagoras, who about 520 B.C. set up a school at Kroton, where mathematics and music were studied. His famous theorem is only one of the discoveries he, or his school, made. He was also a mystic, who believed that souls moved on to other bodies, animal or human, after death. The Pythagoreans were therefore vegetarians: you could hardly run the risk of eating your grandfather!

4.6 A Corinthian wine-jar of about 600 B.C.: it is 25 cms high and is decorated with real and imaginary animals.

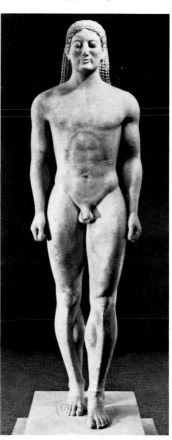

4.7 *kouros* (youth): early days of Greek sculpture, about 530 B.C.: the underlying structure of the body is becoming more correct, but the figure is still stiff and immobile.

Early Athens

Athens during these years experienced the same sort of progress as the rest of the Greek world, shown in her case especially in painting, in sculpture and in politics. By 600 B.C. her fine pottery had taken over from Corinthian ware as the most prized in the Greek world. In Athens, too, sculpture began to free itself from the stiffness that it had taken over from Egypt and to move towards naturalness. About 600 B.C. the long series of statues of naked young men begins (see fig 4.7), and is followed later by the quiet, charming statues of young girls, clothed and half-smiling. A large number of these was found in the pit on the Acropolis where the Athenians had put them when they were tidying up after the sack of Athens by the Persians in 480 B.C.

Athens had escaped the Dorian invasion (see p. 25), and somehow—the legend said that Theseus was responsible—in the Dark Ages she had peacefully brought all Attica under her control (see fig 4.8). The result was that like Sparta she had a quite unusually large area of land, but unlike Sparta all the original inhabitants became Athenians, having equal rights with those who lived in the city itself. Her political development was at first much the same as that of other Greek city-states: first, after kings had disappeared, rule by an aristocratic oligarchy, a Greek word meaning 'rule of the few'; second, an attempt at a tyranny in 632 B.C. which failed; thirdly, the writing down of laws, said to have been done by Drako. Although they may have been harsh, as our word 'draconian' indicates, and indeed a later Athenian said they seemed to be written in blood, the very fact of their being written meant that ordinary people could know what the law said and not be totally at the mercy of aristocratic judges.

The next century (600–500 B.C.) was decisive for Athens and made her different from all other Greek states. Three men particularly are associated with this rise to pre-eminence. The first, Solon, was chosen in 594 B.C. to put right the evils of debt and enslavement, into which many of the poorer Athenians had fallen. This he did by cancelling all debts and forbidding enslavement of free Athenians ever again. But he did more: among many other reforms, two were particularly important for the future: he encouraged industry and commerce, and he paved the way for the later democracy. Industry he helped by welcoming foreign craftsmen to Athens, and by making it compulsory for fathers to teach their sons a craft. Politically, he reduced the power of the aristocratic families by various means, and increased the status of the Assembly, the body to which all free Athenians belonged. He himself was no democrat; as he said in one of his poems, 'I gave the people as much power as was sufficient for them. . . They will follow their leaders best if they are neither too free nor too restrained.' But by establishing a People's Court and by setting up a new Council to prepare business for the Assembly, a job which had before been done by the aristocratic Council of the Areopagus, he deserved the reputation he had throughout later Athenian history as the founder of its greatness.

Yet within forty years it looked as though Solon's work had failed: for the unrest he had tried to stop continued, there was rivalry between different parties in Athens, and finally, after several attempts, a noble named Peisistratos became tyrant. But he was a restrained and successful ruler, and became so popular that his reign was later looked back to as a Golden Age. Among many other benefits, he made loans to poor

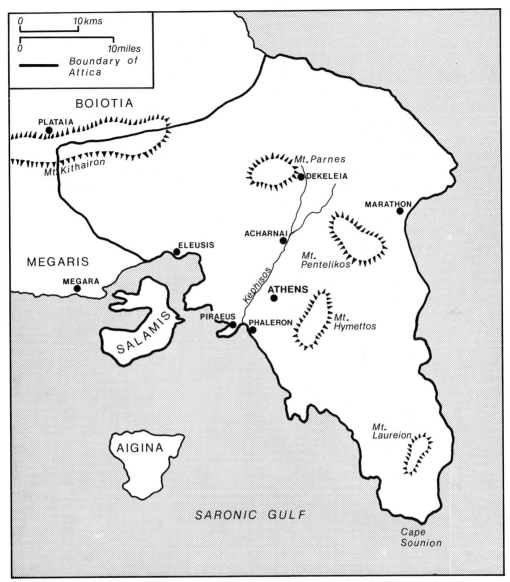

4.8 Attica.

47

farmers, built aqueducts and temples, and expanded festivals. These not only increased Athens' prestige but directly encouraged the development of drama: Thespis is said to have produced the first tragedy in 534 B.C., and comedy appeared a little later.

But, as happened in so many other Greek *poleis*, the tyranny deteriorated in the second generation. His sons ruled jointly for a time; but, after one had been assassinated, the other, Hippias, became progressively harsher until he was expelled. This opened the way for the third great figure, Kleisthenes.

His aim was a unified state, democratically run. He achieved this in two main ways: he broke down local groupings so that antagonism between city and countryside ended; and he increased the size of the Council to five hundred, annually elected. This meant that, since no one could be on it more than twice in his lifetime, a large number of citizens had practical experience of politics and administration. Kleisthenes also provided a useful safety-valve for times when political feelings rose high—ostracism. If a man became unpopular, he could be exiled for ten years, with no loss of property, if enough votes were cast against him. These votes were written on broken pieces of pottery, *ostraka*, which littered classical streets (fig 10.8). An odd arrangement, it may seem to us, but it was infinitely preferable to civil war. Thus by 500 B.C. Athens, through these developments, was ready for the huge achievement of the next century.

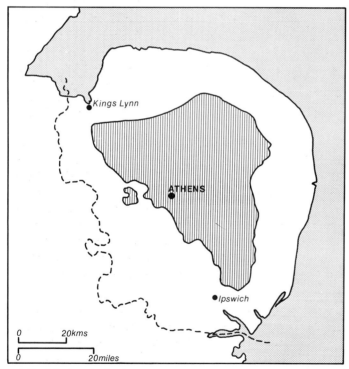

4.9 In this map Attica is superimposed on East Anglia to show their relative sizes.

CHAPTER FIVE

Sparta

Helots

There is a story about a Spartan boy who, in order to conceal a fox which he had stolen, hid it beneath his cloak and allowed the fox to gnaw him rather than let the theft be revealed. He died of the wounds. If he had been discovered, the disgrace would not have been in the stealing, but in allowing it to be detected. The boy's action illustrates the main purpose of the Spartan educational system, which was to produce men capable of showing such bravery as soldiers. Military strength was felt to be essential to Sparta for her very survival.

Sparta was the ruling city of the area of Lakonia in the southern Peloponnese. It lay in the valley of the river Eurotas. Of the people in the towns and villages which she controlled, some were free, known as *perioikoi* or neighbours, although they were inferior in status to the Spartans themselves. Others, because they were felt to be a greater threat, were kept in a state of slavery as publicly owned agricultural labourers. These were called helots. Furthermore, around the end of the eighth century B.C., when other Greek states were obtaining the extra land which they needed by sending out colonies (see Chapter 4), Sparta took over the adjacent area of Messenia and made the Messenians helots as well. Not long afterwards the Messenians revolted, and it is clear that the Spartans only just managed to retain their control.

At the battle of Plataia in 479 B.C., five thousand Spartiates, as the genuine Spartans were called, fought against the Persians, according to the historian Herodotus. With them were five thousand *perioikoi* and 35 000 helots. The Spartiates were determined to remain a select group, not inter-marrying with the rest of the population, nor sharing privileges with them. With their subjects vastly outnumbering them, as the figures for Plataia indicate, it can be seen why Sparta felt it essential to have enough military strength to ensure internal security. Every year the Spartans made a formal declaration of war on the helots, so that it did not count as murder to kill any. On one occasion, in 424 B.C., as we read in the *Histories* of Thucydides, the Spartans

'issued a decree that the helots should choose from amongst themselves those who claimed that they had done best service to Sparta in battle, giving the impression that they would set them free. The idea was that those who were most determined and came forward first to seek freedom were the ones most likely to cause trouble to Sparta. About two thousand were chosen. They put garlands on their heads and went round the temples in the belief that they were to become free. Not long

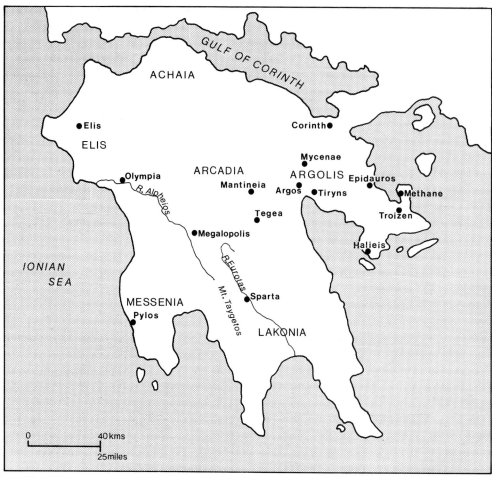

5.1 The Peloponnese.

afterwards the Spartans eliminated them, and no one ever knew how they each met their death.'

(IV, 80)

It was primarily because of this undying fear of a helot uprising that Sparta had deliberately chosen, during the seventh and sixth centuries B.C., to develop into a city-state very unlike others, especially her great rival, Athens.

Previously Spartan life had not been greatly different from that elsewhere. Ruled over by two kings, the aristocratic society had been typical, importing luxury goods, employing skilled craftsmen, enjoying art and poetry. The changes which took place were traditionally ascribed to Lykourgos. Here, rather as in the case of King Minos and Homer, is a figure of shadowy identity, not only to us, but to the Greeks as well. To some he was a man, to others a god. Plutarch, the Greek biographer, wrote a 'Life' of Lykourgos, valuable for its description of Spartan ways, but he was writing a long time after the period in question. Even the Delphic oracle was puzzled, according to Herodotus, saying,

> 'I do not know whether to speak of you as a man or a god, but rather, Lykourgos, I think you are a god.'
>
> (I, 65)

At all events the Spartans themselves attributed the institutions of their society to Lykourgos, although it is in fact unlikely that one person at one time can have been responsible for all of them.

Upbringing

Everything was now dedicated to making each Spartiate a superb and unquestioningly loyal soldier. The process started at birth. Newly-born babies were inspected by a committee of elders, and, if considered too weak, they were left to die by exposure on the slopes of Mount Taygetos. Those who survived were carefully brought up, as Plutarch describes:

> 'The women did not bathe the babies with water, but with wine, making it a sort of test of their strength. For they say that the epileptic and sickly ones lose control and go into convulsions, but the healthy ones are rather toughened like steel and strengthened in their physique. The nurses displayed care and skill: they did not use swaddling-bands, making the babies free in their limbs and bodies; they also made them sensible and not fussy about their food, not afraid of the dark or frightened of being left alone, not inclined to unpleasant awkwardness or whining. So even some foreigners acquired Spartan nurses for their children.'
>
> (*Lykourgos* xvi)

At the age of seven, a Spartan boy came directly under the control of the city, and remained so in effect until the time of his death. From this age boys were brought up in packs, which had a prefect system, and were under the general charge of a state director of education, the *paidonomos*. The military emphasis is explained by Plutarch:

> 'They learned reading and writing for basic needs, but all the rest of their education was to make them well-disciplined and steadfast in hardship and victorious in battle. For this reason, as the boys grew older, the Spartans intensified their training, cutting their hair short and making them used to walking barefoot and for the most part playing naked. When the boys reached the age of twelve, they no longer had tunics to wear, but got one cloak a year. Their bodies were tough and unused to baths and lotions. They only enjoyed such luxury on a few special days in the year. They slept, in packs, on beds which they got together on their own, made from the tops of the rushes to be found by the river Eurotas. These they broke off with their bare hands, not using knives.'
>
> (*Lykourgos* xvi)

The smallest offences were punishable by whipping, and food was deliberately rationed, so that the boys were forced to steal to get more—'if they are caught they are whipped severely, for stealing carelessly and unskilfully.'

The packs of boys were matched against each other in violent games with a ball and

5.2 Swans, cockerels and guinea-fowl decorate this Spartan vase.

5.3 A Spartan girl: bronze figure, about 11 centimetres high.

5.4 Bronze statuette of a ban-queter, believed to have been made in the Peloponnese in the sixth century B.C.

in straightforward fights. As they approached the age of twenty and manhood, the training grew more and more severe and military. At the festival of the goddess Artemis Ortheia, the older boys had to take part in a contest in which they snatched as many cheeses as possible from the steps of the altar to the goddess. To do so it was necessary to run the gauntlet of guards, with whips, who were instructed to use them as hard as they could. Some youths died as a result. Another test was the *krypteia*, or 'period of hiding', during which the boy had to live alone and under cover in the countryside, killing potentially dangerous helots.

The boys were taught music and poetry as well, but these were mostly military in tone—army songs were useful in helping them to keep time in their drill— and based on religious or patriotic themes, in keeping with the rest of their education.

As far as the girls were concerned, Lykourgos, according to Plutarch,

> 'took all possible care. He made the girls exercise their bodies in running, wrestling and throwing the discus and javelin, so that their children, taking root in the first place in strong bodies, would grow the better, and they themselves would be strong for childbirth, and deal well and easily with the pains of labour.'
>
> (*Lykourgos* xiv)

In athletic activities and in processions the girls, like the boys, were nearly naked, which shocked some other Greeks.

Adult Life

At the age of twenty came the most critical time in a Spartan man's life. He now tried to get election to one of the dining clubs, rather like an army 'mess', to which the men belonged. There were about fifteen members of each *syssition* of this kind. In the ballot each member of the mess dropped a pellet of bread into an urn, and if a single man squeezed his pellet flat, the candidate was rejected. To fail to win election to any mess at all meant becoming a social outcast. Members of the mess ate all their meals communally, and each man had to provide monthly a fixed quota of barley, wine, cheese and figs. The diet was plain, including usually a type of broth or porridge, which was well-known outside Sparta for its nastiness. It was apparently dark grey in colour.

The *syssition* was a military section, and the Spartan was now no less at the beck and call of the state than he had been as a boy.

> 'Their training continued right into manhood. For nobody was free to live as he wished, but the city was like a military camp, and they had a set way of life and routine in the public service. They were fully convinced that they were the property not of themselves but of the state. If they had no other duty assigned to them, they used to watch the boys, either teaching them something useful, or learning themselves from their seniors. For indeed one of the fine and enviable things which Lykourgos achieved for his citizens was a great deal of leisure. He forbade them to practise any manual trade at all. There was no need for the troublesome business and efforts of making money, since wealth had become completely without envy and prestige. The helots worked their land for them, supplying the fixed amount of produce.'
>
> (*Lykourgos* xxiv)

One reason why wealth was less desirable lay in the fact that Sparta's authorities refused to adopt the system of making silver into coins in the manner of other Greek cities. Instead she continued to use unwieldy iron bars for money. The historian Xenophon commented that 'a thousand drachmas' worth would fill a wagon'. Nevertheless, there seem to have been some rich families—rich enough, for instance, to breed race-horses which won victories on several occasions at the Olympic Games. Later on, too, the Spartans acquired something of a reputation among other Greeks for being greedy and susceptible to bribery.

Spartans were also forbidden to travel abroad, except on state instructions, and foreigners were not admitted to Sparta without supplying a very good reason for doing so. This was to prevent the citizens from being corrupted by foreign ideas and morality.

Marriages were no less unusual than everything else. The husband continued to live in his mess, only meeting his wife at dead of night in complete secrecy. Wives could also be lent: for instance an oldish man with a young wife might lend her to a young man in order to have a child by him. Plutarch says that Lykourgos thought it extraordinary for other people to spend so much care and interest on the breeding of dogs and horses, yet allow children to be born of unsuitable parents.

5.5 A Spartan soldier.

The Constitution

The constitution was organized so that individual power was closely checked and change by peaceful means very difficult. The fact that there were two kings meant that, as in the case of the two Roman consuls, one could prevent the other from becoming too powerful on his own account. The original powers of the kings were greatly restricted, and they became principally generals. When the army fought outside Sparta, however, one king only was allowed to go as its commander, as the possibility of a disagreement or the loss of both kings was too great a risk. At home they had some powers but were, in fact, less important than the *ephoroi* or 'overseers', five magistrates elected annually from the people. Each month the kings and *ephoroi* exchanged oaths, the kings swearing that they would govern according to the laws, and the *ephoroi* that, as long as the kings obeyed the laws, they would see to it that the kingship was unharmed.

The *ephoroi* kept a close watch on the kings: two went along on any foreign campaign, and they had the power to call the kings before them to explain their conduct. They could even fine or arrest them. The *ephoroi* were generally responsible for the discipline of the state, acting as judges, dealing with foreign ambassadors, presiding over meetings of the council and the assembly. It was they who annually declared war on the helots, and on beginning their years of office they issued a decree that all citizens should 'shave their top lips and obey the laws'.

The council (*gerousia*) was another strong influence in the city. Consisting of twenty-eight men over the age of sixty, elected for life from certain ancient families, its number was brought up to thirty by the two kings. Finally there was the assembly or *apella*, the members of which were the people, or at least the adult males. Although this *apella* had the right to approve or reject proposals put before it, there was an important law to the effect that 'if the people make a crooked decision, the kings and elders shall have the power to withdraw the matter'.

The Spartans had their own method of voting too. This is how Plutarch describes the election to vacancies in the *gerousia*:

'The election took place in this way. The assembly gathered, and picked men were shut in a building nearby, neither able to see or be seen, only hearing the shouts of the people in the assembly. For as in other matters they judged the candidates by the volume of shouting. They were not brought in all at once, but individually by lot, passing in front of the assembly in silence. Those who were shut up had writing-tablets and for each candidate recorded the quantity of applause, not knowing for which one it was, other than that he was the first or the second or third or whichever it was of those brought in. The one who got the most and loudest shouting was the one they elected.'

(*Lykourgos* xxvi)

This was the method of voting which the philosopher Aristotle could only consider as 'very childish'.

The Spartan Achievement

Many of Sparta's ways seem curious to us, but the fact remains that the system was on the whole remarkably effective. Internally she was free from unrest except on isolated occasions, such as the revolt by the Messenian helots in 465 B.C., when they took advantage of the chaos caused by a great earthquake. Externally, by virtue of her military strength and sound diplomacy, she was able to build up for a long time an importance in the Greek world rivalled only by Athens. Sparta soon realized that to continue enslaving her neighbours, as she had done in the case of the Messenians, was a policy which could only create more anxiety. So she turned to a policy of alliances with other cities in the Peloponnese, such as Corinth, Tegea, Argos and Elis. In this way she was, by the end of the sixth century B.C., the leader of the Peloponnese.

When it was necessary to fight, the effectiveness of the training was proved many times. The army was not beaten in a straight fight from the period of the Messenian Wars (see page 49) until the battle of Leuktra in 371 B.C. Plutarch's account of their preparations for, and conduct in, a battle makes it easy to see why they were such fearsome opponents:

5.6 Spartan hounds, like this one on an Athenian cup, were the most popular breed of hunting dog in Greece.

'In times of battles the officers relaxed the harshest aspects of their discipline, and did not stop the men from beautifying their hair and their armour and their clothing, glad to see them like horses prancing and neighing before races. For this reason they took care over their hair from the time when they were youths, especially seeing to it in times of trouble so that it appeared sleek and well-combed, remembering a saying of Lykourgos about the care of hair, that it makes the handsome better-looking and the ugly more frightening. They also had less rigorous exercises, and they allowed the young men a regime in other respects less restricted and supervised, so that for them alone war was in fact a rest from the preparation for war... It was an impressive and frightening sight to see them advancing in time to the flute and leaving no space in the battle-line, with no nervousness in their minds, but calmly and cheerfully moving into the dangerous battle to the sound of music. For men in this frame of mind are unlikely to suffer from fear or excessive excitement, but rather to be steady in their purpose and confident and brave, as if their god were there with them. The king when he marched against the enemy always had with him someone who had been crowned victor in the Olympic Games. There is a story that one man was offered a great amount of money to lose at the Olympics, but refused it. When he had thrown his opponent after a great struggle, someone asked him, "Spartan, what good have you gained from your victory?" and he replied with a smile, "I shall fight by my king against the enemy."'

(*Lykourgos* xxii)

It is easy to gain an impression of the Spartans as a totally dour and joyless people—all that is indicated by the word 'spartan' as it is used in English. There was, however, another side. There is no evidence that the Spartans as a whole ever became restless over their way of life although, of course, there are examples enough of Spartans who failed to live up to the ideal standards expected of them. For many the communal spirit and dedication to the state must have been very satisfying. It was also a feature of life in the messes that there was a great deal of banter, which was neither to be resented nor repeated outside the mess. Another Greek adjective for Spartan—*lakonikos*—has also passed into our language in the word 'laconic', used of a dry wit which says much in a few words. This was the style which the Spartans encouraged and for which they were famous.

When a Spartan was asked why it was that Lykourgos had made so few laws he replied, 'Men of few words require few laws.' Another, in reply to someone who was praising the people of Elis for their fairness in the management of the Olympic Games, answered, 'Yes, they deserve a lot of praise if they can do justice one day in five years.' The retort of a Spartan to an Athenian who had said that the Spartans had no learning was, 'You are right. We alone of all the Greeks have learned none of your bad qualities.'

It can be seen from such remarks that the Spartans were both intensely patriotic and sure of their superiority over others. They had chosen to remain a select minority dominating a majority of inferiors in the form of the helots and the *perioikoi*. The helots did all the everyday work, so that the Spartans could be free to become exceptional soldiers. Curiously, in order to preserve their privileged position, they adopted a system of living in which their individual freedom was very slight.

Nevertheless, there were many people from other parts of Greece who greatly admired Sparta. Among these was the philosopher Plato, and when in the course of his philosophical enquiries he constructed an imaginary 'ideal state', it had many points of similarity to Sparta. Most of the admirers were people whose political views were in favour of aristocracy. Living very often in city-states which had reached democracy by a series of upheavals, they looked enviously at Sparta with her order and discipline. Sparta had avoided the total democracy of many other states by compromising at an early stage and adopting a constitution which had some of the features of monarchy, some of aristocracy (the *gerousia*), some of democracy (the *ephoroi* and the *apella*).

Once Sparta had begun to develop her peculiar ways, the climate became unfavourable for much in the way of artistic achievement, especially in comparison with Athens. This fact was reflected in the very appearance of the city, as Thucydides says in the introduction to his history of the war between Athens and Sparta in the fifth century B.C. (see Chapter 9):

> 'For if the city of the Spartans were to become deserted and only the temples and the foundations of the buildings were left, I think that as time went by there would be few who would believe in Sparta's reputation—and yet it controls two-fifths of the Peloponnese, and is the leader of the rest and of many cities outside it. The fact is that it is not a co-ordinated city and has not got elaborate temples and buildings, but is formed of villages in the old Greek manner and would seem too insignificant. Yet if the same thing were to happen to Athens, one would imagine its power to have been double what it was from the superficial appearance of the city.'
>
> (I, 10)

CHAPTER SIX

Wars with Persia

The Ionian Revolt

In 560 B.C. Croesus, to this day proverbial for his wealth, came to the throne of
Lydia in Asia Minor, with its capital at Sardis. He conquered the Greek cities on the
coast of Asia, but he had a strong respect for the Greeks—he used to consult the
Delphic oracle—and they were able to continue prosperous under the rulers of his
choice.

To the east of Lydia the kingdom of Media, which had previously included Persia,
had been now taken over by the Persians under Cyrus the Great. This is the reason for
the name 'Medes', which the Greeks frequently applied to the Persians. In 546 B.C.
Croesus marched over the river Halys against Cyrus, encouraged by the oracle at
Delphi—'if Croesus crosses the Halys he will destroy a mighty empire.' The mighty
empire soon turned out to be his own; for when he withdrew to Sardis for the winter
Cyrus unexpectedly came after him and, catching him off his guard, took Sardis. So
the Greeks of Asia had a new master. Cyrus then moved on to further conquests,
most notably the capture of Babylon, with its magnificent fortifications built by
Nebuchadnezzar.

Cyrus was wise and tolerant in his reign; his son Cambyses was less impressive,
though he did manage the conquest of Egypt. He in turn was succeeded by Darius, a
distant cousin and an expert administrator. Darius' rule over his subjects, including
the Greeks, was quite reasonable and mild.

Under Darius the Persian Empire, which by now stretched from the Black Sea to
the Persian Gulf and from the Mediterranean to the edge of India, was organized to a
far greater extent than anything previously known. Twenty satrapies or provinces
were created, ruled by satraps; taxation was properly administered, and a fine system
of roads spread all over the empire from the capital at Sousa, an aid both to efficient
government and to trade. The most important, the 'Royal Road', ran for about 2400
kilometres between the capital, Sousa, and Sardis. Herodotus, the fifth century
historian who is the main source of our knowledge of the wars between the Persians
and the Greeks, describes the way in which the official Persian couriers used these
roads:

'There is no faster system in existence than that of these Persian messengers,
which was an invention of the Persians. According to the number of days in a
journey, an equivalent number of men and horses is posted at intervals along the
road, a man and a horse for each day. Neither snow nor rain nor heat nor darkness
can prevent these men from completing their stage in the quickest possible time.
The first, at the end of his stage, passes the dispatch to the second, the second to the

third, and so it is handed on and on in relays down the line. The Persians call this system of courier-horsemen the *angareion*.'

(VIII, 98)

The great war between the Persians and the Greeks began with the revolt against Persia of the Ionian cities in 499 B.C. Perhaps the strongest reason was the Greeks' immensely powerful love of freedom. All their cities in Asia were governed by tyrants who were puppets in the hands of the Persians. Their rule, and the fact that in any case the local satrap could interfere as he wished, was becoming steadily more annoying. The irritation was increased by the existence by this stage of democracies in many of the cities in the rest of the Greek world. However well the Persians might rule, the Greeks just did not want to be ruled by foreigners.

The unrest came to a head as the result of the actions of Aristagoras, the self-seeking tyrant of Miletos. He persuaded the Persians to send an expedition to restore the aristocratic government on the island of Naxos, promising that it would be well worth their while in terms of increased wealth and empire. The expedition failed, and Aristagoras, embarrassed by his promises, saw that his own power in Miletos, dependent on the Persians, was now in danger.

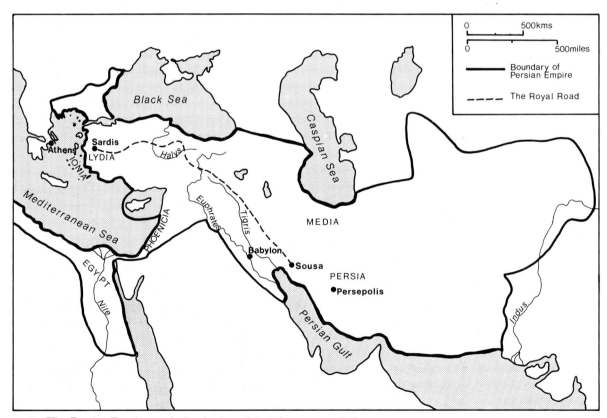

6.1 The Persian Empire, at the beginning of the fifth century B.C.

His best hope lay in an Ionian revolt, and he was encouraged in this by a message from his father-in-law, Histiaios, formerly tyrant of Miletos and now held by the Persians at Sousa as a possible danger to them. The message was written on the shaved head of a slave, who was sent off to Miletos when his hair had grown again.

Aristagoras stirred up the revolt, resigning from his position as tyrant to gain popular support. For help he set off to Sparta. According to Herodotus:

'Aristagoras, the tyrant of Miletos, arrived at Sparta when Kleomenes was still in power. The Spartans say that he went into conference with him taking a bronze tablet on which was engraved a map of the whole world and all the sea and all the rivers.'

(V, 49)

Aristagoras appealed to the Spartans as the leaders of the Greeks to rescue the Ionian Greeks from slavery. The Persians, he said, went into battle wearing turbans and trousers, so the Greeks would easily be able to beat people like that, and the enormous wealth of Persia would be theirs for the taking. He made, however, a crucial error:

'Aristagoras, who had otherwise been shrewd and managed Kleomenes well, now slipped up. For when he shouldn't have told the truth, if he wanted to get the Spartans to Asia, he told him that the march inland took three months. Kleomenes interrupted the rest of what Aristagoras was on the point of saying about the journey, and said: "Stranger from Miletos, be out of Sparta by sunset. You are suggesting something of no interest to the Spartans when you want to take them on a march of three months from the sea."'

(V, 50)

Aristagoras did not give up yet, trying to tempt Kleomenes with increasing sums of money, until Kleomenes' small daughter, the only witness of the interview, exclaimed, 'Father, the stranger will corrupt you if you don't get away from him.' Aristagoras left empty-handed.

6.2 A Persian carving of King Darius holding an audience.

6.3 Persian soldiers on glazed bricks from the palace of Darius at Sousa.

6.4 Trumpeters from the Greek and Persian armies.

The Athenians were more sympathetic. Traditionally the original migration to Ionia (see Chapter 3) had started out from Athens; in addition there was the fact that the Persians had recently supported an attempt to restore Hippias as tyrant in their city. Athens now, in 498 B.C., sent twenty ships, and Eretria, in Euboia, sent five. 'These ships,' said Herodotus, 'were the beginning of trouble, both for the Greeks and the Persians.' (V, 97)

Ionians and allies marched inland from Ephesos and captured Sardis, which was accidentally set on fire. Under increasing Persian pressure the Greeks withdrew, but were caught and badly beaten at Ephesos. This was the signal for the allies to depart in disillusion. The revolt continued, but the might of the Persians made it hopeless. A sea-battle and the capture and sack of Miletos in 494 B.C. brought the uprising to an end. After some early reprisals the Persians were extremely sensible. Tyrannies were abolished and democracies allowed. Measures were taken to ensure fairer taxation and less friction amongst the Ionian cities.

Yet Darius did not forgive the Athenians. He vowed to punish them and is said to have ordered a slave, whenever his dinner was ready, to say three times 'Master, remember the Athenians.'

The First Expeditions

In Athens, meanwhile, the anti-Persian party was gradually becoming stronger than those who favoured reconciliation with the Persians. Herodotus says:

'The Athenians made it apparent that they were very upset at the capture of Miletos in many ways, especially when Phrynichos wrote and put on a play called *The Capture of Miletos*; the whole theatre burst into tears, and they fined him a thousand drachmas for reminding them of their misfortunes. They decreed that nobody ever again should produce the play.'

(VI, 21)

Athens was particularly fortunate at this time in two men, dedicated enemies of Persia. Themistokles was a democrat and a shrewd political leader. (He at this period initiated the construction of a fortified naval base at the Piraeus, which has remained the harbour of Athens to this day.) The other was Miltiades, a refugee from the Persians after the Ionian Revolt. He, despite having been a tyrant in the Gallipoli peninsula, managed to gain the confidence of the Athenians and was elected one of the generals.

The first Persian expedition to punish Athens and Eretria in 492 B.C. was a dismal failure. Under Mardonios, Darius' son-in-law, the army was to move round the edge of the Aegean, with a large fleet sailing in contact with them along the coast. Off Mount Athos the fleet was wrecked in a storm—three hundred ships and twenty thousand men were lost according to Herodotus—and the venture was abandoned.

In 490 B.C. they came again. The leaders were Datis and Artaphernes. This time they sailed straight across the Aegean, taking Naxos and other islands on the way. Eretria was betrayed after a week's siege, and the Persians, full of confidence, sailed on to land at the bay of Marathon, about forty kilometres north-east of Athens.

Persuaded by Miltiades, the Athenians came out to Marathon rather than remain in their city, and with their allies from Plataia camped at the southern end

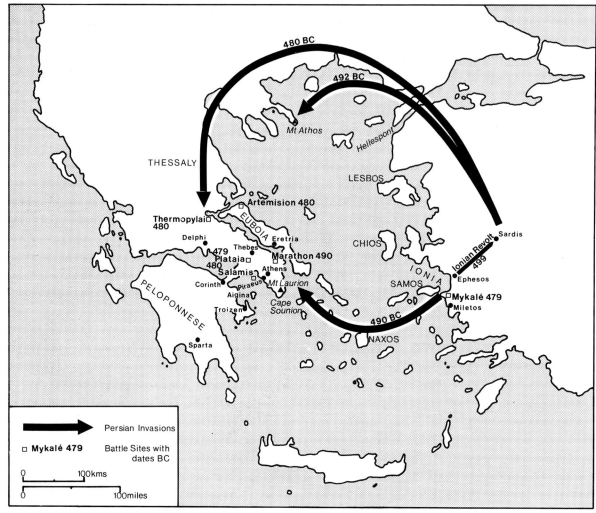

6.5 The Persian invasions.

of the plain. A professional runner called Pheidippides was sent to Sparta to seek help. According to the story he ran 240 kilometres in two days, coming back with the news that, though Sparta was eager to help, troops were unable to come for religious reasons until after the full moon.

For a few days nothing happened: then Miltiades persuaded Kallimachos, the chief Athenian general, to attack. Knowing that the Persians always placed their best troops in the centre, Miltiades strengthened the Athenian wings. Although heavily outnumbered and without any force of cavalry or archers, the Athenians attacked at full pelt, as Herodotus says:

> 'They were the first Greeks of whom we know to charge the foe at speed and the first to stand up to the sight of the Persian dress and the men in it: hitherto even the name of the Medes was enough to make Greeks afraid.'

(VI, 112)

In a long battle the Athenian tactics paid off. Although the Persians broke through in the centre, they were beaten on the wings; the Athenians and Plataians moved towards the centre and trapped those of the enemy who had broken through. They drove them back to their ships, of which they captured seven. The rest sailed off to the south round Cape Sounion, hoping to find the city unprotected. Rumour had it that they went in response to a secret signal, the flashing of a shield in the sunlight. Responsibility for such a signal has never been established. However, the Athenians rushed back from Marathon to Athens and reached it by evening. The Persians gave up at this point and returned to Asia, for the time being.

Next day two thousand Spartans arrived, in time only to visit the site of the battle and to congratulate the victors. A funeral mound, still to be seen, was erected at the battle-ground for the Athenian dead—192 according to Herodotus—and their epitaph was written by Simonides:

> 'Fighting for all the Greeks, the Athenians battled at Marathon and destroyed the power of the gold-armoured Medes.'

Recently another burial place has been identified, that of the gallant Plataians.

Persian losses were heavy, though the figure of 6400 given by Herodotus may be exaggerated. It was a famous victory, and the Persians were not to return for ten years. Meanwhile Athens was safe, and her morale at a peak; the other Greeks had been shown that it was possible and worthwhile to resist the Persians.

Greece in Peril

The next decade was a time of great political activity in Athens as Themistokles—Miltiades had died soon after Marathon—increased his power at the expense of his conservative opponents, aided probably by the process of ostracism (see p. 48).

A most important aspect of Themistokles' policies was his insistence that Athens develop her navy, partly to prepare against another Persian invasion—a policy unpopular with the rich, on whom fell most heavily the burden of paying for it. His greatest success was to persuade the people, when a large new vein of silver was found in the mines at Laurion in Attica, to spend it on building new warships rather than distributing it amongst themselves.

Large-scale preparations were taking place on the Persian side, where Darius had been succeeded in 486 B.C. by his son Xerxes. Cables were ordered which were to hold together two pontoon bridges across the Hellespont. A canal was dug through the peninsula north of Mount Athos to avoid a repetition of the shipwrecks of 492 B.C. Food depots were placed along the intended route of the gigantic army.

In 481 B.C. a congress was held, at the Isthmus of Corinth, of all states prepared to resist the Persians under the lead of Sparta and Athens. By no means all the states were in this alliance; some were indifferent, others were actively pro-Persian. But it was the first time that the Greeks formed any sort of national league. The cause was not helped by the attitude of the Delphic oracle, which clearly thought that resistance was useless and said so.

Xerxes set off from Sardis in the May of 480 B.C., his army so large that it took a week to cross the pontoon bridge at the Hellespont. Once again things had not gone smoothly, as Herodotus records:

'When the strait was bridged, a great storm blew up which smashed and destroyed everything. Learning this, Xerxes was extremely angry, giving orders for three hundred lashes to be given to the Hellespont and iron fetters to be thrown into the sea. I have heard before now that he sent men to brand it at the same time.'

(VII, 34)

Those responsible for building the bridge had their heads cut off. The bridge was then rebuilt. It was a causeway constructed over a great number of ships lashed to each other sideways on.

The Persian numbers quoted by the Greeks are impossibly high—even three million is mentioned. A figure nearer 180 000 is likely to be a more accurate estimate. There were contingents from all over the empire, including Indians, Ethiopians and Arab camel-riders. The fleet, mainly supplied and manned by subject-peoples, Egyptians, Phoenicians, Karians and Ionian Greeks, was said to consist of 1207 ships. Although we need not take literally the claim that 'they drank whole rivers dry', the problems of supplying food and water to such a force must have been enormous.

6.6 The memorial at Thermopylai to the Spartans who died there in 489 B.C.

Thermopylai and Artemision

The first clash took place simultaneously by land and by sea. The Greek plan was to attack the Persian fleet off Cape Artemision at the north of Euboia and at the same time to fight more defensively on land, to protect the coast off which the fleet was to fight. The site chosen was the narrow pass of Thermopylai.

The force of perhaps seven thousand men whose task it was to hold the pass were mainly Peloponnesians, commanded by the Spartan king Leonidas, who had with him three hundred Spartiates. These forces were intended as advance parties, for the Spartans and others were again detained by religious festivals. The main forces, however, did not manage to arrive before the battle.

At sea the Persians were again hampered by storm damage, but by the end of the third day of fighting the Greek fleet was exhausted and forced to head south. At the same time an equally bitter struggle was in progress at Thermopylai. On the first and second days the Greeks, fighting in relays, held off the enemy attacks with relative ease. On the night before the third day a Persian force was led round by a local Greek, Ephialtes, along a mountain track to the far end of the pass. Leonidas saw that the situation was lost and ordered the majority of his troops to depart while he, with his Spartans and the Boiotians, kept up the rearguard. The small force put up a furious resistance—Herodotus says that the Persian officers stood behind their men, whipping any who tried to retreat. Leonidas and his Spartans fell to a man, impressive examples of the Spartan ideals, as their epitaph suggests:

'Passer-by, tell them in Sparta that here in obedience to their laws we lie.'

An anecdote in Herodotus typifies their attitude:

'. . . A Spartan Dienekes is said to have been the bravest. They say that before they joined battle with the Medes, on learning from a man of Trachis that when the Persians fired their bows they hid the sun with their arrows—so many were there—he replied, totally unperturbed, despising the numbers of the Medes, that the stranger from Trachis was giving them excellent news, for if the Medes hid the sun the battle would be fought in the shade rather than in the heat.'

(VII, 226)

Salamis

The Persians were now in control of Greece as far as the Isthmus of Corinth where a defensive wall was built. Many cities, and the Delphic oracle, quickly sided with the Persians. Athens was evacuated except for a few who held out behind the wooden defences of the Acropolis. They did so believing that this was the meaning of the Delphic oracle, which said that a wooden wall was the only hope for Athens. The Persians soon showed this interpretation to be wrong by setting fire to the defences with flaming arrows and slaughtering the defenders. Of the rest of the Athenians, those incapable of fighting went to Salamis, Aigina and Troizen, while all able-bodied men were put on board the ships. These, Themistokles insisted, were the wooden walls of the oracle.

The Greek fleet was assembled in the straits of Salamis (see fig 6.7). To retreat further meant abandoning completely places like Aigina and Salamis, yet

Themistokles found it difficult to persuade the Peloponnesians to hold what was for them a forward position.

He solved the problem by secretly sending a slave to the Persian fleet, pretending that he was on their side. The Greeks, he said, were quarrelling amongst themselves and were on the verge of bolting; a fine victory would be lost unless the Persians attacked immediately. Xerxes, in any case, without this deceitful encouragement, was keen to fight a decisive battle. So he moved his fleet forward and the battle took place in the narrow gulf. The Greeks, although outnumbered, destroyed two hundred enemy ships while losing only forty of their own. Xerxes watched the battle seated on a throne on a hill overlooking the strait, and the whole Persian land army was watching from the shore. The battle is vividly described by Aeschylus in his play *The Persians*. He had fought at Marathon and may have been an eyewitness here. A messenger is reporting to the Persian queen-mother:

'The night passed, and nowhere did the Greeks attempt secret flight; but when the bright horses of the sun covered the earth with dazzling light, first there came from the Greeks the sound of cheerful singing, and the island rocks loudly echoed it. Fear struck all the Persians who had been disappointed in their hopes. For the

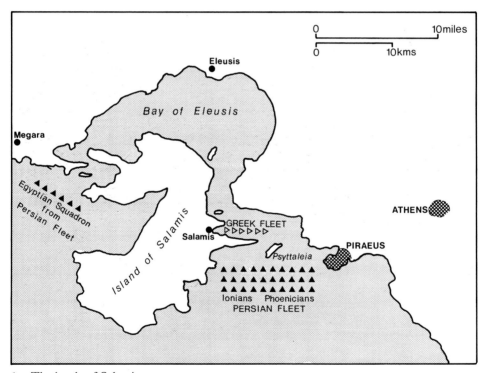

6.7 The battle of Salamis.

Greeks were not singing their hymn like men running away, but like men confidently going into battle. The noise of the war-trumpet on their side inflamed them all. Immediately they dipped their splashing oars in unison and struck the sea at the word of command. Swiftly they came into full view. The right wing took the lead in orderly formation and behind them the body of the fleet advanced. It was possible too to hear shouting: "Sons of the Greeks, forward! Liberate your country, liberate your children, your wives and the temples of your gods, and the graves of your ancestors. The fight is for everything."'

(384ff.)

Later on:

'The sea was full of wreckage and blood. The beaches and the low rocks were covered in corpses. Every ship rowed in a disorderly rout, every one of the Persian fleet. The Greeks struck and chopped with fragments of oars and bits of wreckage as though the Persians were tunny or a shoal of some other fish. Wailing and shrieking covered the sea until dark night put an end to it. I could not finish telling you of the terrible happenings even if I were to relate them for ten days. Of one thing you can be sure, never in one day did such a multitude of men die.'

(420ff.)

6.8 A Greek portrayal of an oriental archer, like those who fought in the Persian army.

6.9 From an Athenian vase, made at the time of the Persian wars, showing a warrior about to depart for battle.

69

Victory Completed

Xerxes ordered his fleet to withdraw to the Hellespont. He himself went home, leaving the land army under the command of Mardonios, who spent the winter in Thessaly. Greece was still far from safe. Mardonios worked hard by diplomacy and had some success in winning allies, but not in the case of Athens, which rejected his attractive promises. In the spring Mardonios re-occupied Attica and Athens, causing as much damage as possible. Sparta and the rest of the Peloponnesians were reluctant to risk themselves beyond the Isthmus of Corinth, but eventually they came north under the command of Pausanias.

The last battle on Greek soil was fought near the small town of Plataia in Boiotia. Pausanias was forced to withdraw from his original position and he was not helped by the poor discipline in his allied forces. Yet, owing mainly to the bravery of the Spartans, the enemy attacks on the withdrawal were not only held off, but the tables were turned. In the rout Mardonios and large numbers of Persians were killed and their camp captured. Thebes, the chief Greek ally of the Persians, was soon taken, and the leading pro-Persians were put to death. It took a long time for the Thebans to be forgiven for 'Medizing', as helping the Persians was called.

A great wealth of plunder was left for the Greeks in the captured camp. After dedications had been made in various temples, the rest was divided among the troops, with Pausanias getting ten of everything—'women, horses, precious metals, camels and everything else'. He was astonished at the luxury of Mardonios' tent, the gold, the silver, the tapestries, the coverlets. He ordered the captive cooks to prepare a meal as they would for Mardonios, and his own servants to get ready a typical Spartan meal:

> 'The food was made ready, and the difference was astonishing. Laughingly he sent for the Greek generals, and on their arrival pointed out the two meals, saying: "Men of Greece, I called you here because I wanted to show you the stupidity of the Persian, who when he had this way of life came to rob us who are so poor."'
>
> (Herodotus IX, 82)

The last action of the war was at Cape Mykalé in Ionia, where the Greeks attacked what remained of the Persian fleet, routed at Salamis and now beached at Mykalé. The Greeks landed and set fire to the entire fleet. Tradition claimed that this happened on the very same day as the battle at Plataia, but this seems improbable. The Mykalé engagement was the signal for many of the Ionian cities to rise against the Persians.

The Greeks had completed a victory of which they and their descendants were justly proud. Nevertheless, although they had driven the Persians out of Greece, Persia remained a powerful nation and a force to be reckoned with by the Greeks for a long time yet.

CHAPTER SEVEN

Religion

After the defeat of the Persians at Salamis, Themistokles, the Athenian admiral, is said to have used his position to extort money from various Greek states who had gone over to Persia.

'The Andrians,' says Herodotus, 'were the first of the islanders to refuse Themistokles' demand for money; he had put it to them that they would be unable to avoid paying because the Athenians had the support of two powerful deities, one called *If-you-please* and the other *Oh-but-you-must*. And the Andrians had replied that Athens was lucky to have two such useful gods, who were obviously responsible for her wealth and greatness; unfortunately, however, they themselves, in their small and inadequate island, also had two deities in permanent possession of their soil—and by no means such useful ones. For their names were *Haven't-a-penny* and *Sorry-I-can't*. Consequently no money would be forthcoming; for, however strong Athens was, she could never turn Andros' "can't" into "can".'

(VIII, 3)

This lighthearted anecdote shows one side of the Greek attitude to religious matters. Another sort of mockery is seen in *The Frogs*, a play by Aristophanes, in which the god Dionysos is shown as a coward, a glutton and a lecher (see Chapter 12). And this play was not only produced at the Great Dionysia in Athens, a festival held in honour of that very deity, but won the first prize. So, clearly, most Athenians did not regard this mockery as blasphemous.

But there was another side to Greek religion. They knew that gods abounded everywhere: these powers could be friendly, but they could equally well be indifferent or positively hostile. You had to be careful: to avoid arousing a god's opposition was as important as winning his support. This helps to explain why religion played such a large part in Greek life. Prayers, sacrifices, omens, oracles, festivals, buildings, all were reminders of the gods. This religion was more concerned with ritual than morals. What was important was to make the right sacrifices to the right god at the right place with the right words. If you did, you could, as Plato complained, be wicked and get away with it. Of course good behaviour was desirable; but it was more for the sake of your family, friends and fellow-citizens than for the gods.

Greek children grew up in houses which had a little statue of Hermes outside, and in the courtyard there was probably some sort of altar to Zeus Ktesias, Zeus in his role as defender of family property. Prayers and libations were very frequent, either to get success for a particular event, a journey, a business deal, even a bet, or for the god's favour in general. The poet Hesiod, talking about the farmer's day, advises him to

'appease the immortal gods with offerings and sacrifices, when you go to bed and when the holy light returns. So they may have kindly feelings towards you, and you may buy other people's land, not have someone else buy yours.'

(338–41)

The great events of family life, birth, coming of age, marriage, death, were all marked by appropriate religious rituals. If they lived in the country, children would know that their parents were careful to sacrifice and pray to Demeter for good crops, to Pan for healthy flocks, to the Nymphs for sufficient water. Town children would see their fathers honouring Hephaistos (smiths), or Prometheus (potters) or other gods associated with crafts and industry.

The reason for these sacrifices is clear from Hesiod's words above: you give to the gods so that they may give to you. An inscription found on the Acropolis in Athens reinforces this *quid pro quo* relationship between man and god: 'Telesinos dedicates this statue to you; rejoice in it, and grant him to dedicate another', a polite hint that Athena's help will be appreciated and that this appreciation will be shown in material form!

7.1 The woman is pouring a libation from a jug (*oinochoé*) onto an altar in the shape of an Ionic capital (see page 120). The other figure may represent the god, perhaps Zeus, being honoured.

Festivals

Outside the immediate family, there were festivals. At least sixty took place in the official Athenian year, and this figure ignores a large number of local ones. It is easy to think of festivals as being crowded, grand affairs like the Olympic Games at Elis in the Peloponnese or the Great Panathenaia in Athens. But there were many smaller ones, for members of the same clan or *deme* (parish). These were religious functions, to make sure the gods were on your side. But they were also social occasions, holidays very welcome in a calendar that did not have weekends.

The sacrifices held at these festivals were carefully conducted: priest and victims, usually sheep and cattle, wore garlands, the altar and the audience were purified with holy water, silence was ordered. In this silence prayers were made, according to a set formula. It was important that this should be done correctly: incorrect prayers would be neither acceptable nor effective. Then, after sacred grain had been sprinkled round the victim, some hair was cut off its head and thrown in the fire. It was then stunned with a club, and its throat cut. The blood was caught in a bowl and, later, poured on the altar. The thigh-bones and fat were burnt as an offering to the god, the entrails were inspected for omens, and the meat eaten. Meat was very rare in the normal diet (see p. 143); and so sacrifices were enjoyed not only by the god but by his worshippers, too.

The great festivals also, which brought together people from all over the Greek world, were in honour of and under the patronage of the gods. Athletics, chariot-races, musical competitions, the production of plays, processions, all provided interest, colour and excitement. But the religious character of the festival was very clear: the Pythian games at Delphi were in honour of Apollo; Zeus was the patron of the Olympic Games; and the dramatic festivals at Athens were sacred to Dionysos.

Religion was obviously a great part of the inspiration behind art and architecture, too. By far the most common public building, and usually the most impressive, in Greek cities was the temple. Most Greek sculpture of the fifth century B.C. was religious: Pheidias' statue of Zeus at Olympia and the Parthenon sculptures (see Chapter 11) are outstanding examples of this. On a more domestic level, much of the decoration on Greek vases is based on the mythology of the gods: one of the earliest vases in the British Museum shows the wedding of Peleus and Thetis, the parents of Achilles, and all the gods who came to that feast.

Gods

So gods were inescapable. And this was at least partly because there were so many of them. There were, first, the Olympians, those twelve brilliant, strong-willed, quarrelsome gods, who are both like and unlike human beings. They are like them in their violent loves and hates, their feasting, their different characters; they are unlike them, not only because they are immortal and much more powerful, but also because they lack moral principles.

This divine family has a head, Zeus, father of gods and men, who was originally a sky-god and still retains his traditional weapon, the thunderbolt. He has the final decision about what shall happen; but he can be won over by charm, gifts or deception. Hera, his sister and wife, is goddess of marriage and childbirth; and his brother Poseidon is god of the sea. There are two other older deities, sisters of Zeus and Hera, Demeter, the Earth-mother, the giver of fertility and crops; and Hestia, goddess of the hearth. The other Olympians are children of Zeus, but have different mothers: Athena, the goddess of wisdom and skills; Apollo, god of light, music and oracles; Artemis, his full sister, the virgin huntress, goddess of the moon; Hermes, the messenger of the gods; Aphrodité, goddess of beauty and sexual love; Hephaistos, the lame smith, patron of metalwork, the only handicapped figure; and Ares, the god of war.

There are two important gods outside these twelve—Hades, brother of Zeus and Poseidon, god of the Underworld, and Dionysos, who traditionally was a late arrival in Greece, but who became rapidly and widely accepted. He was god of wine and of drama; and his worship was associated with fierce emotion and wild dancing, with the whole irrational and instinctive side of the human personality.

Such were the great powers of Olympos. But the number of other deities was very large, some minor but widely known like Pan, Eros, Hekaté, some very local deities. The Olympians were the gods of a fighting aristocracy, and their magnificence made them splendid gods for the state. But the ordinary Greek was probably more concerned with those rituals that were linked with the natural year, since the majority of Greeks lived, and still do live, directly or indirectly off the land. They therefore

7.2 Poseidon: this life-size bronze statue of the god was made about 460 B.C. and found in the sea off Cape Artemision in 1928. The trident he is about to hurl has not been found.

may well have felt more in need of, and closer to, the traditional deities worshipped in those festivals that marked sowing and harvest: the Thesmophoria in late October to bless the sowing; the Anthesteria in early spring to celebrate its arrival and the hope it brought of harvest (the middle day of the festival, which ended with a drinking competition, was suitably called the Day of Jugs); and the Kronia in July, when masters and slaves feasted together, to give thanks for the harvest. The popularity of the names Demetrios and Dionysios perhaps makes the same point: these two deities were vital for good harvests.

The Mysteries

These gods and their festivals, whether state or local, were public and shared by all Greeks, or at least by all the people in a particular *polis* or clan or village. But many Greeks felt a need for personal and individual involvement in religion and for consolation and hope. They found this in what were called 'The Mysteries'. These were ceremonies, originally fertility rites, by which the participant felt himself renewed and purified, and in which he was offered some sort of immortality. Moreover, in some cases, this promise seems to have depended on leading a good life, so that here, if nowhere else in Greek religion, morality was a necessary part of it.

There were many different Mysteries: the most famous were those celebrated at Eleusis, twenty kilometres west of Athens, held in September in honour of Demeter and her daughter Persephoné. The celebrants purified themselves in the sea, walked in a great procession over Mount Aigaleos to Eleusis, and there fasted and roamed about in the night. They were then admitted to the brilliantly lit Hall of Mysteries in a high state of religious emotion, and saw the Mysteries. What these were is not clear; they were probably some sort of sacred drama, retelling the story of the carrying off of Persephoné by Hades and her return to earth in spring, a symbol of

7.3 Aphrodité and Pan playing five stones; Aphrodité is being advised by a small Eros. The picture is incised on the back of a mirror case; the position of the original handle can be seen at the bottom.

75

7.4 Hermes, Apollo and Artemis: Hermes, as the messenger of the gods, is wearing travelling clothes. He is looking back at Apollo, who is playing the *kithara*. Artemis, whose flesh is painted white to show her sex, holds the bow and has a deer beside her.

7.5 A bronze head of Apollo, slightly over life size, cast about 465 B.C. The eyes were originally inlaid with glass and marble, and the eyelashes projected.

death and resurrection. At any rate, the initiates—and there were elaborate rites of initiation before anyone was allowed to be present at the ritual—felt themselves joined with the processes of the universe and were promised life hereafter. The promise is vague:

> 'Blessed is he, whoever of men upon earth has seen these things; but whoever is uninitiated in these rites, he has always a different fate down in the murky darkness when he is dead.'

But it was enough to make Eleusis one of the greatest centres of Greek religion.

Omens

The mysteries were, then, a rather private, individual way of getting in close touch with the gods. But, in general, the most common way of discovering the will of the gods was through omens and oracles. The fact that the Greek word for omen is derived from the word for bird shows how important birds were in this respect. Plutarch, a later Greek writer, says,

> 'One large, well-known and ancient part of prophecy is bird-lore. For their sharp perception and quickness in reacting to whatever they see means that the god can use them as his agents. He directs their movements, their cries and their twitterings—which, like winds, can sometimes be contrary, sometimes favourable—to check or to encourage men's activities and initiatives. That is why Euripides (the playwright) calls birds in general "the messengers of the gods".'
>
> (*On the Intelligence of Animals* xxii)

Two other highly-regarded sources for omens were the entrails of sacrificial animals, and dreams. Xerxes, for example, decided to attack Greece, so the story in Herodotus runs, because he had a dream twice repeated; and his decision was reinforced when the only opponent of the scheme was persuaded to sleep in the king's bed—and had the same dream with the same threats of disaster if the vision was not obeyed! And 'it was after he had inspected the sacrificial victims' that, later in the same war, Megistias, the prophet with Leonidas at Thermopylai, 'announced to the Greeks their coming doom'. Leonidas wanted to send him away with the allies; but he refused and perished at his post.

But any slightly odd happening could be taken as an omen: a sneeze, a word taken out of context, thunder, an eclipse. What was needed was correct interpretation of the omen. Some things were obvious—omens on the right were lucky, those on the left bad—and anybody could interpret them. But some were harder; and so there were prophets or seers who built up a reputation for skill in explaining omens. Kalchas in the *Iliad* was such a man—'past, present, and future held no secrets for him; it was his second sight, a gift he owed to Apollo, that had guided the Achaian fleet to Troy'. So was Teiresias, the prophet of Thebes in Sophocles' play *Oedipus the King*, 'who stands nearest to the lord Phoibos Apollo in divination'. In historical times, Lampon, a friend of Pericles who helped found the colony of Thurioi in southern Italy, had a great reputation as a seer. Plutarch has a story about him which is an interesting example of the confrontation between religion and philosophy:

'The head of a one-horned ram was once sent to Pericles from his estate in the country. When Lampon, the prophet, saw that the horn had grown strong and solid from the middle of the forehead, he said that victory in the rivalry between the two parties in the state, led by Thucydides (not the historian) and Pericles, would go to the man to whom this sign had been given. Anaxagoras, however, had the skull dissected and showed that the brain had not filled its proper cavity but had been displaced in a pointed, egg-shaped formation to that place in the cranium from where the horn grew. At the time Anaxagoras won the admiration of the people there. But a little later it was Lampon's turn to be admired when Thucydides was ostracized and the entire control of state affairs passed to Pericles.'

Plutarch's own comment is perceptive:

'However, there was nothing, in my opinion, to prevent both scientist and prophet being right, the first correctly explaining the cause of the omen, the second its meaning. For it was the job of the first to observe why it came to be and how it developed into what it was; whereas the second was concerned to declare what its purpose was and what it signified. There are people who say that to discover the cause of a happening robs it of any significance. But they do not realize that this argument does away not only with divine portents but with all artificial symbols like the noise of gongs, the light of fire-beacons and the shadow on sundials. Each of these has been deliberately used to convey some meaning. But this is perhaps a subject for another essay'!

(*Pericles* vi)

Oracles

Finally, you could inquire directly of the gods through their oracles. There were, indeed, collections of past oracles. Before his dream mentioned above, Xerxes had been put under pressure by people who employed a collector of oracles

'to recount selected oracles; if any suggested failure for the Persians, he made no mention of them. Instead, he picked out the most favourable and told them to the king; he foretold the expedition and said that it was fated that the Hellespont would be bridged by a Persian.'

(*Herodotus* VII, 6)

But these collections might clearly be suspect. Indeed, the man mentioned here had previously been expelled from Athens for forging oracles! So, if you could afford the time and money, you went to ask for yourself. You went to Dodona in north-west Greece, where the leaves of Zeus' oaks gave his oracles; or to the cave of Trophonios in Boiotia, where, after a terrifying crawl into a black, subterranean hole, you heard or saw the future; or, of course, to Delphi.

Delphi was, and is, one of the most striking places in the world. It is not surprising that among its mountains people felt the gods particularly near. The shrine of Apollo there, together with the Games in the stadium and theatre higher up the mountain, became a focus for the whole of the Greek world. Many *poleis* showed their respect

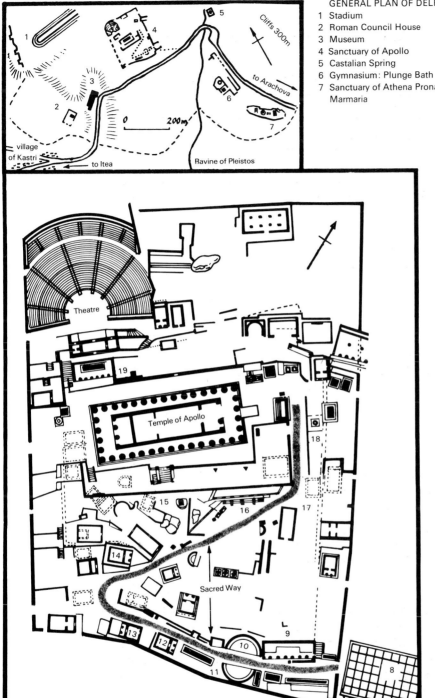

GENERAL PLAN OF DELPHI
1 Stadium
2 Roman Council House
3 Museum
4 Sanctuary of Apollo
5 Castalian Spring
6 Gymnasium: Plunge Bath
7 Sanctuary of Athena Pronaia—The Marmaria

SANCTUARY OF APOLLO
8 Roman Agora
9 Spartan Monument
10 Monument of the Kings of Argos
11 Monument of Argos
12 Sicyonian Treasury
13 Siphnian Treasury
14 Treasury of the Athenians
15 Base of column of the Naxian Sphinx
16 Athenian Portico
17 Ionic Capital
18 Base of Tripod of Plataia
19 Position where the Charioteer was found

7.6 Plans of Delphi.

79

for the god—and their wish for his support—by building treasuries in which their gifts accumulated. Its reputation grew so much that foreigners, too, asked the oracle's advice, as we have seen (Chapter 6) in the story of king Croesus of Lydia.

The ambiguity of the oracle's replies might seem to throw doubt on its value. But it is quite clear that, despite apparent mistakes—as when Delphi advised surrender to the Persians—it had enormous influence. Enquiries ranged from large matters of state—where should the Athenians found a new colony in Italy in 443 B.C.? should Sparta attack Athens in 431 B.C.?—to individual affairs. Chaerephon asked whether anyone was wiser than Socrates ('no'), while Xenophon enquired which god he should sacrifice to in order to ensure success for his expedition (Chapter 17) into Asia with Cyrus (wrong question; it should have been, 'Ought I to go or not?'). To all enquirers the god's answer came, first through the priestess, the Pythia, sitting on the sacred tripod in a frenzied trance, and then interpreted by the priests who were in charge of the shrine. Moreover, whatever you made of this specific answer, his two well-known pieces of general advice remained, carved on the front of the temple: 'Know yourself' and 'Nothing too much'.

Critics

There were doubters, of course. Xenophanes of Kolophon in Ionia complained that 'Homer and Hesiod have attributed to the gods all those actions that are shameful and blameworthy among men, stealing, adultery and deception of each other.' He pointed out that men make gods in their own image—'the Ethiopians say their gods

7.7 The temple of Apollo and the valley at Delphi looking east.

80

are snubnosed and black, while the Thracians think theirs are blue-eyed and red-haired'—and that 'if cattle and horses and lions had hands and could draw and make things like men, horses would draw their gods in the shape of horses, cattle theirs in the shape of cattle.' He himself believed that 'there is one god, not like men in body or thought. He remains perpetually in the same place, utterly unmoved. It is not fitting he should go to different places at different times. Without effort he causes everything to move by the thought of his mind'—a definition of God that would satisfy many Christian theologians. Lucian, a later novelist and writer of science fiction, one of whose books is called *Voyage to the Moon*, laughed at the traditional ideas about the gods in a comic speech he puts into the mouth of Zeus:

'Apollo, too, has taken on a dreadful job. He is practically deafened by people disturbing him with demands for prophecies. One minute he has to be at Delphi, the next he rushes over to Kolophon, goes on from there to Xanthos, then off at full speed to Delos or Branchidai. In fact, wherever the priestess, after drinking from the holy spring and chewing laurel leaves, writhes about on her tripod and calls on him to appear, he must immediately and with no delay present himself and spin out oracles—or disgrace the whole profession!'

7.8 The Pythia: the priestess sits on the sacred tripod, holding the laurel of Delphi.

Euripides doubted whether any god could have ordered a son to kill his mother, as, according to the myth, Apollo did to Orestes.

But these were the doubts of a relatively few writers and poets. They were probably shared by other educated people, who turned to philosophy for an understanding of the universe and man's place in it. But gods and oracles, mysteries and omens went on in ordinary people's belief, were absorbed by the Romans into their religious thought, and continued, despite the official acceptance of Christianity, until after the fall of the Roman Empire.

7.9 The Treasury of the Athenians at Delphi: this was built from the spoils of the battle of Marathon soon after 490 B.C. and re-erected (with four-fifths of the original stones) in 1906.

CHAPTER EIGHT

The Games

If you travel south from Corinth to Argos and then turn westwards, you pass first through the gaunt mountains of the Peloponnese. Then the road begins to drop down, and soon you reach what Pausanias, who wrote a *Guide to Greece* in A.D. 175 called 'the greatest of rivers in its volume of water and the most pleasant to look at'. It is the river Alpheios, and it flows past Olympia. This whole region is green and fertile; it was, and still is, one of the most highly cultivated areas in Greece, and produces one of the best Greek wines. Here, in this delightful valley, from very early days Zeus was worshipped, Zeus Olympios, Zeus who lives on Olympos (see Chapter 7). And so his shrine was called Olympia, and it gradually become the most important in Greece. A festival was instituted in his honour; and part of that festival was athletics.

To us, the Olympic Games are a series of sporting events. But for the first thousand years of their history they were part of what was primarily a religious occasion. This was clear in various ways. Sacred heralds were sent out to all Greece to proclaim the Games. A sacred truce was declared for a month before and after the Games, to ensure that they could proceed without interruption and that people who attended them were unmolested by rival states. The focal point of the whole site was the altar to Zeus; and this was flanked by his temple on one side, by the temple of Hera, his wife, on the other. Even fines on athletes who broke the rules were often paid in the form of statues of Zeus: a whole line of them stood on the north side of the enclosure. And, once the Games started, two and a half out of the five days of the festival were devoted to religious activities.

This combination of religion and athletics may seem odd to us. But it was not strange to the Greeks for at least three reasons. First, funeral games at the burial of heroes were traditional—Homer describes those for Patroklos in the *Iliad* (XXIII). Athletics were therefore linked with the spirits of the dead and the deities of the Underworld, and this was easily extended. Secondly, skill and achievement of any kind were a proper offering to the gods. The gods were thought of as graceful, powerful beings: they would naturally appreciate these qualities in men. Thirdly, the whole of Greek society was marked by competitiveness—part of the reason, perhaps, for its excellence (and for its cruelty?). Since, as we have seen in Chapter 7, religion was associated with most areas of Greek life, it was inevitable that competitiveness, too, should be linked with religion.

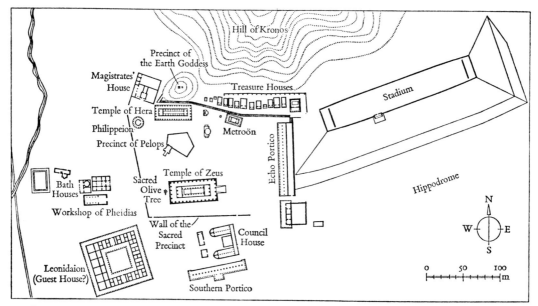

8.1 Plan of Olympia in the fourth century B.C.

8.2 A chariot at full speed, apparently just on the point of winning. The charioteer holds one pair of reins in each hand and a goad in the right. This picture is painted on one of the large jars (*amphorai*) given as prizes in Panathenaic Games. Other examples are figures 8.3, 8.6 and 8.7.

The programme at Olympia was as follows:

Day 1: sacrifices, oaths, checking of athletes
Day 2: morning: equestrian events
     afternoon: the pentathlon
Day 3: morning: religious observances
     afternoon: boys' events
Day 4: morning: 'track' events
     afternoon: wrestling, boxing, *pankration*, race in armour
Day 5: banquet and sacrifices

Events

The first event, the chariot race, was the most spectacular: the four-horse two-wheeled chariots had to cover twelve laps of a straight course 200 metres long, with a 180° turn at each end. There was an elaborate mechanical starting gate, which allowed the outside charioteers, who had the furthest to go to reach the far post, something of a start. Cutting in in front of a rival was forbidden; but collisions and crashes were very frequent. Pindar, the fifth-century lyric poet, tells us about one winner in a similar race at Delphi, the king of Kyrene in North Africa, whose chariot was the sole survivor, and therefore the winner, of forty-one starters!

The horse-race followed immediately. It was over the same course in the hippodrome, and the difficulties of the jockeys, who rode bareback and without stirrups, can be easily imagined. A curious fact about these first two events was that it was the owner who won the prized garland of olive leaves, not the driver or jockey whose skill and courage had brought the victory.

The rest of the events were held in the stadium, where there were seats for the judges and an embankment for the spectators. The ground between was broken up by pickaxes and covered with a deep layer of sand. The pentathlon, the first event there, had five parts—discus, long jump, javelin, 200 metres and wrestling. These events were much the same then as now, with two exceptions: the javelin was hurled with the aid of a thong, which had a rifling effect and probably increased the distance; and the long-jumper held two weights which somehow were used to lengthen the jump or to achieve a clean landing (see fig 8.4). It was almost certainly a standing long jump.

The boys' events, 200 metres, wrestling, boxing, were restricted to competitors aged between twelve and eighteen, although how the judges could be sure of the entrants' ages is not clear. But they were not an unimportant part of the games, to judge at least from the fact that a quarter of Pindar's surviving poems are addressed to boy victors. One of them, to a young Thessalian named Hippokleas, who had won the 400 metres at Delphi, shows that success was sometimes a family tradition: his father, Pindar says, had won one of the foot-races at Delphi, and the race in armour at Olympia twice.

The final day of athletics had the three running races in the morning, probably with heats. They were the 200 metres, a single length of the stadium, the 400 metres, a double length, and a longer race, probably twelve double lengths. The starting line was a marble stone with two long slits in it, although later a sort of starting gate seems

8.3 Two young competitors in the horse-race at full speed.

8.4 Long jump practice.

8.5 A discus-thrower and his trainer on a red-figured *amphora* of about 430 B.C.

to have been used. But there were no lanes, apparently, and so obstruction was not uncommon.

The most popular events came on the last afternoon, the violent body-contact sports, wrestling, boxing and the *pankration*. There were no time-limits, no ring and few rules. There were judges; but there were also deaths—and a law which treated such deaths as accidents and not manslaughter! Wrestling was much like ours today. But boxing was more brutal: not only were there no gloves (indeed, the leather thongs worn round the hand caused more damage than a naked fist would have done—see fig 8.7), but open-handed blows were also allowed. And the *pankration* was, in the words of one modern scholar, a vicious 'combination of wrestling and judo with a bit of boxing thrown in, in which the contestants punched, slapped, kicked, wrestled, much of the time on the ground, and even—although illegally—bit and gouged each other.' Pausanias describes a statue he saw of one pankratist who

'was fighting his last remaining rival for the wild-olive. This opponent, whoever he was, caught Arrachion and held him with his legs in a powerful scissors grip; at the same time he started to throttle him with his hands. Arrachion then broke one of his opponent's toes. Arrachion died from the strangling, but at the same time the strangler gave in because of the pain in his toe. The Eleians (Elis was the *polis* which controlled the games) crowned Arrachion's corpse with the wreath and proclaimed it the winner.'

(VIII, 40)

The final event of all was the race in armour; a surprising end, perhaps, but one that reflects both the emergence of the hoplite as the main defence of the state (see Chapter 4) and the Greek liking for a quiet end to excitement, whether in the theatre or in the stadium.

The prizes for all this effort were what Pindar calls 'the olive's pale-skinned ornament', simple garlands of olive leaves. The prestige, however, for the winners was enormous, and more rewards awaited them at home: they were often given money prizes or pensions, or at least free meals in the town-hall, for the rest of their lives. Yet it was for the winners only: there were no silver or bronze medals. Winning was the only worthwhile thing, and defeat was bitter. Another of Pindar's victory odes, for a young wrestler from Aigina, shows this very clearly:

'And now four times you came down with bodies beneath you,
(You meant them harm),
To whom the Pythian feast has given
No glad home-coming like yours.
They, when they meet their mothers,
Have no sweet laughter around them, moving delight.
In back streets out of their enemies' way
They cower; disaster has bitten them.'

(*Pythian* VIII, 5)

The Non-athletic Side

The traveller to the festival, however, as he came down to Olympia, would see very much more than just athletes. Spectators came in their thousands; and with them all

8.6 The foot-race: the artist has shown considerable skill in the positioning of the figures and in making slight variations of detail.

8.7 Two boxers fight, and a third looks on, while tying the thong on his left hand. The goddess Niké (Victory) on the right is acting as judge.

8.8 The *pankration*: the fighter on the left is about to strike his opponent, while the man on the right is trying to gouge out his opponent's eye. The trainer rushes forward to prevent the foul.

the sorts of people who have attended fairs in every age and country: drink-sellers, showmen, pastry-cooks, gamblers, pedlars, thieves, singers, prostitutes, travelling actors. One later account says that

'Many miserable "professors" could be heard shouting and reviling each other round the temple, while their so-called pupils fought with one other. Writers were reading their rubbish aloud. Many poets were reciting their verses to the applause of others, many conjurers were showing off their tricks, fortune-tellers theirs. There were countless advocates perverting the law, and not a few pedlars hawking everything and anything.'

Women were there, although they were not allowed into the central area. They competed in their own, rather minor, games, held in honour of Hera. But they were not permitted even to watch the main games. One lady who did so in disguise to watch her son box gave herself away when she leapt over the fence in her excitement; but 'the judges,' says Pausanias, 'let her off out of respect for her father and her brothers and her son, all of whom were Olympic victors'! (V, 6, 7) 'But,' he goes on, 'they made a law for the future that trainers, too, should enter the arena naked' as, of course, did all the athletes.

What was remarkably absent at Olympia was anything like the facilities provided nowadays at Olympic Games. A hostel and a gymnasium were built fairly late in the history of the games, and there were two small bath-houses. But for competitors and spectators alike life was open-air and uncomfortable. As one writer put it:

'Unpleasant and difficult things happen in life. Don't they happen at Olympia? Aren't you burnt by the sun? Aren't you crowded and tight-packed? Aren't washing facilities bad? Aren't you soaked to the skin whenever it rains? Don't you get more than enough noise and shouting and other unpleasantnesses? Still, I expect you tolerate all this because you offset it against the marvellous spectacle.'
(Epiktetos, *Discourses* I, VI, 26)

Pausanias even speaks of the Eleians sacrificing to Zeus Apomyios (Averter of Flies), to protect Olympia!

What was also to be seen was great religious architecture and art. The temples of Zeus and Hera have been mentioned already. And in the fifth century B.C. the Eleians commissioned Pheidias, the famous Athenian sculptor, to make a huge statue of Zeus, covered with ivory and gold. So important was this work that Pheidias had his own permanent workshop at Olympia; and the statue of Zeus soon became one of the seven wonders of the world.

The Games, then, were primarily religious and athletic occasions. But politics were not absent. Official delegations from many Greek *poleis* were sent to Olympia. They brought gifts for Zeus, but doubtless took advantage of the huge gathering to pursue diplomacy. Treaties and other public documents were often set up at Olympia, a practice that gave them publicity as well as divine protection. The treasure-houses, built by various states, and the statues, donated by individuals, had the same double purpose. And it is quite clear that success at Olympia was used by individuals to further their political ambitions. Alkibiades, a young Athenian aristocrat, argued that

'the Greeks regarded our city as having even greater power than it in fact did have because of my success at the Olympic games, although earlier they thought they had exhausted us completely in the war. I entered seven chariots, more than any private individual had done before, and I gained first, second and fourth places. The rest of my arrangements, too, were in keeping with this victory. Such success rightly earns praise, and as a result of it people think more highly of the city's power, too.'

(Thucydides VI, 16)

So effective was this argument that the Athenians made him joint commander of their enormous, and ill-fated expedition to Sicily (p. 103).

Several tyrants (see Chapter 4) used the Games to win public support for their regimes. Hiero of Syracuse, for example, won three times, but chose carefully to do so in the equestrian events, where he did not have to compete in person. And in the fourth century Philip of Macedonia publicized his intervention in Greek politics by winning in three successive Olympics. It was characteristic of his son, Alexander (the Great), that, when asked to run in the Games, he replied 'only if kings will be my opponents.'

The Olympic Games continued in their original series for over a thousand years, from 776 B.C. until at least A.D. 261. They were held every fourth year, and these Olympiads, as the four year periods were termed, were the only way of identifying years common to all Greeks. Thus 255 B.C. was known as the second year of the 131st Olympiad. The Olympic programme reached its final form by 520 B.C. Thereafter there were one or two short-lived innovations, like the mule-cart race of which only fourteen races were held, and, a little strangely, the addition of competitions for heralds and trumpeters. But generally speaking they continued for nearly eight hundred years unchanged. So did their status. Many other games were established, as we shall see. But none of them equalled the Olympic Games in prestige. This is clear from the records that individual athletes published. These lists, sometimes of great length with hundreds of victories mentioned, gave their successes, but always put Olympic victories first. They also included draws at Olympia and even 'having fought for the wreath', that is, a beaten finalist.

Professionalism

With such prestige at stake, it is not surprising that training became very important. It was, of course, usually the sons of the wealthier citizens who had the time to indulge in these activities and the money to pay the trainers. But most cities were willing to help finance promising athletes, and so the net for potential winners was spread fairly wide.

Trainers played a large part in the development of winners, and Pindar mentions them in several of his victory odes. As athletes became more professional, diet was seen to be important. Pausanias speaks of one man who

> 'was so successful at the long-distance race that he won twice at Olympia, twice at the Pythian Games, three times at the Isthmian Games and five times at Nemea. It is said that he was the first to have a meat-diet. Until then athletes' food had been cheese straight from the basket.'

(VI, 7, 10)

8.9 The stadium at Delphi, at 640 m. above sea-level: the presidents' seats can be seen half way along on the left. The starting- and finishing-line was at the far end. There was room for 7000 spectators.

A Spartan winner of the 200 metres in 668 B.C. is said to have had a special diet of dried figs. Training manuals, too, were produced, even do-it-yourself booklets. And by Roman times, perhaps earlier, a sort of athletes' trade union was set up, which not only worked to secure privileges for its members, such as freedom from taxation and from military service, but also looked after dependants and made block travel arrangements.

These developments were brought about by the great increase in the number of games. The traditional 'Circuit' had consisted of four: the Olympic Games and the Pythian Games (at Delphi) every fourth year, the Isthmian (at Corinth) and the Nemean (near Argos) every other year. These were 'sacred' games, where the prizes were mere wreaths, laurel at Delphi, wild celery at Corinth and Nemea. But gradually more and more 'prize' games were established, where money prizes were given; in the end there were probably more than three hundred of them. There was therefore a great deal of prize money to be won, and distinguished athletes did very well. This explains Pausanias' story about an Alexandrian boxer named Apollonios who blamed head-winds in the Aegean for his late arrival for the compulsory month of training at Olympia before the games. A rival gave his game away: Apollonios had been busy winning cash prizes in games in Ionia and so set sail too late. . . . And one Olympic victor was paid a huge fee merely to appear at a local games festival.

The system was criticized, of course. Xenophanes in the sixth century B.C. tried to discredit athletic prowess:

'If a man is victorious in speed of foot or in the pentathlon, where the precinct of Zeus lies beside the streams of Pisa at Olympia, or in wrestling, or in the painful art of boxing, or in that terrible contest called the *pankration*, he is looked up to with honour by his fellow-citizens, and is given a high seat at festivals and maintenance at public expense and a gift to have as his treasure. He gets all this, too, if he wins with horses. But he is not as deserving as I. For my wisdom is better than the strength of men or horses. . . For even if a good boxer is one of the people or a man good at the pentathlon or at wrestling, the city is no better run because of this nor are her store-houses enriched.'

Aristotle later doubted the value of professional athletics for a proper education:

'The athlete's training neither produces a good condition for the general purposes of civic life, nor does it encourage ordinary health and the procreation of children. . . Some amount of exertion is essential for the best state of body, but it must be neither violent nor specialized, as is the case with the athlete. It should be rather a general exertion, directed to all the activities of a free man.'

(*Politics*, 1335b)

And Galen, the distinguished second-century A.D. doctor, complained bitterly of the 'malpractice' of trainers, whose 'fraudulent art' produced mindless, ugly, distorted men. But these writers were an intellectual minority. Ordinary people liked festivals for their holiday atmosphere, the crowds, the entertainment, the excitement; the popularity of athletics as part of them was assured.

CHAPTER NINE

Imperial Athens

The history of the fifth century B.C. in Greece is dominated by two wars. The first, against the Persians, has been described already in Chapter 6. This enormous and unexpected victory gave the final impetus to Greek self-confidence to create the unparalleled achievements of the following fifty years. But the second war, the Peloponnesian War (431–404 B.C.), in which Athens fought Sparta and in which, as allies to one side or the other, almost the whole of the Greek world was involved, ruined Athens and ended the period of high culture. The huge, exciting promise of the *polis* ran out, and the Greeks became merely another talented people instead of unique and startling innovators.

Athenian Expansion

So the fifth century B.C., with its marvellous but brief flowering, demands attention, and much of the rest of this book is about various aspects of it. This chapter is concerned with its political and military history; and this, after the Persian wars, is largely the account of the growth and the collapse of Athenian power. Her dominance began with the setting up of a league of Greek states to protect the Ionians and, indeed, all Greece against any further Persian attacks. Athens was offered, and willingly accepted, the leadership. Thucydides the historian says that she

> 'decided which states should supply money for the war against Persia and which should provide ships. The purpose of the league was to take revenge for what they had suffered by ravaging the Great King's territory.'
>
> (I, 96)

The league had considerable success: Persian garrisons were evicted from the cities along the north Aegean, piracy was suppressed and, most remarkable of all, in about 468 B.C. the Persian fleet was annihilated on the river Eurymedon in southern Turkey. The leader of the allied expeditions was an Athenian named Kimon. He was the son of Miltiades, the winner of Marathon, and his aristocratic flair and generosity were an immense asset during these years.

Sparta meanwhile had troubles. Two of the states in the Peloponnesian League which she led (see p. 56) turned democratic, Argos led a rebellion against her leadership, and finally, after an earthquake had destroyed much of the city, she was faced with a helot revolt. She asked for help from Athens, which was given reluctantly and only after a passionate appeal from Kimon 'not to allow Greece to go lame, or their own city to be deprived of its yoke-fellow.' But Kimon's support of

9.1 'The Mourning Athena': in a statue of about 460 B.C. Athena leans on her spear, looking at what is thought to be a monument to fallen soldiers.

Sparta proved unwise: the Spartans grew frightened of an Athenian presence in the heart of the Peloponnese and asked them to withdraw. This snub was deeply felt in Athens, and shortly afterwards Kimon was ostracized.

Spartan ingratitude, however, was only one cause of his ostracism. The more important one was a major change in the whole political climate at Athens, which made him and his policies unpopular. Since the reforms of Kleisthenes (Chapter 4), Athens had been democratic. Now the democracy became more radical. The Council of the Areopagos, the traditional aristocratic body, lost its political importance; the ancient and honourable office of *archon* was opened to any Athenian citizen; and, perhaps most significant of all, pay was introduced for a wide range of state duties (Chapter 10).

There was a new foreign policy, too, directed against Sparta: an alliance was made with Argos, Sparta's traditional rival in the Peloponnese, and soon Corinth, Sparta's leading ally, was attacked. Operations were mounted on land and sea, and by 457 B.C. Athens had control of the whole of central Greece. The amazing vigour and

9.2 Part of an inscription on a block of marble which records a treaty, made in 433 B.C., between Athens and Rhegion in southern Italy.

resilience of Athens are shown best, perhaps, by the fact that, concurrently with these campaigns in Greece itself, she also sent a fleet of two hundred triremes to help Egypt break away from the Persian Empire. The cost, however, of this energetic policy is seen in an inscription of 459 B.C.: 'Of the Erechtheid tribe: these men died in the war, in Cyprus, in Egypt, in Phoenicia, in Halieis, in Aigina, in Megara in the same year.' There follows a list of one hundred and seventy-seven names. And this is for only one out of the ten Attic tribes, and for one year only.

Kimon died in 450 B.C. in an attack on Cyprus, still held by Persia, and shortly afterwards peace seems to have been negotiated. Half a century had passed since the Great King had first interfered in the Greek world (Chapter 6); now, by the terms of this peace, Persia was indeed kept out of mainland Greece and the Aegean, but the Greeks in Ionia were left exposed. Still, the peace with Persia gave Athens what she wanted, greater freedom to pursue her ambitions inside Greece. But they were not realized: for, within three years, her land empire in central Greece had collapsed; her leaders had had to bribe the Spartans to abandon an attack on Attica; and some of her island allies were in revolt. And so in 445 B.C. a peace was made with Sparta which restored their original possessions to each side, but did at least recognize Athens' right to her maritime empire.

For this was what the anti-Persian league had become.

'We have done nothing surprising, nothing contrary to human nature, if we accepted leadership when it was offered and are now unwilling to give it up. There are three very strong reasons why we should not do so, honour, fear and self-interest. Nor are we the first people to be in this position: it has always been a law of human society that the weak are controlled by the strong.'

(Thucydides I, 76)

95

Here is the voice of imperial Athens, in the words of her envoys defending her policies before the Peloponnesian League. It can be heard, too, in the treaties which Athens made with various of her subject-allies in these years.

> 'The people of Chalkis are to swear as follows: I shall not revolt from the people of Athens in any way or by any means whatever, either in word or in deed; nor shall I follow anyone who revolts; and if any person causes a revolt, I shall denounce him to the Athenians . . . and I shall be as good and honourable an ally as I am able. . .'

Similar regulations have survived for Samos and other allies: in many cases they impose on the allies constitutions that were miniatures of the Athenian one, with a supreme assembly, people's courts, appointment by lot and other typically democratic features (see Chapter 10). The harsh ruthlessness that lay behind these diplomatic documents is seen, too, in various decrees Athens passed to regulate her control of the empire: a decree to tighten up the collection of the tribute, and another to make Athenian coinage, weights and measures obligatory on all her allies. Her rule was reinforced by the fleet, by garrisons, by the confiscation of land and the establishment on that land of Athenian colonists, whose task it was to ensure Athens' continuing control of the area.

9.3 The Panathenaic Way: along this road went the annual procession in honour of Athena. It ran from the Kerameikos, through the *agora* (here) and up to the Acropolis, seen in the background.

Was all this merely to increase Athenian power and wealth? Her enemies said so; and some of her own citizens were doubtful of the morality of her policy. But her allies gained something: relative peace, freedom from piracy, encouragement of trade, some sort of justice. And the democrats in these *poleis* may well have preferred to be ruled by democratic Athens than by their own aristocrats. Whether this was enough to balance the loss of independence, especially in Greek eyes, is doubtful. Certainly, when war came again, Sparta claimed that her purpose in fighting was to liberate the Greeks from Athenian tyranny.

Athens' energy, that 'busybodiness' that the Spartans complained about, took her everywhere: she founded a colony, Amphipolis, at a strategic junction on the north Aegean coast road; she sent a fleet to the extreme north-east corner of the Black Sea to show the flag—and to keep the vital corn-route open; she made valuable alliances with *poleis* in Sicily and Italy; and there, too, she established Thourioi, a city open to all Greeks (Herodotus joined the emigrants), but intended as an Athenian strong-point in Magna Graecia. Thus her influence extended from Asia to Italy, and all this from a city where there may have been 40 000 citizens and a total population of 300 000—roughly comparable with that of Nottingham. It is little wonder that her enemies were alarmed.

Pericles

These middle years of the fifth century are often regarded as the high summer of Greek culture. Most of this was, of course, centred in Athens, and there the presiding genius was Pericles. Thucydides says of this period that 'in what was nominally a democracy, power was in fact in the hands of the first citizen.' (II, 65) But this is unfair to Pericles: he was no dictator, no tyrant in the Greek sense, not even a prime minister in ours. He was general for fifteen years without a break, it is true. But each year he had to be re-elected; and, even when elected, he had to persuade not only his nine colleagues but also the temperamental and changing assembly (see Chapter 10) every time he wanted his policy endorsed and carried out. So his position was due to his intelligence, his rhetorical skills and, perhaps most impressive to his contemporaries, his incorruptibility.

The Athens of this period saw the carrying out of an enormous building programme (see Chapter 11), which included the Parthenon and the temple of Poseidon at Cape Sounion. Pericles' enemies used this as an opportunity to attack him, as a later historian, Plutarch, tells us:

'"The Greeks," they shouted, "must consider this an unendurable insult, they must regard themselves as subject to open and flagrant tyranny, when they see that we forcibly exact contributions from them for the war against Persia and then use these moneys to gild and beautify the city, like some vain woman, all dolled up with precious stones and statues and temples worth millions of pounds." In reply, Pericles said to the people that they did not have to provide their allies with any account of how the money was spent, provided they continued to fight the war for them and to keep the Persians away.'

(*Pericles*, xii)

It was a tough line to take.

During these years, too, Herodotus published his history in Athens, and Sophocles, the tragedian, wrote his plays. And the new learning and ideas were spread through the teaching of the sophists, the travelling professors (Chapter 15) who were later blamed for most of Athens' ills. Pericles had friends among this intellectual company, Pheidias the sculptor (of the Parthenon and Olympia), Protagoras the sophist, and Anaxagoras the scientist who was exiled for, among other things, saying that the sun was a lump of molten stone, somewhat bigger than the Peloponnese. His mistress, Aspasia, too, was of the same calibre: it is reported that, young, non-Athenian and woman though she was, Socrates, that formidable philosopher, enjoyed arguing with her.

One of Pericles' supporters was Thucydides. He was, it seems, no lover of radical democracy. But he recognised how much that democracy had achieved under Pericles' leadership. And so he decided to write the history of the war which in the end destroyed the Athens he knew and loved. It is surprising, perhaps, that such a small war between tiny states should still reverberate down the centuries. But Athens has given modern Europe half its heritage; and Thucydides' grave and sombre history has become what he intended it should be, 'a possession for ever'. Fighting broke out in 431 B.C. and continued, with short interludes, for twenty-seven years. Virtually the whole of Greece was caught up in it.

Athens at War

The effect of the war was made worse by the frequent civil wars going on at the same time inside many *poleis*. Democrats looking to Athens for support and oligarchs looking to Sparta were at each other's throats; the misery caused was immense. The violence of these internal disputes was matched by that between the two sides: the Athenians, for example, passed a decree, towards the end of the war, it is true, to cut off the right hand of every enemy taken alive. The Spartans captured Plataia, a small city in Boiotia which was allied to Athens, killed all its male inhabitants and sold the women and children into slavery. The Athenians did the same to the island of Melos, which chose to stay with Sparta rather than join the Athenian empire. The war may have been small by modern standards; but it was no less harsh and cruel.

Pericles had foreseen the war and told his compatriots where their best chance lay.

'It was unwise to go out of the city and fight a pitched battle. Instead, they should all come inside the walls and guard them. The fleet, in which their strength lay, was to be thoroughly fitted out. The allies, too, should be kept under firm control, since Athens depended on the income from their contributions. It was, he argued, intelligent planning and adequate finances which usually led to success in war.'

(Thucydides II, 13)

Pericles had taken care to build up Athens' reserve fund on the Acropolis to an unprecedented amount. Seaborne attacks could be made against the Peloponnese, and so Spartan strength would be gradually reduced. Athens was invulnerable behind her walls and the Long Walls that joined the city to the Piraeus (see fig 9.5), and so should be confident of ultimate victory.

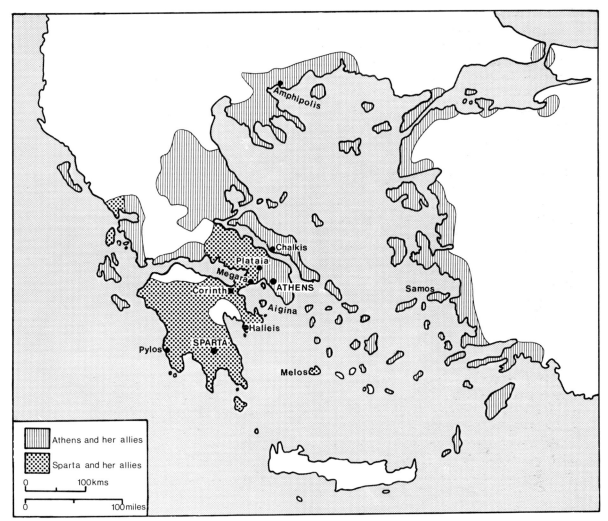

9.4 The Peloponnesian War: the division of Greece.

The first part (431–421 B.C.) of the war bore out Pericles' analysis exactly. The annual Spartan invasions of Attica achieved very little; the Athenian fleet operated successfully around the Peloponnese; and although Athens lost, decisively, the only land battle she fought—as Pericles had warned—it brought Sparta no nearer winning the war. But what he did not foresee was the plague, a savage epidemic that struck Athens twice (430 and 427 B.C.) and killed a third of her population. Thucydides himself caught it, survived it and observed it:

'People who were fit and healthy suddenly felt hot, feverish pains in the head: the eyes became red and inflamed, bleeding took place in the throat and tongue, and the breath was abnormal and fetid. Sneezing and hoarseness followed, and the disease soon moved down to the chest with painful coughing. When it settled in the abdomen, it produced stomach upsets and vomiting of every type of bile known to doctors, with great distress to the sick. Most people suffered from empty retching and strong spasms; for some, the retching ended at this stage of the disease, for others much later.

The surface of the body was not particularly hot to the touch, nor was the patient pale; the skin was somewhat red, blotched, and covered with small pustules and ulcers. Internally, however, the fever was so great that not even the lightest clothing was tolerable, and people wanted only to be naked, and most of all to plunge into cold water. Many actually did so, if they were not looked after, flinging themselves into water-tanks because of their unquenchable thirst—although it made no difference whether they drank much or little. Worst of all was the inability to stay still and the lack of sleep.

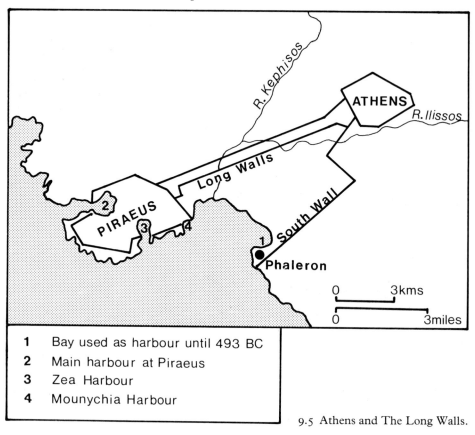

1	Bay used as harbour until 493 BC
2	Main harbour at Piraeus
3	Zea Harbour
4	Mounychia Harbour

9.5 Athens and The Long Walls.

As long as the disease was at its height, the body did not waste away but showed unexpected resistance to the pain. Consequently, most died on the sixth or eighth day from the internal fever with some strength still left in them; or, if they survived beyond this, mostly died from the weakness caused by the disease affecting the bowels with ulceration and excessive diarrhoea.'

(II, 49)

Then Pericles himself died. This was crucial: for not only did Athens lose his experience and skill, but his successors 'who were more on a level with each other and each of whom aimed at occupying the first place, adopted popularity-seeking methods which resulted in their losing control over the internal conduct of affairs.' (II,65) They abandoned his strategy and in the end lost the war. There were at first, however, some notable successes: one of them was when the Athenians, in the most unexpected action of the whole war, managed to capture two hundred and ninety-two Spartans (who 'never surrendered'), after they had been besieged on the island of Sphakteria on the west coast of the Peloponnese, despite elaborate attempts to help them:

'The Spartans had offered large rewards to those who were willing to take bread, wine, cheese and other sorts of food, which would be useful under siege, across to the island. They promised freedom, too, to any helot doing so. Despite the danger many attempted the crossing, and especially helots, who put to sea from various parts of the Peloponnese and sailed in by night to the seaward side of the island. They watched in particular for nights when the wind blew from the sea. For it was then easier to slip past the Athenian triremes on guard, who under such conditions found it impossible to anchor. The helots, too, had no concern about their boats: they had had them valued and so ran them ashore without anxiety at the landing places where the soldiers awaited them. On the other hand, all those attempting the landing when it was calm were caught. Underwater swimmers, too, swam across to the harbour side of the island, pulling behind them on cords skins containing poppy-seed mixed with honey and crushed linseed.'

(IV, 26)

9.6 This drain was built by Kleisthenes about 500 B.C. It runs along the west side of the *agora*, taking water from the hills in the south-west to the Eridanos (see fig 10.1).

9.7 The temple of Athena Niké *c.* 420 B.C.

Shortly after this there were three years of uneasy truce, and then the war broke out again.

The Sicilian Expedition

The second part of the war saw the most spectacular of the Athenian campaigns, the one that most completely reversed Pericles' cautious strategy, and the one that made inevitable Athens' final defeat. In 415 B.C. she sent an enormous expedition to capture Sicily, supported it with large reinforcements—and lost the whole force. Thucydides devotes nearly a quarter of his whole history of the war to this one campaign; for he clearly saw it as the supreme example of that arrogant self-confidence which he considered to be the cause of Athens' ultimate defeat. He describes at length the debate on it in the Athenian assembly; he discusses the various strategies proposed by the different commanders on their arrival in Sicily; he gives us the Sicilian reaction, their plans and defences; he goes into great detail on the size of the rival forces, the engagements, the camp-sites, the manoeuvres. All leads to the final battle in the Great Harbour at Syracuse in 413 B.C., where the Athenians had to break the boom across the mouth of the harbour to escape.

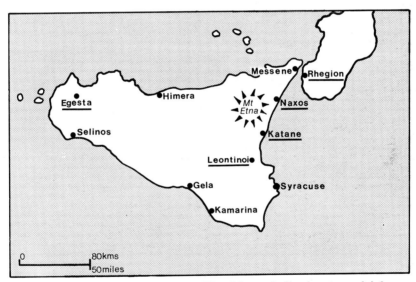

9.8 Sicily in the Peloponnesian War. The cities underlined supported Athens.

'Everything for the Athenians depended on their fleet, and their fear for the future was quite indescribable. As they watched the even balance of the battle, the struggle going on and on with no final decision, their bodies swayed to and fro, reflecting the great fear in their minds. They felt huge terror; for they were perpetually on the verge of escape or destruction. In this same Athenian army, as long as the sea-battle was indecisive, all kinds of shouting could be heard, groans of "we are losing", cries of "we are winning"—all the various noises that a great army in its great danger was driven to make. The same sorts of feelings were shared by the crews of the ships, too, until in the end, after the battle had lasted a long time, the Syracusans and their allies clearly routed the Athenians and fiercely, with loud shouts and cheers, drove them to the land.'

(VII, 71)

So the Athenians failed, and after a few weeks of wretched indecision and attempts to escape overland, most of the expeditionary force was killed. The few who were captured mostly died from maltreatment in the quarries of Syracuse. There is an interesting note in Plutarch's biography of Nikias, one of the Athenian commanders on the expedition who was killed by the Syracusans, that

'some Athenians were saved because of Euripides (the tragedian). For the Sicilians, it seems, were more fond of his poetry than all the rest of the Greeks who lived outside Greece itself. This is the reason, people say, why many of the survivors, when they got home, went to see Euripides to thank him. Some of them explained that they had been set free when they had taught their masters all they could remember of his poetry. Others said that they had been given food and water in their wanderings after the battle because they recited some of his lyrics.'

(xxix)

Athens Defeated

The blow to Athens was enormous. Many of her allies revolted, and Sparta persuaded Persia to provide her with a fleet. This last part (412–404 B.C.) of the war was fought in the Aegean and Ionia, and mostly at sea. At first, in fact, Athens recovered remarkably well, and it almost seemed at one stage that she might win the war. For she won several major battles and brought many of the allies back under her control. But Persian help to Sparta, which Sparta obtained at the price of surrendering the Ionian Greeks to their old rulers, and Athenian incompetence brought about her ultimate defeat. Harsh terms were imposed on her: the Long Walls and fortifications of the Piraeus were to be destroyed, all ships except twelve were to be surrendered, and Athens was to lose her own empire and become a Spartan subject-ally. After this, according to Xenophon, who completed the history of the war from the point at which Thucydides stops,

'Lysandros (the Spartan admiral) sailed into the Piraeus, the exiles returned, and they began to pull down the walls to the music of flute-girls and with great enthusiasm, since they thought that day was the beginning of freedom for Greece.'

(*Hellenika* II, 2)

It did not, unfortunately, turn out like that, as Chapter 17 will show.

CHAPTER TEN

Democracy and Law

One of the difficulties in trying to understand Greek society is that words have changed their meanings. One obvious example is democracy. We all think we are democrats and that we know what the word means. Yet look at how the Greeks used it: 'In a democracy there is, first, that most splendid of virtues, equality before the law. Secondly, it has none of the vices of monarchy: for all offices are assigned by lot, all officials are subject to investigation, and all policies are debated in public.' This is Herodotus talking (III, 81) about different types of government. Most of what he says about democracy we would accept. The fact that 'all offices are assigned by lot', however, makes it sound a haphazard, even dangerous, way of running a state. Then Euripides makes one of the characters in his play *The Suppliants* say that 'this city is free and not ruled by one man. The people rule, as year by year new men succeed to office.' Year by year? Is such a frequent change of government a necessary part of democracy? The Greeks seemed to think so.

Aristotle, too, who collected the constitutions of over one hundred and fifty states and who knew more than most about Greek politics, adds to the picture:

'The same man is not to hold an office twice, or only rarely, with a few exceptions, notably military. Jury service on all, or most, matters is open to all, and always in the case of the most important decisions, such as the annual investigations into officials' conduct of their office, questions of citizenship, and contracts between individuals.'

(Politics, 1317b)

An annual check of officials and only one term of office make it all very different from our sort of democracy.

Direct Democracy

To see how Greek democracy worked in practice we must look at Athens. A contemporary writer, who did not like Athenian democracy at all, admits

'It is right that in Athens the poor and the common people should have more power than the nobles and the rich, because they provide the rowers for the fleet and thus give the *polis* its strength.'

(The Old Oligarch 1, 2)

Athens was the largest democracy, the most influential and the one we know most about. The key fact about it is that everybody could take a direct part in government. We elect members of Parliament to govern the country, the Athenians governed it themselves. This could happen there because of the size of the *polis*: there were probably about 40 000 citizens—a biggish football crowd—in Athens at the beginning of the Peloponnesian War. And so it was quite possible for them all to come to the public meetings at which the major political decisions—of peace and war, of finance, of alliances—were made. Of course, not everybody did. Some would be working, others uninterested, many lived too far away to make frequent visits to Athens a practical possibility. But the principle remained: all Athenian citizens had the right to speak and vote at the meetings of this general assembly or *ekklesia*, the body which had final and supreme power in the state.

The involvement was direct and immediate. It is early 415 B.C. The *ekklesia* is debating whether the fleet should be sent to attack Sicily. You go along, but hardly as a spectator. If you and your fellow-citizens vote in favour of it, you are voting, in all probability, to send yourself or your son or nephew as a rower or a hoplite. Voting becomes rather important in such circumstances.

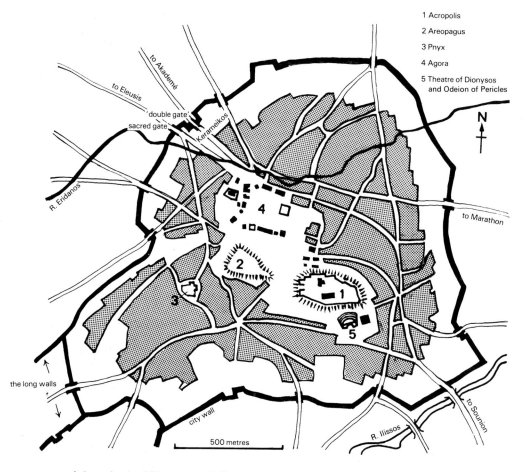

1 Acropolis
2 Areopagus
3 Pnyx
4 Agora
5 Theatre of Dionysos and Odeion of Pericles

10.1 Athens in the fifth century B.C.

Its Leaders

Here, then was direct democracy in action. Decisions were taken by the citizens themselves, But, like most mass meetings, the *ekklesia* could be swayed by skilful speakers. So oratory was important: you became a political leader only if you were able to persuade the *ekklesia*. There was no party to make you its leader, because parties in the modern sense did not exist. Obviously various groups, the farmers, the sailors or shopkeepers, might join together to support a particular proposal. But these groupings changed from meeting to meeting. The only way to exercise political power was by convincing a majority of your fellow-citizens that your proposals were the best for the state. So to stay a leader meant that you had to continue to win the approval of the *ekklesia*, meeting after meeting. It must have been a wearing business.

There was a lot of criticism of the demagogues, as these leaders were called (p. 101). One of them in particular, Kleon, who became the leading politician in Athens after Pericles' death, always gets a bad press. Plutarch attacks him for his vulgarity:

'He was offensive and conceited. . . It was thanks to him that decent behaviour was no longer seen at meetings of the *ekklesia*. For he was the first popular leader to bellow his speeches, to throw open his cloak and slap his thigh, and to stride up and down on the platform while haranguing the people.'

(*Nikias* viii)

And Aristophanes' play *The Knights* is a savage ridiculing of him. He is the 'filthiest, most blatant, lowest-down liar of all time: . . . he sucks-up, smarms, and

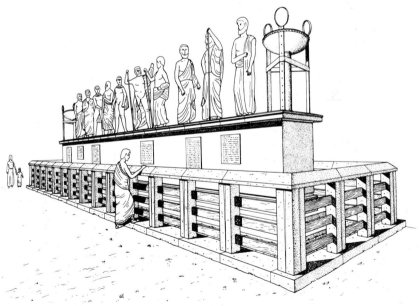

10.2 The notice-board in the *agora*, built round the shrine of the Eponymous Heroes (after whom the ten Athenian tribes were named). Here appeared notices like drafts of proposed laws and lists of men required for military service.

soft-soaps the Assembly until he has it where he wants; . . . he's the tax-extorter, the bottomless pit, the Charybdis of rapacity', who 'helps himself to public money', who 'has a squad of muscle-men, tough young leather-sellers . . .' And the rest of the demagogues are of the same sort: 'It's no use thinking decent or educated men can be leaders of the people—that's left to the illiterate and dishonest these days.' Aristophanes did not like demagogues, and in any case this is comedy. But it shows one weakness of democracy.

10.3 The *agora* at Athens: view from the south east today, and a reconstruction of the same area as it was about 400 B.C.

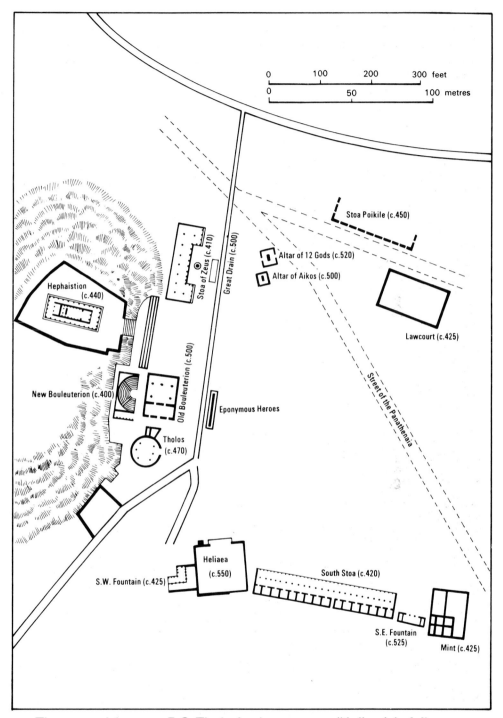

Scale:

| 0 | 100 | 200 | 300 feet |
| 0 | 50 | | 100 metres |

Stoa Poikile (c.450)

Stoa of Zeus (c.410)

Great Drain (c.500)

Altar of 12 Gods (c.520)

Altar of Aikos (c.500)

Hephaistion (c.440)

Lawcourt (c.425)

Old Bouleterion (c.500)

New Bouleterion (c.400)

Eponymous Heroes

Street of the Panathenaia

Tholos (c.470)

Heliaea (c.550)

S.W. Fountain (c.425)

South Stoa (c.420)

S.E. Fountain (c.525)

Mint (c.425)

10.4 The *agora* at Athens, 400 B.C. The *bouleterion* was a council hall and the *heliaea* was a courthouse.

Its Officials

The *ekklesia* normally met three or four times a month. But government business required regular attention, and this continuity was provided by the *boulé* (Council). This consisted of five hundred citizens, fifty chosen by lot from each of the ten tribes. It was in office for a year, and nobody was allowed to serve on it more than twice. This meant that a large number of Athenians must have had a direct and practical experience of government. For the councillors of each tribe served as a *prytany* (standing committee) for a tenth of the year; during that period all state business came in the first place to them. To enable them to fulfil their duties, they lived in the *tholos* (see fig 10.4) and were fed at public expense. Each day one member became chairman of the *prytany* and, if there was a meeting of the whole *boulé* or of the *ekklesia* that day, he acted as chairman of that meeting, too. In his hands were the keys to the treasuries and the seal of Athens.

The duties of the *boulé*, which met every day that was not a holiday, were many. It received embassies and dispatches; it decided what matters should be put to the *ekklesia* and published the agenda; it was in overall charge of triremes, dockyards and cavalry horses; it supervised officials; it scrutinized the candidates for coming elections; it checked the accounts of all officials once in each *prytany*; and, in general, as Aristotle says, 'it co-operates with the other magistrates in most of what they do.' So its members must inevitably have developed a considerable understanding of the problems of running a *polis*.

In Athens, then, there were no M.P.'s and no political parties; there was no permanent civil service either. Necessary administration was done by various officials, often in boards of five or ten. The *agoranomoi* looked after the markets, *metronomoi* inspected weights and measures, and the *sitophylakes* were in charge of the corn-supply. There were five *hodopoioi* 'whose duty it is to ensure that the workmen provided by the state repair the roads'; *hieropoioi* were chosen to make sacrifices and be in charge of certain religious festivals; and the duties of the ten *astynomoi* (city commissioners) included ensuring

> 'that none of the dung-collectors dump dung within two kilometres of the city-wall. They also prevent the extending of houses into, and the building of balconies over, the streets, and the constructing of pipes with outfalls over the roads and of doors opening outwards into the road. And they see to it that the girls who play the flute, the harp and the lyre are not hired for more than two drachmas.'
>
> (Aristotle, *The Constitution of Athens* 50)

All these officials were chosen by lot and usually for a single year. For, again, it was felt that it was more democratic for a large number of citizens to take part in rotation in running public affairs than that there should be long-serving experts who might use their experience and skill for their own advancement or to victimize others. All these officials had to undergo the investigation Aristotle speaks of at the end of their year of office. If they were found to have been negligent or dishonest, they were fined or even exiled. So you were encouraged to do the job as well as you could.

For only two offices was voting still retained—military leaders (*strategoi*) and those in charge of finance. And in the case of the generalship, a man could be re-elected, as Pericles was for fifteen years. Here, at least, it was recognized that skill and

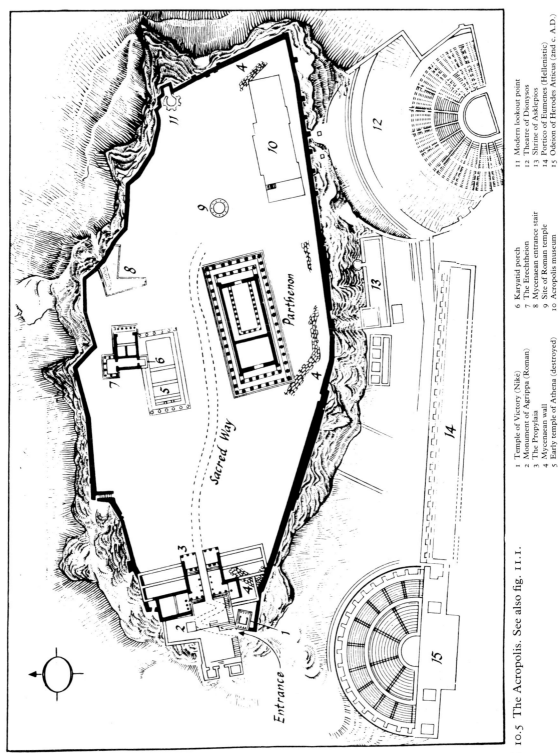

10.5 The Acropolis. See also fig. 11.1.

1 Temple of Victory (Nike)
2 Monument of Agrippa (Roman)
3 The Propylaia
4 Mycenaean wall
5 Early temple of Athena (destroyed)
6 Karyatid porch
7 The Erechtheion
8 Mycenaean entrance stair
9 Site of Roman temple
10 Acropolis museum
11 Modern lookout point
12 Theatre of Dionysos
13 Shrine of Asklepios
14 Portico of Eumenes (Hellenistic)
15 Odeion of Herodes Atticus (2nd c. A.D.)

experience were essential; otherwise citizens' lives could be lost. Thus the generalship became the most influential of all offices.

Its Finances

There was one other way in which the generalship was different from all other state duties: it was not paid. And this is the second of the principles the Athenians thought were essential for democracy. It was not enough to make the vast majority of public appointments open to every citizen. It had also to be possible for a man to do them without losing his earnings. Otherwise only the wealthy would be willing to undertake them. It was easy for the enemies of democracy to sneer at this 'distribution of public money' whereby the people 'became extravagant and undisciplined instead of restrained and self-sufficient.' But it was necessary if Athens was going to be a thorough-going democracy.

As well as this payment to officials in Athens, the state paid jurymen, citizens on most military and naval duties, and officials employed on state business abroad. But the pay was small, hardly more than a subsistence wage; it was certainly only half

10.6 The Karyatid porch on the south west corner of the Erechtheion, the temple sacred to both Athena and Erechtheus.

that which we know from a surviving inscription was paid to skilled workmen building the Erechtheion (see p. 112). There were other people helped or maintained at state expense: war casualties who were unable to work, orphans of men killed in war, victors at the major games, and, an interesting example of what a democratic *polis* gave in return for the contributions of its members, 'anyone whose property is less than three *mnai* (see p. 116) and who is incapable of working because of physical disability.'

The money for this came from the contributions paid by her allies, from taxes paid by *metoikoi* or resident foreigners, and from customs dues on exports and imports. And, since this trading was largely in the hands of non-Athenians, it will be seen that citizens did not tax themselves. There was one exception; and even that was hardly a tax. Rich citizens were required to undertake an expensive public service, called a liturgy—a word we restrict to a set form of religious worship. The two most common were the equipping of a trireme—the state provided the hull and paid the crew—and the production of a play or the training of a choir for the annual festivals. This, clearly, was a kind of super-tax. But at least it must have given rich citizens somewhat more satisfaction than their modern counterparts get from sending a cheque to the Inland Revenue. You could be proud of 'your' elegantly completed trireme or the magnificence of the costumes in 'your' play.

10.7 Water-clock: a copy of the means used to time speeches in the law-courts.

Its Legal System

The last, and perhaps most important, aspect of Athenian democracy was the law-courts. We try to separate law and politics; the Greeks and the Romans did not. The result was, as Aristotle says, that 'when the people have the right to vote in the courts, they control the constitution.' Hence this right 'contributed most to the strength of democracy.' All disputes, public and private, had to be settled in these people's courts, which were quite different from our courts. There was no judge, no prosecuting or defending counsel, no deliberation by the jury. Instead of a judge there was a chairman, whose job was simply to ensure that the proceedings were conducted in an orderly fashion. With no counsel, both the plaintiff and the defendant had to make their own speeches, although they could use professional speech-writers to write them. Indeed, most of our knowledge of Athenian law comes from surviving speeches of this sort. The jury was given no guidance about similar cases in the past, no indication of relevant laws, and no advice on how to evaluate—or reject—the evidence presented. When the two speeches, timed by a water-clock, were finished—and all cases had to be decided within a day—they decided the verdict by a simple majority vote. If the verdict was guilty and there was no fixed penalty, the plaintiff and defendant proposed two different penalties, and again the jury chose one by a simple majority vote.

Enormous trouble was taken to ensure that no influence or bribery could be used. The juries were, first, very large: juries of five hundred were normal, juries of a thousand not uncommon. Secondly, they were chosen in the morning, from the six thousand enrolled each year, for the cases to be heard that day. There was also a very elaborate system of tokens and tags, so that no one could predict which juryman would go to which court.

Two other surprising features of Athenian law arise from the fact that there were no police. Some Scythian slaves were, indeed, employed by the *polis* to keep order at meetings of the *ekklesia* and to sweep idle citizens from the *agora* (town centre) to the Pnyx by means of a rope covered with red chalk—anybody so discoloured was fined! But there were no police as we know them. There was therefore, first, no official prosecution of criminals, and so all cases had to be brought by private individuals. This was real democracy, perhaps, where the responsibility to check crime rests on everybody; but it encouraged the emergence of an unpleasant crowd of informers—people who made a profession of sniffing out breaches of the law and blackmailing those concerned. Secondly, there were no means of ensuring that victory in the courts led to your getting stolen property back or your damages paid. You could only threaten another prosecution—or use persuasion.

But it was the political use of the courts which the Greeks themselves thought most important. One critic of democracy said that 'in the law-courts, the Athenians are more concerned with self-interest than with justice. . . They use the courts to protect members of the *demos* (ordinary people) and to ruin their opponents.'

This attack could either be made directly, by bringing a specific case of illegal action against someone, or indirectly, by using any case as a chance to smear and denigrate him, since anything, relevant or not, could be said in court. So the courts were both part of radical democracy in Athens and a means of consolidating and extending that democracy.

Its Drawbacks

One vital thing remains to be said. The Athenian system may have been a thorough-going democracy, but participation in it was strictly limited to adult, male citizens. Here, of course, is another major difference from our society: the Athenian system, so complete and embracing in its political and administrative aspects, was exclusive in social terms. Women, slaves and *metoikoi*, that is, perhaps three-quarters of the population, were allowed no part in the running of the state. It was an oddly partial democracy.

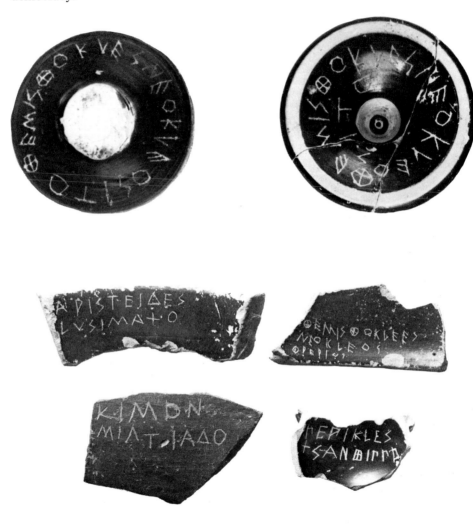

10.8 Ostraka (see page 48); you can see the names of Aristeides and other leading Athenian politicians. ITO means 'Out with . . .'

However, there was not much opposition in Athens to it. There were aristocrats, of course, and wealthy citizens who might have preferred a different system. We hear of one leader who 'grouped the aristocrats into a single body' in the *ekklesia* so that their united voice could be heard. But there was no chance of their overthrowing the democracy. Only twice did Athens have a non-democratic government: first, after the disaster in Sicily (p. 104), and secondly, following her capture by Lysandros in 404 B.C. On the first occasion, democratic excesses were blamed for the catastrophe, and so a group of oligarchs was able to seize power for a few months. But, as soon as the fleet started to have some success off Ionia, full democracy was restored. And it was only the Spartan garrison that enabled the Thirty Tyrants, as they were called, to rule after the end of the war. But they conducted such a reign of terror that they were soon attacked by exiled democrats and removed; and even Sparta refused to help them. So Athens stayed democratic.

How successful was it? It lost the war, of course. And we know of some emotional and rash decisions it made. For example, it condemned—illegally—the generals who failed to save the crews of sinking triremes after a victory in 406 B.C.; and it executed Socrates (p. 167). But these actions were taken under the stress of war and defeat, when, too, Pericles' successors 'were so concerned with their own private intrigues to secure the leadership of the people that they allowed the affairs of the *polis* to fall into disarray.' And there is the other side. Pericles' view of Athens as an 'education to Greece' and of Athenians as 'lovers of beauty without extravagance, and cultivators of the mind without being soft' may be idealized. But it is hard to deny that the Athenian way of life attracted, encouraged, perhaps caused, a flowering of genius in literature, mathematics, philosophy and art that is probably unique.

10.9 An Athenian four-drachma coin, with the head of Athena on the obverse, her owl and an olive sprig on the reverse.
Athenian coinage: 6 obols = 1 drachma
               100 drachmas = 1 mna
               60 mnai = 1 talent

ecture, Sculpture and
y

the fifth century B.C., when Athens was at the peak of her political
a wealthy city. As was mentioned in Chapter 9, this wealth now
to initiate in the city a building programme of astonishing intensity
here was a need both to replace the many temples which had been
ersians in their invasion of 480 B.C. and to give adequate thanks to
the gods for saving Greece at that time. Pericles saw, too, that the prestige of the city
would be greatly increased by such beautiful and impressive public buildings. That
employment was thus provided at the state's expense for a vast number of workers
was also sound policy for a statesman relying on popular support.

Plutarch, in his *Life of Pericles*, tells of the energy and enthusiasm which went into
the project:

> 'So the works arose, towering in size, unsurpassed in shape or grace, with the
> workmen competing to excel themselves in the beauty of their craftsmanship. The
> most remarkable thing was the speed. Men thought that each building would only
> be completed after many successive generations, but all of them reached perfection
> in the peak period of a single government.'

(xiii)

The centre of activity was, of course, the Acropolis, where a new temple was
needed for the city's patron goddess, Athena. So the Parthenon was begun in 447
B.C. The architects were Iktinos and Kallikrates, and Pericles put his friend
Pheidias, whose later work at Olympia has been described in Chapter 8, in charge of
the sculptured decorations of the building. Pheidias was already famous for his
statue on the Acropolis of Athena Promachos—Athena the Champion. Put up to
celebrate the victory over the Persians, this was an enormous bronze figure of the
goddess, which could be seen by sailors far out to sea as it gleamed in the sun.
Pheidias supervised the work of other sculptors on the Parthenon, but he himself
made the great gold and ivory statue of Athena inside the temple, destroyed long ago
and now only known to us imperfectly from written descriptions and Roman copies.

At the western end of the Acropolis the architect Mnesikles designed an approach
and gateway—the Propylaia—of suitable dignity for the sacred area. Work began on
it in 437 B.C. After Pericles' time, in about 420 B.C., the tiny but perfect temple of
Athena Niké, Athena as goddess of victory—again to celebrate victory over the
Persians—was built on a high platform at the side of the gateway (fig 9.7). Finally,
towards the end of the fifth century B.C., came the Erectheion, a temple both of Athena
and of Erectheus, a legendary king of Athens (see fig 10.6).

Elsewhere in the city, the temple of Hephaistos, overlooking the agora and still remarkably well-preserved, also belongs to Pericles' period. Hephaistos was the craftsman of the gods, and his temple was by the part of Athens where many craftsmen had their workshops. Of non-religious buildings the most important was the Odeion, a concert-hall which Pericles had built near the Theatre of Dionysos. Further afield in Attica, the temple of Poseidon overlooking the sea at Cape Sounion to the south of Athens and, to the north, the new hall for the celebration of the Mysteries at Eleusis (see p. 75) were further parts of Pericles' building programme.

Although other places and other times produced many fine buildings, the temples built during this second half of the fifth century B.C. in Athens exemplify the best of all Greek architecture. They reached an amazing degree of beauty in their simple elegance, achieved by a fine understanding of proportion in design, and by great technical skill.

The Greek Temple

Consideration of Greek architecture will inevitably be mainly concerned with temples. These were the most important buildings in any city, so that the most care was taken over them. Temples form a very large proportion of the buildings which have survived into our time.

A Greek temple for many people means the gleaming white marble of the Parthenon. It is often a surprise to discover that parts of the temples, and sculptures as well, were painted by the Greeks. Although nearly all the paint has now disappeared, sufficient traces are left for this to be known with certainty.

11.1 The Acropolis at Athens.

The characteristic straight outlines of a temple were partly dictated by practical considerations. Since the technique of building arches or vaults was not perfected until Roman times, in a Greek building the roof had to take the form of horizontal beams and slabs supported at right angles by vertical walls or columns. Above these the temple's roof usually rose gently from either side to a ridge running from the front to the rear of the building. This left a shallow triangular space, or pediment, above the end columns.

The purpose of the temple was not, as in a Christian church, to hold large congregations. The altar was outside, and any gathering of worshippers, perhaps for a sacrifice, would take place there. The temple was to house the statue of the god or goddess, and the central feature was a rectangular room (*naos*) for that purpose, in which suitable offerings to the deity could also be kept. In the Parthenon this was where Pheidias' gold and ivory statue of Athena stood. Sometimes there was a second chamber to the rear of the *naos*, used as a treasury for offerings. The windowless *naos* opened out on to a porch with columns. Around all or part of the building were rows of columns forming covered walks or colonnades. Their arrangement and number varied from temple to temple, though, as one would expect, there was a steady trend away from the simplicity of early times towards more complicated designs. Yet the basic rectangular ground-plan remained standard, with very few exceptions. Their great love of symmetry often led the Greeks to place a dummy porch at the back of the temple to match the real one at the front. The whole building was on a platform of stone, rising in steps from the ground level.

11.2 The Parthenon.

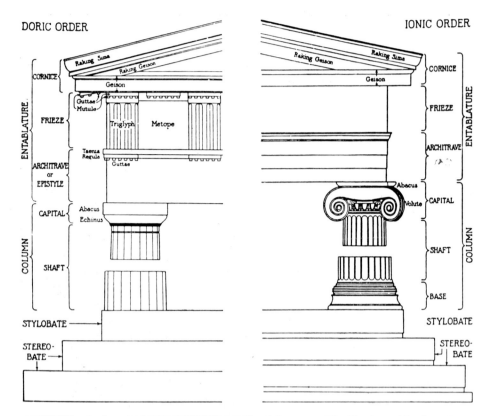

DORIC ORDER

CORNICE

Raking Sima
Raking Geison
Geison
Guttae
Mutule

ENTABLATURE

FRIEZE

Triglyph   Metope

ARCHITRAVE
or
EPISTYLE

Taenia
Regula
Guttae

CAPITAL

Abacus
Echinus

COLUMN

SHAFT

STYLOBATE

STEREO-
BATE

IONIC ORDER

Raking Geison   Raking Sima
Geison

CORNICE

FRIEZE

ARCHITRAVE

ENTABLATURE

Abacus
Volute

CAPITAL

SHAFT

COLUMN

BASE

STYLOBATE

STEREO-
BATE

11.3 The Doric and Ionic orders.

11.4 The capital of a Corinthian column.

120

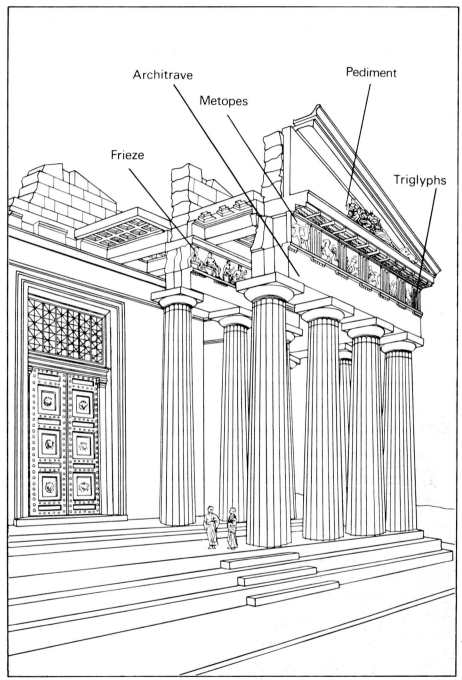

Architrave

Metopes

Pediment

Frieze

Triglyphs

11.5 A cross-section of the front of the Parthenon.

The columns of a temple were in one of three standard styles, or 'orders'—Doric, Ionic and Corinthian. Other features of the buildings are associated with each style, and so the temple as a whole can be classified as being of one or other of the three orders. The easiest way to distinguish them is by the top, or 'capital', of the columns. The Doric is plain, the Ionic has a ram's horns pattern, and the Corinthian is more ornate, with carvings of acanthus leaves as though they were growing from the top (see fig 11.4). Although their invention was in the sequence given above, they did not entirely replace each other, and indeed elements of more than one style could be combined in the same building. The columns taking the form of statues of young women in one of the porches of the Erechtheion (see fig 10.6) were very unusual. Columns of the three common Greek styles have always been much used in architecture, right up to modern times.

Between the top of the columns and the roof itself was an area decorated by stone carvings (the frieze), which might either be a continuous strip, even stretching around the whole building, or, if the temple was Doric, a series of individual panels, called metopes. The latter were separated by stone slabs decorated with three vertical grooves cut in them, known as triglyphs. These were the equivalents of the ends of the wooden cross-beams of early temples. When stone replaced wood as the principal building material, they were kept as a traditional element of the temple's appearance. In the case of the Parthenon, there was both a continuous frieze and one of metopes.

11.6 The Parthenon metopes show the battle between Lapiths and Centaurs, a legend which also symbolized the struggle of Greeks (=Lapiths) against barbarians (=Centaurs) in the wars with Persia.

The triangular pediments formed by the shape of the roof at the ends of the temples were also filled with sculptures. It was difficult to fit the carvings naturally into the area available, and great skill was sometimes shown in finding ways of filling the awkward corners (see fig 11.8).

The sculptures in the pediments and friezes depicted subjects connected with the deity of the temple. For instance the Parthenon, being the temple of Athena, showed an idealized version of the Great Panathenaic procession in its continuous frieze. That procession, in which once every four years a specially new-woven sacred robe was offered to the goddess, extended around all four sides of the temple. One of the pediments showed the birth of Athena, and the other showed Athena and Poseidon fighting for ownership of Athens.

Many of the sculptures from the Parthenon are now in the British Museum, and are known as the Elgin Marbles. The temple became at one point a Christian church, then a Turkish mosque, for Greece was long under the rule of Turkey. In the seventeenth century A.D. the Turks, when besieged by a Venetian army, stored gunpowder in it, and so great damage was caused when artillery blew it up in 1687. Later Lord Elgin, British ambassador to Turkey, obtained permission to bring many of the carvings from the Acropolis to Britain to save them from further damage. More recently the buildings of the Acropolis have been conserved and repaired as far as possible, but there is still very great concern over damage caused by air pollution and the enormous crowds of tourists.

Although other material, such as limestone, was used, marble was the favourite for the Greek temple of classical times. There was a good supply of this available in both mainland Greece and in the islands, as well as in Asia Minor. Particularly good stone came from the marble-quarries on the islands of Naxos and Paros and on Mount

11.7 A section of the Parthenon frieze: a cow being led to sacrifice.

Pentelikos near Athens. Blocks of marble were joined to each other not by mortar, but by bronze or iron clamps and pins, set in lead. Great care was taken to ensure accuracy, and in some of the best work the joins, for instance between the drums which made up a column, were virtually invisible.

There were many technical refinements used to improve the appearance of the buildings and to correct optical illusions. Thus very slight upward curves were used to make horizontal lines appear straight—if left actually straight, they would have given the illusion of sagging. For similar reasons the columns tapered a little and were slightly convex. The height, width and length of temples were in carefully calculated proportion to each other.

Sculptures

By the time of Pericles, Greek sculptors, like the architects, had reached a high degree of skill. Apart from the great amount of carving used in architecture, there were many free-standing statues, religious and otherwise. Gravestones also inspired some fine work. Earlier carvings, for all their beauty, showed the human form and animals in awkward, and very often physically impossible, poses. Such features as hair and folds of drapery had at first been represented by a few lines or a pattern on the stone. Gradually over the centuries the sculptors had developed their techniques and by now they were able to produce an effect of natural movement and appearance, and understood the rules of perspective (see fig 11.7). Despite this, the expressions on the faces remained almost invariably dignified and serene, even in scenes of fighting or mourning. As time went on, in the fourth century and later, faces showed more emotion, and sculptors concentrated on showing what was real in life rather than

11.8 Horse's head from the corner of a Parthenon pediment. One of four horses represented as drawing the chariot of the moon as it sets below the horizon.   *Reproduced by Courtesy of the Trustees of the British Museum.*

124

what was ideal. There gradually developed as well, some would say, an excessive emphasis on technical skill for its own sake.

The development of the art of bronze-casting was highly important in the history of Greek sculpture, since it allowed sculptors to show a much wider range of subject. Thus statues could be cast in several pieces and later joined. Balancing weights could be placed in the hollow sections for poses which heavy and breakable stone would not allow.

Only a very small percentage of genuine Greek sculpture has survived until the present. Of the two most common materials, stone and bronze, the former has the disadvantage of being relatively brittle, and the latter of being a desirable metal to melt down and re-use.

A further hazard to the original statues lay in collecting and looting. Wealthy Romans, especially, thought it highly fashionable to decorate their houses and estates with original Greek statues, acquired sometimes by dishonourable means. On the other hand, this same practice has given us many of the statues we do still have. Some statues have been recovered from shipwrecks, which occurred when they were being transported from Greece. Furthermore, those Romans who were unable to

11.9 A famous bronze statue from the fifth century B.C.—'the charioteer of Delphi'. The chariot and horses are lost.

125

Storage jars

Amphora Neck-amphora Peliké Stamnos

Bowls for mixing wine and water   Water-jars

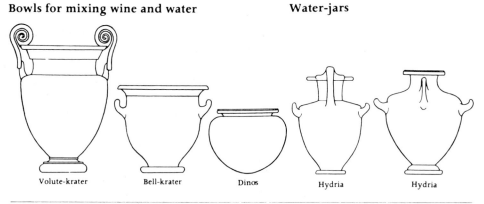

Volute-krater Bell-krater Dinos Hydria Hydria

Jugs   Perfume bottles

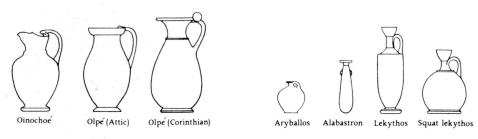

Oinochoé Olpé (Attic) Olpé (Corinthian)   Aryballos Alabastron Lekythos Squat lekythos

Drinking cups   Cosmetic pots

Kylix Stemless kylix Kantharos   Pyxis (Geometric) Pyxis (Classical) Pyxis (Classical)

11.10 Greek vase shapes and their uses.

afford or obtain original statues settled instead for copies of masterpieces. A number of these have come down to us and, although inferior, they are an important source of knowledge of lost originals. Many statues popularly thought of as Greek are really Roman copies.

Consequently the names of the great Greek sculptors are well known to us. Pheidias and Polykleitos lived in the fifth century B.C., and Praxiteles, Skopas and Lysippos in the fourth, but virtually none of their works survives.

Pottery

Another important area of Greek art is pottery, which, in addition to its artistic merits, is of great significance to us as historical evidence.

Vases in those days were the main type of container for commercial products, whether liquid, like wine or olive-oil, or dry, like grain. In fact pottery fulfilled the functions carried out by a whole range of materials nowadays, such as cardboard, plastics, tin and glass. Obviously pottery had many domestic uses, and it was widely employed in matters of religion—to hold wine at ceremonies or for ornamental vases in temples or tombs. Because pottery does not decay, even if it frequently breaks, an

11.11 Mounted archer wearing Persian, or perhaps Scythian, dress: a red-figured Athenian plate of about 510 B.C.

enormous quantity has been found, and a great amount of historical knowledge is based on its interpretation by archaeologists. The place of discovery, the depth at which it is buried and the nearby objects are all valuable information, especially since a good deal is known about the dating of styles and types of pottery.

Vases were painted with religious, mythological or everyday subjects. These paintings, unfortunately almost the only kind of Greek painting which has survived, thus provide information over a wide field, as can be seen from the frequency with which they are used as illustrations in this book.

Potteries existed in every town and village of Greece, many with their local characteristics. Yet for about a century and a half, starting in the sixth century, Athenian pottery dominated all others. Found all over the Mediterranean area, in places as far apart as Spain and Asia, it shows clearly the commercial and political power of the city, as well as the high quality of its pottery. Previously, vases from Corinth had been the most widespread.

The clay used in Athens contained a high level of iron, so that it produced a reddish colour when fired in the kilns. At first this was left as the background to figures drawn in black. From about 525 B.C. the reverse came to be more popular; the background was glazed black and the figures left in the red colour, with details shown by black lines. In style and skill Greek pottery, like the other kinds of art, reached its climax during the fifth century B.C.

In some cases the painter or potter signed the vase, writing in the former case 'X decorated it', or in the latter 'X made it'. Sometimes the same man 'decorated and made it'. Writing on the vase was also commonly used to indicate the names of figures shown, the subject-matter, words spoken by the figures, or even a greeting to anyone looking at the vase. The shapes of the vases fell into a number of standard types, depending on their practical purpose (see fig. 11.10).

Another form of pottery very common throughout the Greek world, many examples of which have been found, was that of small terra-cotta or 'baked earth' figures. Used as offerings to gods, toys, ornaments, or buried with the dead, they too were originally painted, although the colours have mostly gone from surviving pieces. Like vases, they have a wide variety of styles and subjects and are valued both as works of art and as historical evidence.

11.12 Terra-cotta figures.

Reproduced by Courtesy of the Trustees of the British Museum.

CHAPTER TWELVE

The Theatre

The City Dionysia

The invention of drama is among the most important of the many Greek contributions to European civilization. One of the greatest events of the Athenian year was the festival of the City Dionysia, held in the spring and attracting many visitors to the city. The main feature of this was the dramatic competition. In a world where entertainment of this kind was not readily available, the Athenian citizen must have looked forward greatly to the occasion. He was fortunate, in the fifth century B.C. especially, in the quality of the plays produced. In Aeschylus, Sophocles and Euripides, the tragedians, and Aristophanes, the comic poet, Athens had outstanding playwrights.

The dramatic competition lasted for four days, taking place in the open-air theatre, which can still been seen, though with subsequent alterations, on the southern slope of the Acropolis (see fig 12.1). Quite a few other Greek theatres survive, such as that at Delphi, high on the hillside, and, perhaps the finest of all, that at Epidauros in the Peloponnese (see fig 12.2). Some of these theatres are still used. However, the structures which survive are of stone and therefore belong to the fourth century B.C. or later, for in the fifth century the stage building and seating were wooden, only later being made more permanent by the use of stone. A sloping site was chosen, since it created a natural auditorium with the audience on banked tiers of seats. This was the *theatron* ('viewing-place'), rather more than a semi-circle in shape.

No doubt the audience brought cushions with them, and food and wine as well, for this was not going to the theatre as we know it. They watched four or five plays in a day—perhaps ten hours of performance, with intervals between, but not during, each play. A capacity audience seems to have been about 17 000, although we are told of one of more than 30 000. Its exact composition is a vexed question, since it is uncertain to what extent, if at all, women, children and slaves were allowed to attend. Certainly the bulk of the audience was made up by the adult male citizens, sitting in the block of seats allocated to their tribes. There were also large numbers of *metoikoi* (see p. 113) and visitors from other cities.

As its name implies, the City Dionysia was held in honour of the god Dionysos, and its religious aspect was highly important. The festival opened with a procession and sacrifices, after which the statue of Dionysos was carried by torchlight into the theatre to attend the performances. In the front rows were special seats for distinguished visitors and important officials, at the centre of whom sat the priest of Dionysos. An altar to the god was situated in the middle of the circular area between the audience and the stage building.

The Chorus

The very notion of a play originated from religious choral dances, when one member of the chorus began to speak on his own in dialogue with the rest of the chorus. The Athenians attributed this development, from which drama grew, to Thespis in about 534 B.C. Little is known of this figure, but he was traditionally regarded as the father of tragedy. In the beginning this first actor was the poet himself—the plays were entirely composed in verse—but later there were professional actors.

Although Aeschylus added a second actor, and later Sophocles a third, the chorus remained essential to Greek plays and is one of the most obvious differences from modern works. There have however been instances, as in T. S. Eliot's *Murder in the Cathedral*, where its use has been imitated. The chorus performed in the circular area in the middle of the theatre, originally just of earth, but later paved with stone. Called the *orchestra*, or 'dancing-place', its name reflects the fact that the chorus danced as well as sang. They were fifteen in number and accompanied by a flute-player. Cast perhaps as a group of sailors, local citizens, or slaves, according to the story of the play, they sang and danced choruses at intervals throughout the play, and at other times conversed with the actors. Usually the choruses took the form of comment on events in the play. Gradually their importance declined and sometimes they seem little more than interludes.

The Stage

To the rear of the *orchestra* stood a low stage and a stage building (*skené*). In the latter the actors could change, and properties could be stored. In fact little scenery was used, for no attempt was made to produce a realistic set. The stage building itself,

12.1 The theatre of Dionysos at Athens.

which had a central door and probably others to the sides, usually represented a palace or a house or a temple. Some use seems to have been made of painted screens and backcloths to suggest, for instance, rocks and the sea, or a city in the distant background. Portable statues of gods and goddesses could also be used to indicate the setting—such as Apollo for the temple at Delphi, Athena for Athens.

Generally, however, such properties were kept to a minimum—perhaps just a single statue or a throne or an altar. What was said in the theatre was far more important than what was seen, and the author relied principally on the power of his words to set the scene in the imagination of his audience. This was particularly true of the many descriptive speeches made by messengers in the plays. The objects on the stage were intended merely to suggest in a traditional way the setting which the audience was supposed to visualize. Similarly, the spaces between the sides of the stage and the seating—the *parodoi*—had an established significance. An actor arriving through the one on the right would immediately be known by the audience at Athens to have come from the city or the harbour, while entry from the left denoted arrival from the country.

In addition to the ordinary low stage, the flat roof of the stage building was sometimes used as an acting area. Furthermore a crane (*mechané*), probably a jib operated by ropes and pulleys, was available for characters to be shown airborne, flying to and from the stage, often in winged chariots. Naturally both the upper stage and the crane were especially suitable for gods and goddesses, who commonly appeared in the plays. They often arrived at a timely moment, usually the end, to sort out human affairs. The Latin phrase for this—*deus ex machina*—has become a standard way of describing such a convenient arrival.

12.2 Aerial view of the theatre at Epidauros in the Peloponnese.

Other stage equipment included trap-doors and a device known as an *ekkyklema*. This was a platform on wheels which could be rolled forward through the central door of the stage building. It enabled such scenes to be shown as the aftermath of a murder in a palace which the stage building represented. Scenes of violence were never shown happening on the stage.

Costume

The actors in tragedies were usually portraying heroes of legend or remote history, or deities. To do justice to these rôles, they wore majestic flowing robes, rather like a priest's, richly coloured and patterned. They wore special boots, called *kothornoi*, which became symbolic of tragedy as a whole. Known in English as buskins, they were loose enough to fit either leg—Theramenes, a politician who kept changing sides, earned himself the nick-name of 'the Buskin'. Later on, so that the tragic actors might look even more impressive, their *kothornoi* were given a much thicker sole, and their bodies were padded under the costumes.

In the comedies, the costumes of the actors were intentionally ridiculous. A great deal of padding was used to distort their figures, and they wore short tunics, beneath which they often had, strapped to their bodies, symbolic representations of the male organs, called *phalloi*. Comic actors wore flat slippers.

Strange as it seems to us, all the actors wore masks made of linen, cork, or wood. There were only three actors and, since the leading actor only played one part, the other two had to take all the remaining rôles, including those of females. Masks obviously made this simpler, and, as they were the only part of the costume which was changed, a switch of character could be made very quickly indeed. Also, in a

12.3 Special seats for priests and officials in the theatre of Dionysos: cushions and canopies added to the comfort.

large open-air theatre—it was a hundred metres or more from the back row to the stage at Athens—subtle facial expressions would have been lost to a great part of the audience, but the exaggerated features of a mask could be seen. Hair was attached to the masks, and so there were no separate wigs. After the fifth century B.C. the hair was sometimes built up into a conical shape to give the impression of extra height.

The masks served an important purpose by becoming traditionally of a standard appearance for a certain type of character, so that the audience, who had no programme, would be able to recognize quickly a new character as a hero, a priest, a slave and so on. In comedies the masks were naturally much more distorted and exaggerated than in tragedies, and sometimes were ludicrous caricatures of living persons, whom the poet was making fun of in the play.

As a further help to the audience in identifying characters, appropriate symbols were used. So a king would hold a royal sceptre, Herakles would carry his traditional club and Poseidon his trident.

Tragedy

Disasters, deserved or undeserved, bloody revenge, agonizing problems of conscience are among the more common themes of tragedy. The plots often involve 'dramatic irony'—situations where the audience recognize the facts before the characters on the stage do so—and there are a great many remarkable coincidences. These factors, as well as the often despairing songs of the chorus, the absence of much action on the stage itself and the many speeches made by messengers, combine to make these plays strange affairs to those living in a different age. They are not very relaxing entertainment, perhaps, but the philosopher Aristotle considered that the

12.4 The chorus in a modern production of a Greek play.

fear and pity which they aroused had a cleansing effect (*katharsis*) on the minds of the audience. The plays discussed the most profound questions of human life.

The same stories were quite often used by different writers. The audience in any case had usually known from childhood the outlines of the legends involved. They did not expect to hear a new story, but a new treatment of a familiar story. In early times the three tragedies put into the competition by each playwright were linked in subject matter, forming a 'trilogy', but the practice died out, and we have only one surviving set of this nature, by Aeschylus.

Probably the most famous of all Greek tragedies is *Oedipus the King*, by Sophocles. Admired by Aristotle, it is, in many ways, typical. Like almost all tragedies it was taken from ancient legend. The play involves the gradual discovery of terrible facts about Oedipus which are not entirely his fault.

Oedipus was brought up in Corinth as the son of its king, but left the city when the Delphic oracle told him that he was fated to kill his father and marry his mother. He came to Thebes, killing on the way a stranger who arrogantly ordered him out of the way at a remote crossroads in the hills near Delphi. Thebes was being persecuted by the Sphinx, a monster which asked riddles and killed those who answered incorrectly. For Thebes the riddle was, put briefly:

'Which creature has two feet, three feet and four feet, but is weakest when it has four?'

By giving the simple answer to this, Oedipus saved Thebes, and was rewarded with the throne and the hand of the queen, Jokasta, as the previous king, Laios, had been murdered on the way to Delphi.

Oedipus the King opens with Thebes again in distress, some years later. There is a terrible plague, in which the cattle are dying, the crops are failing, no children are born. Oedipus, who by now is the respected king with four children by Jokasta, discovers that the trouble is caused by the presence in the city of the murderers of Laios, which is angering the gods. He decrees awful punishment to them unless they give themselves up, and to any who shelter them.

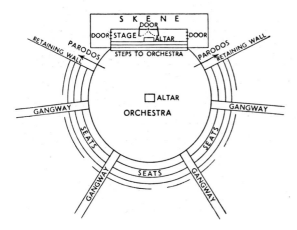

12.5 Plan of a Greek theatre.

As the play proceeds it becomes apparent to Oedipus, relentlessly seeking out the facts, that not only did he himself commit the murder of Laios, in the violent encounter he had on his way to Thebes, but also that he is in reality the son of Laios and Jokasta. It emerges that when Oedipus was born the oracle foretold that he was destined to kill his father and marry his mother. To avoid this Laios gave the child to a shepherd to leave it out to die on the mountainside, but the shepherd had from pity given the baby to a Corinthian shepherd. The child was taken to Corinth, where he was brought up as the son of the king. At last Oedipus can have no further doubt:

'Alas! Alas! All is clear. Oh light of day, may this be the last time I see you, I who am shown to be the child of those whose child I should not be—married to the woman I should not have married, killer of the man I should not have killed.'

(1182ff.)

He rushes into the palace, where Jokasta, already realizing the truth, has hanged herself. Seizing her brooch, he gouges out his own eyes. The play ends with Oedipus' life in ruins. The chorus comments:

'Alas, generation of mortals, I think your life is as nothing. What man earns more happiness than merely to seem so, and after seeming so, to fall? Seeing your example, unhappy Oedipus, and your fate, I consider no mortal happy.'

(1186ff.)

Agamemnon, by Aeschylus, is the story of the murder of Agamemnon when he returns to Mycenae after the Greek expedition to Troy (see Chapter 2). The treacherous killing was the work of his own wife, Klytaimnestra, and her lover. Other plays describe the revenge taken on these two by Agamemnon's children, Orestes

12.6 Mask of a tragic actor.

and Elektra. *Medea*, by Euripides, concerns the killing by a foreign princess, Medea, of her own children, when her husband Jason takes a new wife. She also kills the new bride and her father. *Iphigeneia at Aulis*, by the same author, deals with the sacrifice by Agamemnon of his own daughter in order to obtain a favourable wind from the gods for the Greek fleet to be able to sail to Troy—Iphigeneia is led to believe that the ceremony is to be her marriage to Achilles.

With themes such as these, we can see that the plays are indeed powerful tragedies. The characters in them are on a larger scale than ordinary humans, and the events and situations are not those of ordinary life.

The Tragedians

Of the plays of Aeschylus, seven survive from about ninety. Aeschylus, who lived from 525 until 456 B.C.—there was a story that he died when an eagle dropped a tortoise on his bald head—wrote on grand and often terrifying subjects in a correspondingly grand manner. He was intensely religious and patriotic. He fought in the battle of Marathon, and his description of the later battle of Salamis (see p. 68) is so vivid that it is likely that he was at least an eyewitness of that.

Sophocles, whose long life from 496 to 406 B.C. we have already mentioned (see p. 11), wrote about one hundred and twenty plays, of which we still have seven. He won twenty-four victories in the drama contest, and never dropped lower than second place. Uncontroversial in his private life, he played the full part of an

12.7 Terra-cotta statuettes of comic actors.

Athenian citizen, serving as general at least twice and holding public office on other occasions. His plays are orthodox in their moral and religious beliefs, and written with a polished skill.

Euripides concentrated more than Aeschylus and Sophocles on normal human life. He lived from about 480 until 406 B.C. His plays often reflect the questioning of traditional religious and moral beliefs which was current at the end of the fifth century B.C. (see Chapter 15). For this he was criticized by some, as also for his frequent use of convenient coincidence and the *deus ex machina* in his plots. Nevertheless he won the first prize five times and was also much admired, as is indicated by the story of the Athenian prisoners after the disaster at Syracuse (see p. 104), who were able to gain their release by reciting to their captors from Euripides' poetry. Euripides, like Aeschylus, is said to have met a sad end—torn to death by the hunting dogs of the king of Macedonia. Nineteen of his ninety-two plays remain.

Comedy

The Frogs, a comedy by Aristophanes (about 448–385 B.C.), gives us exaggerated but instructive parodies of the styles of Aeschylus and Euripides. In that play the god Dionysos, ludicrously disguised as Herakles and accompanied by a slave called Xanthias, goes down to the Underworld to bring back a tragic poet to Athens, where there is none left of any worth since the death of Sophocles. Arriving in Hades, after various farcical adventures, they come upon a contest for the throne of Tragedy, which Dionysos is invited to judge. Aeschylus and Euripides are the only competitors, because with typical modesty Sophocles has declined to challenge Aeschylus. The poetry of Aeschylus and Euripides is weighed and measured, and the former wins because he is the heavier and grander. In this passage the chorus describes in advance what the contest will be like:

'Aeschylus the Thunderer will have terrible anger in his heart, when he sees his opponent sharpening his fangs. His eyeballs will be rolling then, in his terrible rage.

There will be helmet-crashing clashes of words with horse-hair crests, and scrapings of splinters and carvings of works when the man Euripides defends himself against the high-stepping sayings of the poet of genius.

Aeschylus bristling his shaggy mane of hair—it's all his own, home-grown— with a frightful scowl will roar and hurl phrases built with bolts, ripping them off like timbers of a ship with his giant blast.

But from the other side the craftsman of words, Euripides, the smooth examiner unrolling his tongue and shaking malicious reins, will cut to pieces the sayings and wear away by his quibbles the great labour of the other's lungs.'

(814ff.)

In the Greek the alternate paragraphs not only describe, but also imitate the styles of the two poets.

The Frogs takes its name from a chorus of frogs (not the main chorus which sings the passage above), whose harsh cries of 'brekekekex koax koax' torment Dionysos as he is forced by Charon, the ferryman of the dead, to row his own way across the marshy river into Hades. Such a chorus also provided the title for some of

137

Aristophanes' other plays, like *The Wasps* and *The Birds*. Eleven of his plays survive, which are our only examples of the 'Old Comedy' of the fifth century B.C. This, unlike tragedy, referred openly and frequently to the political situations and issues of the time—attacking the new-fangled thinking of the sophists (see Chapter 15), pleading for the end of the war with Sparta, frankly attacking politicians. Its serious intention was achieved by ridicule of those with whom the poet disagreed. There was also a passage in each play when the action stopped, and the chorus delivered an address to the audience expressing the views of the poet on some topic of current interest in Athens. This was known as the *parabasis* of a play.

Many of the constant references to the events and personalities of Athens in the fifth century B.C. are bound to be lost on a modern audience. Yet the plays also contain a great deal of slapstick comedy and cheerful obscenity. This, and the fact that a good few of the themes are of universal appeal, mean that revivals of the plays nowadays are quite frequent and successful. Here is a scene from *The Frogs* during the journey down to Hades. Dionysos has been scared out of his wits by the threats made to him when he has knocked on the door of the palace of the king of Hades and, because of his disguise, wearing a lion-skin and carrying a club, has been taken to be Herakles himself. The latter is not entirely welcome—one of his Twelve Labours was the stealing of Kerberos, the three-headed watchdog of the Underworld. However, as the scene shows, he clearly managed to get on well with the queen, Persephoné.

XANTHIAS (sarcastically): By Poseidon, you were brave.
DIONYSOS: By Zeus yes, I think I was. But weren't you afraid of the shouts and threats?
XANTHIAS: Heavens no! I didn't even take any notice.
DIONYSOS: Come on then, since you're so confident and brave, you be me and take this club and lion-skin, if you're so fearless. And I'll take a turn as your baggage-carrier.
XANTHIAS: Give me them quickly then—your word is my command—and take a look at Heraklexanthias to see if I'm cowardly and chicken-hearted like you.
DIONYSOS: You look a proper sight. Come on then, let's have the baggage.
    (A servant-girl comes out of the palace.)
GIRL: Sweetest Herakles, are you back again? Do come in. When our queen Persephoné heard you were coming, she started to bake some cakes, and put on two or three pots of pease-porridge, and started to roast a whole ox and to make scones. But do come in. (Herakles was notorious for his huge appetite.)
XANTHIAS: Most kind of you, thank you, but. . .
GIRL: By Apollo, I shan't allow you to go—she was stewing up the birds and toasting the savouries, and mixing the sweetest of wine. Do come in with me.
XANTHIAS: You're very kind, but. . .
GIRL: You are being silly, but I shan't let you go. There's the most gorgeous flute-girl waiting for you inside, and two or three dancing-girls. . .
XANTHIAS: What's that you say? Dancing-girls?
GIRL: Beauties, all tarted up. Do come in. The cook was just starting to take the fish off the stove and the table was being laid.
XANTHIAS: In you go and tell those dancing-girls in there that I'm on my way. Boy! Follow me here and bring the bags.

DIONYSOS: Hang on there! Surely you're not taking me seriously just because I kitted you up as Herakles for a joke? Don't be so stupid, Xanthias. Pick up the baggage and carry it again.

XANTHIAS: What's going on? Surely you're not meaning to take away what you gave me yourself?

DIONYSOS: I'm not meaning to. I'm already doing it. Take off the lion-skin.

XANTHIAS: I protest. I call on the gods.

DIONYSOS: What gods have you got in mind? You must be a crazy half-wit to expect to be Herakles when you're just a slave and a mortal.

XANTHIAS: All right then, take them. Perhaps one day you'll want a favour from me, god willing. . .

(491–533)

Gods, as Dionysos here, were frequently shown in comedies as cowards or thieves, although there was far from being any suggestion that they did not really exist or should not be worshipped. Plots and events in the plays were fantastically

12.8 Scene from a comedy in which a lover pleads with a girl at a window.   *Reproduced by Courtesy of the Trustees of the British Museum.*

139

impossible. In *The Peace*, by Aristophanes, a character flew up to heaven on a giant beetle; in *The Clouds*, Socrates was depicted as spending much of his time suspended in a basket in the sky, seeking philosophical inspiration (see also p. 116); in *The Birds*, the characters, tired of life in Athens, went off to create a new home in an imaginary kingdom of birds, between heaven and earth. There were unexplained jumps in time and place, and suddenly the actors would turn and speak directly to the audience, which happily accepted all these absurdities. The chorus was quite likely to appeal directly to the audience for loud applause, so that their play would win the prize.

Comedies were performed in the City Dionysia at Athens, but they were particularly associated with another festival, the Lenaia, held earlier in the year when there were likely to be fewer outsiders present. To compete in the City Dionysia, the comic poet supplied one play, but the tragedian four—three tragedies and a satyr-play. Satyr-plays were performed after the tragedies. So named because of their chorus of satyrs, partly human, partly goat, who were attendants of Dionysos, these wild and uproarious plays dealt with grotesque and humorous episodes in ancient legend. The only complete example left is *The Cyclops* by Euripides, about the blinding by Odysseus of the one-eyed monster, the Cyclops.

The Organization

We may judge the importance attached to drama by the Athenians from the degree to which the state was involved. As official religious festivals the competitions were organized and considerably financed by the city. Even the members of the audience from the time of Pericles seem to have had their admission charge paid by the state. A 'Theoric Fund' was set up for this purpose, and later on a law was passed punishing by death anyone who suggested that the money be used for military reasons in time of peace.

Applications by poets to compete had to be made to the chief magistrate of the year, the *archon*. He was said to 'grant a chorus' to those whom he selected, which meant that the playwright was supplied with actors at the city's expense and was assigned a *choregos*. The latter was a wealthy citizen who as a public service (see page 113) undertook the payment for the training and costumes of the chorus. His willingness or otherwise to spend could make all the difference to a poet's chances. If successful the *choregos*, like the writer and the actors, won a prize and might put up a monument or inscribed stone in the city to commemorate the victory. He would probably also have to spend some more money on a celebration party for his cast.

The competitions in the City Dionysia were judged by panels of ten citizens, and final decisions rested on the votes of five of these drawn by lot. Then the victorious poets and *choregoi* were presented by the *archon*, in the crowded theatre, with crowns of ivy.

CHAPTER THIRTEEN

Every Day

The Greeks did not, it seems, take houses very seriously. This was partly because of the climate: life out of doors is much more possible and enjoyable in Greece than in northern Europe. It was also because they thought that public buildings—temples, theatres, law-courts, fountains—were more important than private houses. It was left to the Romans to develop luxurious domestic architecture.

Houses

The normal Greek house, in both town and country, was made of sunbaked bricks on a stone foundation, with walls often so flimsy that burglars were known as 'wall-piercers'! It often had a partial second storey, and was roofed with tiles. Blank walls usually faced on to the street; there was a courtyard in the middle where many household jobs were done in the open air, and a number of not very large rooms off it. The courtyard sometimes contained a well, and, if the owner was rich, there might be a bathroom. The two main rooms were the *andron*, where the men held their supper parties, and the loom-room, where the women worked and spent a good deal of time. One room was sometimes a small shop, with its own entrance onto the street; and the rest were bedrooms and store-rooms. There were, of course, bigger houses: Plato the philosopher speaks of one belonging to Kallias, one of the richest men in Athens, where the courtyard had two colonnades around it, each of which was large enough to allow seven men to walk abreast (see p. 166). We hear too, of houses with their own gymnasium and baths. But normally they were much more modest.

Inside the rooms things were equally simple. There were only four sorts of Greek furniture: chests, couches, chairs and stools, and tables. Cupboards do not seem to have existed. Floors were beaten earth, and windows were high, small and unglazed. Wealthy houses might add a stone floor, sometimes with mosaic decorations, and tapestries on the wall. So, although some of the furniture shown on Greek vases is elegant, we should have found it all rather uncomfortable.

Clothes and Cosmetics

The day started early. Socrates, in one of Plato's dialogues, is woken by a young and keen friend who has heard that Protagoras, the famous sophist, is in Athens and wants to go and see him as soon as possible. Socrates persuades him to wait until it gets light! So they talk for a while in the bedroom, the visitor sitting on Socrates' couch. This couch, with its woollen blankets but no mattress, might well have been the only furniture in the room. Getting up was a rapid business: shaving and washing were left for later in the day; and dressing meant only putting on a linen *chiton* (a sort of shirt), sandals, and perhaps a square of woollen cloth on top as a cloak (*himation*).

Women's clothes were equally simple. They wore a longer version of the *chiton*, which was often patterned and looked rather like a very loose-fitting dress. It was held in place by brooches at the shoulder and a belt at or above the waist which produced the folds so often seen in Greek sculpture. Women, too, wore the *himation* out of doors. Hair styles for wealthy women were elaborate, and jewellery and make-up were much used. Xenophon, the historian and sociologist, tells us of one husband who complained—gently—about his wife's wearing of powder and rouge. He pointed out that 'these deceits may in some measure take in strangers, but it is inevitable that people will be found out when they constantly associate with each other'—in the morning, when sweating or crying, or in the bath! He goes on to say that 'as the gods have made horses the most agreeable things to horses and oxen to oxen, so also mankind think the human body in its natural state to be the most agreeable thing.' (*Oikonomikos*, 10, 2) One wonders whether his wife was really convinced! Perfume, too, in charming little bottles called *aryballoi* was common, sometimes imported, more often made locally from olive-oil and herbs.

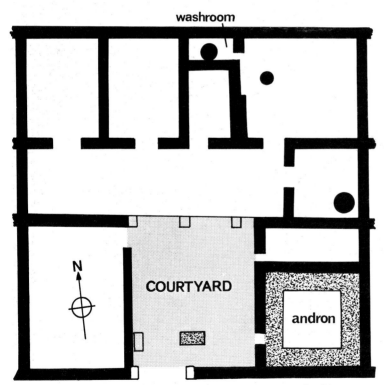

13.1 House at Olynthos: plan. This is one house in a block of ten.

Food

Food for most people was simple and sparse. The staple diet in towns was bread (for Athenians, mostly from imported corn) and fish. Eggs, vegetables (especially lentils, celery, radishes, beans), olives, grapes and figs were also available. Meat was rare, usually eaten only at the feast after sacrifices. Milk and cheese came almost entirely from goats. Cattle were uncommon, and so therefore were beef and cow's milk, as our word 'butter' shows: *turon* is cheese in Greek; *bou* (ox)+*turon* (cattle-cheese) is special enough to have a different word. There was no sugar, of course, in the classical world; honey was therefore very important. One well-known kind came from Hymettos, a mountain five kilometres east of Athens.

In the morning and at midday meals were hardly more than snacks. The main meal of the day (*deipnon*) was in the late afternoon and usually consisted of two courses: poultry or fish, cheese perhaps, with vegetables and sauces first, followed by figs, olives, nuts, grapes and other fruit. Although knives were used, fingers took the place of forks; and a lot of scraps seem to have collected on the floor. Often, no doubt, the whole family ate together. But what we hear most about are the formal dinner parties, to which male guests only were invited.

13.2 Women wearing the *himation* over the long *chiton*. These terracottas, which come from Tanagra in Boiotia and are 20 and 26 cm high, were made probably in the third century B.C.

Dinner-Parties

For these, the walls were decorated with flowers and long streamers of vine or ivy, and the guests wore garlands and lay on couches round the walls of the *andron*. Beside them stood small, often three-legged, tables for food and wine. The *symposion* (drinking-party) proper began after the food had been eaten and the tables taken out. Greek wine was thick and sweet, and therefore almost always drunk diluted. We are told that 'it gives good cheer to those who mix and drink it moderately; but mix half and half, and you get madness; unmixed, total collapse.'

These *symposia* varied. Some were for conversation. As Plato says:

'When civilized, educated people have a party, you won't see flute-players or dancers or harpists there. They are quite able to entertain themselves, without this sort of facetious nonsense... They talk amongst themselves, speaking and listening in turn—and all quite calmly, even if they have been drinking very heavily.'

(*Protagoras*, 347D)

Plato's own account of one such party has seven long speeches on the nature of love, some witty, some rather boring, some profound. Another *symposion* described by Xenophon is more relaxed—and probably more realistic. It begins with a professional funny man arriving uninvited and trying to amuse the other guests by

13.3 The drinking party: a *symposion*: the man in the centre may be proposing a toast. Notice the cushions, and the flowers on two of the tables. The picture itself is painted round the outside of a flat cup (kylix) similar to the ones shown in it.

telling jokes; when his third one has fallen flat, he covers his head with his cloak and bursts into tears! This raises a laugh, and the party goes on. A sort of cabaret, is brought on, two girls and a boy, who dance and play the flute and the lyre. There are acrobatics, too:

> 'After this, a circular frame was brought in, with upright swords set round its rim. The dancer did somersaults into the frame and out of it again over the swords, so that the spectators were afraid she would injure herself. But she completed the performance confidently and safely.'

(*Symposion* II, 12)

Many vases have pictures of this kind of *symposion*. Some illustrate what Dionysos talks of in one comedy:

> 'Three bowls only do I mix for the sensible, one to health, the second to love and pleasure, the third to sleep. When this is drunk up, wise guests go home. The fourth bowl is ours no longer but belongs to violence, the fifth to uproar, the sixth to drunken revel, and the seventh to black eyes. The eighth is the policeman's, the ninth belongs to vomiting, and the tenth to madness and hurling of furniture.'

But, before these extremes were reached, other entertainments were possible: songs were sung or poetry recited, either what you had made up yourself or passages

13.4 The drinking party: the boy is playing the *diaulos* (a double oboe), while the man lies back on the cushions on his couch. The table, used for the food earlier, has been pushed under the couch.

145

from well-known poets. One favourite game was *kottabos*, in which the last dregs of the wine in your cup were flicked at a mark or to knock off a disc balanced on a stand. Players were judged, it seems, by the elegance of their throwing as much as by its accuracy.

Women and Children

Like Greek political life, social life was for men only, or more or less so. Women's lives were much more restricted, tied closely to the home and family, and with little contact with the outside world. In his famous Funeral Speech over the dead of the first year of the Peloponnesian War, Pericles says to the widows, 'The greatest honour a woman can have is to be least spoken of in men's company, whether in praise or in criticism.' Girls did not go to school like their brothers. They were taught household jobs by their mothers at home, and at about the age of fifteen they were married. Marriages were arranged by the parents; the bride might well not meet her husband, who was usually considerably older, until the wedding. Before it, the bride would be bathed in holy water. A wedding meal was held at the bride's house, when both families, relatives and friends joined in. There was a wedding-cake, and the couple were pelted with sweets. Hymns were sung, the bride was conducted to her husband's house in a procession, and the mothers lit the wedding torches in the bedroom.

When children were born, those who were weak and sickly were often exposed, that is, put in a clay pot and left to die in some bleak spot. But there was much rejoicing over healthy babies, as well as the usual grumbles. As they grew up, they had all sorts of toys—rattles, clay animals, jointed dolls at first, then hobby-horses, tops, yo-yos, swings and five-stones. They kept pets—hares and quails seem to have been popular—and played games such as leap-frog and a sort of hockey (see fig. 15.3).

The mothers had to do the household chores, of course, as well as looking after their children. In most houses except the poorest they had the help of a slave or two.

13.5 The drinking party: a game of *kottabos* being played by a guest and by one of the girls who entertained the men.

146

But there was a great deal to be done: you bought corn, not bread, in the market and therefore had to grind and bake it at home. Water had to be fetched from the public fountains. And you had to buy, clean, card, spin, weave and dye wool and, less often, flax to produce the cloth from which you then made clothes for the household. Add to this shopping, cooking and, in wealthy houses, the organizing of the slaves' work, and it is clear why one of Xenophon's characters says there is no-one to whom he entrusts more of his important affairs than his wife—although he admits in the next breath that there is no-one to whom he talks less!

The affection among members of a family is seen in many gravestones and vase-paintings showing funerals. Epitaphs, too, show the grief that very high infant mortality and shorter lives generally caused. When someone died, the corpse was laid out in the house and mourned by family and friends. They cut their hair and wore black. An obol, a small coin, the traditional fee for Charon, the ferryman on the river Styx on the edge of the Underworld, was placed in the dead person's mouth. A procession of mourners, often with hired musicians, went to the cemetery, where the dead were sometimes cremated, sometimes buried.

Cities

What were the cities like in which all this went on? They would have struck us as a strange mixture of public wealth and private squalor. The houses, as we have seen were small, poorly furnished and dirty. They were crowded together, separated by streets which were usually just stony alleys, winding, narrow and smelly, with a runnel of filthy water down the middle. Yet in the centre of the city the civic buildings would be impressive, large, well-built and expensively decorated.

Most Greek cities, of course, like Athens, just grew up round the *agora*, the town-centre, which was used in early days for the market, the political assembly, and ceremonies. But some cities were carefully planned. The port of Athens, Piraeus, was one of these. The town-planner was a man called Hippodamos, who used the grid-system which New York has made famous in the modern world. But it goes back a long way. Hippodamos himself came from Miletos in Asia Minor where, as a young man, he had doubtless seen the rebuilding of his own city after the Persian Wars. This was on a rectangular plan, used with great subtlety to fit the topography (see fig. 16.1). There were three residential areas, and space was left for the gradual development of commercial, public and religious buildings, all with direct access to the harbours, the housing blocks and landward communications. This grid idea was applied to a good number of Greek cities in the fifth and fourth centuries B.C. and later, of course, was taken over by Roman engineers. Priené in Ionia is a splendid example (see fig 16.2); and Alexandria and Pompeii are well-known.

City Centre

Pausanias defines a *polis* as a place having government offices, a gymnasium, a theatre, an *agora* and a fountain. The *agora* was the most important of these. It was, according to King Cyrus of Persia, in Herodotus' story, 'the special place marked out, where the Greeks meet to cheat each other.' In Mycenaean times the palace had been

13.6 Boy combining work and play: he carries a covered plate of food in his left hand, while trundling a hoop along with the right. It is an early red-figure cup (*c.* 500 B.C.), and the artist has not quite mastered the art of drawing a twisting torso.

13.7 Women at a fountain-house: five fountains fill *hydriai* standing on blocks. Two of the girls, Iopé and Kleo, are apparently offering wreaths, Rhodope turns round to talk, while the unnamed girl on the right is perhaps praying. They all wear the embroidered *chiton*.

the centre of the town; but then those were aristocratic societies. In the more democratic *poleis* it was appropriate that the place where all citizens met should be the focus of city life. The *agora* at Athens was certainly that. Government buildings were put up around it—the *bouleuterion* where the *boulé* met, the *tholos* where the duty *prytany* lived, the law-courts, the mint. The city's regard for the gods was seen in the massive altar to the Twelve Gods—incidentally, the centre of the Attic road system— and the temples of Hephaistos and Apollo immediately to the west of the *agora*. Across the middle of it ran the Panathenaic Way (see fig. 9.3), the route which the procession in honour of Athena at the Panathenaic festival took on its way to the Acropolis and the Parthenon. On the edge of it stood three *stoai*, colonnades where business could be done and friends met.

In the middle was all the hubbub of buying and selling. The whole area was crowded with flimsy stalls ('shops' is a very misleading word), where every kind of business was carried on. There was some sort of rough grouping: fishmongers, barbers and bankers all worked on the north side; olive-oil was sold on the east side; and free men wanting jobs could be found for hire on the west, near the temple of Hephaistos. One character in a comedy says, 'I went round from garlic-sellers to onion-boys, from spice-merchant to haberdashery, and to where books are for sale.' This last was a place called 'The Orchestra', presumably where plays had been performed before the theatre of Dionysos on the south slope of the Acropolis was built. So the *agora* must have been hot, dusty and noisy.

Baths

There were, however, ways of refreshing yourself. Two fountains, so essential in drought-ridden Greece, had been built there, the one in the south-east corner, Enneakrounos (Nine-Springs), erected by Peisistratos, being the most important in the city. There were wine-merchants, too, and food stalls. Or you might take yourself off to the public baths. These were disliked by some people as productive of softness, because hot water was available as well as warmed rooms. But they were good places to gossip in as well as to wash. And it was washing; they were not big enough for swimming. In any case, the Greeks seem to have swum only when they had to, not for pleasure. There was a plunge bath in the establishment at the Piraeus; but most baths probably had only hip-baths. The full-length bath was an invention of the decadent Sybarites in southern Italy. But even hip-baths were better than the font-like basins at home which had to be filled by hand from some outside fountain.

Parks

You might also go off to the suburbs of the city, to the parks. These were known as *gymnasia* because they were used as places where young men exercised naked (*gymnos*). But they were not large rooms as modern gymnasia are. Aristophanes speaks of one, the Akademé, where young men race 'under the olive-trees, sharing the fragrance of leafy poplar and carefree convolvulus and the joys of spring, where the plane tree whispers to the elm.' It was Kimon who had 'turned the hitherto parched and waterless Akademé into a well-watered garden with shady avenues', another of his public benefactions, like planting trees in the *agora*. So these places were parks with sports grounds rather than buildings. There were three in Athens, the Akademé in the north-west, dedicated to Athena, who had twelve sacred olives there, the Lykeion in the east, sacred to Apollo, and the Kynosarges to the south, in honour of Herakles. They had running tracks, sanded areas for boxing, jumping and wrestling, changing rooms and washing facilities. But they were known, too, as places where philosophical talk went on. The sophists (see Chapter 15) often taught there, and later they became virtual universities, with lecture-rooms and libraries. Plato's school at the Akademé and Aristotle's at the Lykeion have given the Scots and the French their words for high schools.

After a day spent like this in work, talking and recreation, you went home, had your supper (on a non-party day) and went to bed. The next day was to start at dawn again.

13.8 Women washing, a red figure vase of about 450 B.C. The girl on the left is rolling up her *chiton* and her boots stand beside her.

CHAPTER FOURTEEN

Work and Trade

'One of the Spartans,' Plutarch tells us, 'happened to be staying in Athens when the courts were in session. He found out that one defendant, who had been convicted on a charge of having no work, (Solon had made it illegal for citizens to have no occupation) was going home very depressed, escorted by his sad and sympathetic friends. So he asked the bystanders to point out this man who had been found guilty "of living like a free man". So convinced are the Spartans that it is fitting only for slaves to be occupied with crafts and money-making.'

(*Lykourgos* xxiv)

This Spartan idea, that work is somehow disgraceful, is found in many Greek writers. Xenophon quotes Socrates:

'Those jobs which are known as mechanical (he means crafts and industry) have a bad reputation. In the *poleis*, quite understandably, they are regarded with contempt. For the bodies of those who do them, workmen and foremen alike, are damaged, since they are forced to sit down to them and to work indoors, and some people even have to spend all day at the fire. As their bodies grow soft, so do their characters, too. For these low-class jobs do not allow people enough time to be with their friends or to take any part in public life, with the result that such workers are obviously bad at social and political activities. Indeed, in some *poleis*, particularly those which are thought to be best at war, no citizen is allowed to do these jobs.'

(*Oeconomicus* IV, 2 and 3)

It was a traditional idea, reflecting an artistocratic society where the nobles used slaves to do the chores—which allowed them to spend their time in war and politics. In fact, of course, most ordinary people had to work. But the notion persisted that it was an infringement on the free man's liberty; the Greeks would not have understood the Marxist idealization of work and the worker.

Still, the Greeks did work, and the majority of them on the land, as small peasant farmers. But crafts and craftsmen flourished, especially in Athens. One of Aristophanes' characters says:

'When the cock sings his dawn song, up they all jump and rush off to work, the bronze-smiths, the potters, the tanners, the shoemakers, the bath-attendants, the corn-merchants, the lyre-shapers-and-shield-makers, and some of them even put on their sandals and leave when it's still dark.'

(*The Birds* 489)

Plutarch, when he is describing Pericles' policies to involve all Athenians in the national prosperity, adds to the list of trades:

'He brought before the people proposals for great public works, plans for buildings that would involve many crafts and take a long time to complete. . . The materials to be used for them were stone, bronze, ivory, gold, ebony, cypress-wood. The trades to be engaged in completing the programme would be carpenters, sculptors, bronze-smiths, masons, dyers, workers in gold and ivory, artists, embroiderers, embossers. . . There would also be rope-makers, weavers, leather-workers, road-builders and miners.'

(*Pericles* xii)

The Greeks were well aware of the advantages of specialization:

'For in small *poleis* the same man makes beds, doors, ploughs, tables, and often this same workman will build houses, too. And he is satisfied if he finds enough employment even like this to earn a living. It is impossible for a man who works at many crafts to be highly skilled in all of them. In large *poleis*, on the other hand, greater demand for each craft means that one skill provides an adequate living for each man. Indeed, often not one entire craft: one man, for example, will make men's shoes, another women's. There are even some places where one man earns his living by stitching the shoes, another by chopping up the leather, another by only cutting out the uppers—and there is one man who does not do any of these jobs but simply assembles all the parts. It is inevitable that the man who specializes in a very specific job will do this job to a high degree of excellence.'

(Xenophon, *Cyropaedia* VIII, 2, 5)

14.1 A carpenter: he is shaping a beam (with a lock?). The head of the adze is lashed on.

One large area of Athens, the Kerameikos, showed how this worked in practice. It was the potters' quarter; and no doubt the exchange of ideas—and the competition—that this grouping of workers in the same craft brought about was one of the reasons why Athenian pottery was so excellent.

It is, however, misleading to talk of 'industry'. All this work went on in very small groups. The largest 'factory' we hear of was one owned by a *metoikos* named Kephalos. This establishment, which made armour, employed one hundred and twenty slaves. Most workshops, however, were much smaller: we have the prosecution speech in a case involving a man called Timarchos who owned a small place where nine shoemakers and one foreman were employed. And Demosthenes' father (see p. 179) had one workshop with thirty-two knife-makers and another with twenty carpenters who made beds.

A good deal of this 'cottage industry' went on in rooms in private houses or outbuildings attached to them. When the state contracted out work, it did so to very many small groups of craftsmen, not to large firms. These craftsmen could be free men, *metoikoi* (resident foreigners) or slaves, indeed often all three worked together. Records have survived of men employed on the Erechtheion (see fig 10.6) in 405 B.C. seventy-one workers were under contract, of whom twenty were citizens, thirty-five *metoikoi* and sixteen slaves. Of the foremen, three were citizens, two were *metoikoi* and one a slave. All, whatever their social status, were paid the same rate. The average wage for a skilled worker was a *drachma* a day, that is, twice what unskilled

14.2 Vase painters: the young man on the left has his paint in a pot on a table beside him, while the man on the right may be going off to fill another with more paint.

153

workers and jurymen were paid, and the same as a soldier or a sailor on campaign. The precise details of the job specification are interesting. Two out of the surviving sections read:

'Stones forming the revetment of the portico, Pentelic stone: length, four feet less one palm; height, two feet; thickness, three palms. To the man who laid them, three drachmas each less two obols. To Simon of Agryle, two stones: five drachmas, two obols. . . .'
To the man who dressed these stones on top: fourteen lengths of four feet. To Phalakros of Paiania and his assistant: forty-nine drachmas. . . .'

Two of the most important crafts were metal-working and pottery. Pottery has been discussed in Chapter 11. In metal-working the main difficulty was to generate temperatures high enough to reduce the ore. The usual fuel was charcoal, and several writers discuss which trees produce the best charcoal. This had to be heated by draughts, and bellows were used in the furnace for this. But the temperatures reached were not very high (1200°C), and the resulting metal was impure and therefore brittle. Delicate, high-quality work was done, but it was achieved by artistry rather than chemistry.

Slaves

Most of this work was done by slaves. But, as we have seen, slaves mixed freely with other people—in Athens, at least. 'Those who can afford it,' says Xenophon, 'buy slaves in order to have fellow-workers'—fellow-workers, not underlings to be ordered about. Indeed, one conservative Athenian complains that

'there is a very great lack of discipline among the slaves and *metoikoi* in Athens. You are not allowed to strike a slave there, nor will a slave step aside for you. The reason for this Athenian custom I shall explain. If there were a law that permitted a

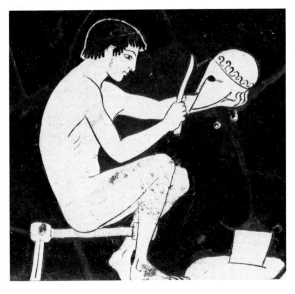

14.3 An armourer is shaping a helmet, with an anvil in front of him.

free man to strike a slave, *metoikos* or freedman, you would often find yourself hitting an Athenian on the assumption that he was a slave. For ordinary citizens there wear no better clothes than slaves or *metoikoi*, and look no different.'

(*The Old Oligarch* I, 10)

Still, the difference was still there. Euripides, the radical playwright, might say that 'one thing only disgraces a slave, and that is the name. In all other respects a slave, if he be good, is no worse than a free man.' Yet legally the slave had no rights: he could not marry nor own anything; and evidence from slaves in lawsuits was considered acceptable only if they were tortured to give it. The same prejudice is shown in Aristotle's definition of a slave as 'a tool that happens to be alive' and 'a possession that breathes'.

There were probably eighty to a hundred thousand slaves in Athens in the fifth century B.C., that is, about one slave to every three of the free population. Where did they all come from? Most were foreign, as can be seen from an auction in 414 B.C. It included sixteen slaves, ten men, five women and one boy. Of these, five were from Thrace, where Herodotus tells us that parents sometimes sold their own children into slavery, three from Karia, two each from Syria and Illyria, and one each from Kolchis, Scythia, Lydia and Malta. Some, on the other hand, were Greek, partly through capture by pirates at sea or brigands on land, most presumably through war. This was the fate of Melos described on p. 98. Others, of course, were the children of slave-parents and thus slaves themselves.

Most households had one or two slaves, some half a dozen or more. This was because slaves were cheap. The average value of those sixteen auctioned slaves was 160 drachmas, that is, roughly equivalent to what it cost to keep a slave for a year (365 × 2 or 3 obols a day; see fig 10.9). They included skilled workers, a goldsmith, a cobbler, a fabric-maker, a maker of cooking-spits—as well as a donkey-driver! So it is not surprising that we hear of slaves being a useful investment. One writer claims that 'the first and most necessary kind of property, the best and most manageable kind, is man. Therefore the first step is to procure good slaves.' Nikias, the fifth century B.C. general who was killed in Sicily (p. 104) owned a thousand slaves which he hired out at an obol a day to work in the mines, the hirer to pay for food and (ominously) 'to fill vacancies as they occurred'. This gave a return of forty or fifty per cent—60 drachmas a year on an initial cost of about 160 drachmas. It is not surprising that other people did the same. Of course, depreciation presumably applied, especially to slaves who worked in the mines.

This was the worst form of slave employment. The silver mines at Laurion were a great advantage to Athenian finance. Her 'Attic owls'—see p. 156—were accepted all over the Greek world. The cost in human suffering, however, was great. Although some of the mining was open-cast, underground seams also had to be worked. These were reached by narrow tunnels, a metre square, with pillars of ore left to support the roof. Unscrupulous contractors sometimes removed these pillars, despite the risk to the miners. They dug the ore out, kneeling or lying flat, small clay oil-lamps beside them; other workers dragged the ore away to the main shaft, carried it up a wooden staircase and took it to the ore-washing workshops. Then the ore was smelted, usually on the same site, with all the unpleasant and toxic fumes that this process involved. Conditions were appalling, and a good number of mining slaves must have been among the twenty thousand slaves who, according to Thucydides, escaped to the Spartans in the last years of the Peloponnesian War.

That was the blackest side of the picture. Many other slaves must have led reasonably pleasant, contented lives. Those who worked in houses often established good relationships with their masters and their families, looked after their children, used and protected their property. They acted as cooks, porters, *paidagogoi* (see p. 161), maids, bodyguards, overseers—and were sometimes set free, after which they had the same rights as *metoikoi*.

They could also buy their freedom. Many of the craftsmen slaves lived apart from their master, paid him a proportion of their earnings (Timarchos' shoemakers handed over two obols a day), and kept the rest towards buying their freedom. Some slaves were very talented people, doctors, teachers, architects. Many were good businessmen, the best known of whom, a man named Pasion in the early fourth century B.C., bought his freedom, made his fortune as a banker, lent large sums to Athens, was made a citizen in return—and left half a million at his death.

Money

Coinage, as we saw in Chapter 4, had come to Greece from Lydia about 600 B.C. Before that, people had done business by barter, by exchange—three sheep for one cow, twenty-five apples for one clay lamp, and so on. In Homeric society oxen had been used to show value: Glaukos in the *Iliad* exchanged gold armour, worth a hundred oxen, for a bronze set, worth nine—'Zeus the son of Kronos must have robbed him of his wits'! And Odysseus' nurse, Eurykleia, had been bought for the worth of twenty oxen. Later, metal had been used by weight, especially iron objects, tripods and bowls, of regular size. The names of later coins show that the iron spit (*obolos*), too, was commonly used, both singly and in handfuls (*drachma*). But, from the sixth century B.C. onwards, coins took over, except in rigorously conservative places like Sparta (see Chapter 5).

Many *poleis* issued coins, but only three currencies were used at all widely outside their own *poleis*—those of Aigina, Kyzikos on the Black Sea, and, of course, Athens. These coins changed very little over two hundred years. Once accepted, their traditional design inspired confidence. So Athenian four-*drachma* coins (the famous 'Attic owls') of 280 B.C. found in Afghanistan are very little different from those of 480 B.C. found in Athens itself. The coins of other *poleis* had a much more local circulation and were issued therefore mostly in small denominations for retail trade. For the same reason, bronze coins were minted from 400 B.C. onwards. Otherwise, the vast majority of Greek coins were silver. Some were very beautiful, particularly those of Syracuse and other western *poleis*. And, beautiful or not, they have a high historical value. It was common to bury coins to keep them safe, and the discovery of such hoards has thrown much light on prosperity in the *poleis*, on trade relations and alliances, and has helped to establish an accurate dating system for the Greek world.

These different coinages made bankers essential as moneychangers. They also accepted money on deposit, and used it to make loans. The interest rate was on average twelve per cent, which compares well with hire purchase arrangements in modern society. The average interest on mortgages on houses in Athens was about

a (obverse)   *a* (reverse)

b

c   *d*

14.4 Coins from Magna Graecia about 400 B.C.: (a) a ten-drachma piece from Syracuse, showing Persephoné and dolphins on the obverse, and a four-horse chariot, whose driver is being crowned by Niké (Victory), on the reverse; (b) a four-drachma silver coin from Rhegion, with a stylized lion's head; (c) a two-stater silver coin from Thourioi, whose symbol, the bull, is kicking up stones with his hooves; (d) a silver stater from Heraklea, whose patron, Herakles, is here shown defeating the Nemean lion.

14.5 A shoemaker: notice the rack of knives and the bowl for holding the water which was used to keep the leather wet and pliable for easy cutting.

157

14.6 Ships: a merchantman under sail is about to be rammed by a (pirate?) galley driven by oars. Notice the steersman and steering oars on the merchant ship; and the boar's head ram, furled sail and two banks of oars on the galley. It is therefore a bireme, an earlier warship than the trireme (see fig 14.7a).

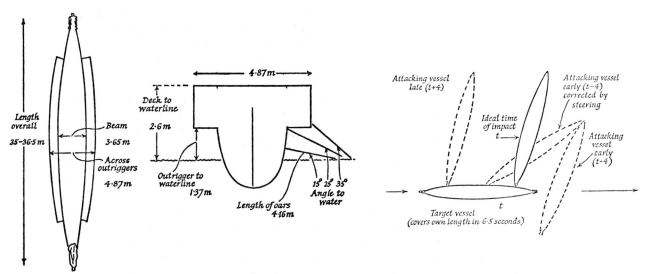

14.7a The trireme.

14.7b Ramming by a trireme.

ten per cent. We hear a good deal, too, about loans for trading overseas. Loans for the corn-run from Athens to the Black Sea and back carried an interest rate of thirty per cent, while a one-way trip from Byzantion or Sestos to Athens had a rate of ten to twelve per cent. It was a risky business, as the many wrecks discovered by marine archaeologists make clear. On the other hand, if your ship came home, you made a large profit.

The ships in which this trade was carried were rounded, with a deep hold, a single mast and a large, square-rigged sail. They were slow, unsafe and small. The average length was probably twenty metres, with a beam of six metres. They could sail at four to five knots with the wind behind, but very much less, if at all, with the wind forward of the beam. So the journey from Brindisi on the heel of Italy to Alexandria, in front of the steady north-west winds, took eighteen to twenty days, while the return often took sixty days or more. Navigation, in any case, was difficult, with no charts, no lighthouses, no buoys and no compasses. Captains therefore hugged the coast and sailed, if possible, only by day. All this explains why Hesiod advises people to 'go to sea, if you must, only from June to September—and even then you will be a fool!' It was under these conditions and in these craft that Athens imported corn, timber, metals, slaves, and luxuries like almonds from Naxos, perfume from Rhodes and ointments from Egypt. She paid for them by exporting oil, wine, silver and pottery.

But the Athenians, and other Greeks, had another type of ship—long (almost forty metres), narrow (four metres) and driven by oars. It had a crew of one hundred and seventy rowers, a boatswain, a helmsman, a few officers and twenty marines. This fast, light craft, armed with a ram, was the Greek warship, the trireme. A mast and sail were used for long journeys, but it was the power and skill of its rowers that made the trireme such a formidable weapon. Its average speed, rowed, was nine knots, with bursts of up to eleven and a half. The exact arrangement of rowers has been much disputed. The most likely is shown in the diagram on p. 158. On the outrigger were the *thranitai* ('stool-rowers'), below and inboard of them the *zygioi* ('thwart-rowers'), below them again and with oar-holes only half a metre above the waterline the *thalamioi* ('hold-rowers'). To co-ordinate all these rowers and to time manoeuvres properly demanded a great deal of training. As Pericles said to the Athenians just before the outbreak of the Peloponnesian War:

'Our opponents will not easily gain experience of fighting at sea. For even you, who have been practising it ever since the Persian Wars, have not yet mastered it. . . Naval warfare is a skill; and, like other skills, it cannot be learned by part-time, random practice. Indeed, it leaves one no time for anything else.'

(I, 142)

The ramming of an opponent was an operation that called for split-second timing and precise steering. 'The "window" during which an effective strike could be made was very short indeed. Assuming the modest speed of nine knots, each ship would travel its own length in about six and a half seconds. If the attacker arrived about four seconds too soon (t-4), he could himself be struck and holed by the target vessel; and, if he tried to avoid this by turning to starboard, his ram would strike only a glancing blow and inflict very little damage. Up to perhaps four seconds after the optimum time (t to t+4) some damage, although less than the maximum, could be inflicted.

After that, the target vessel was virtually safe.' But an attack by a squadron of these ships travelling at ten to eleven knots must have looked impressive and the damage caused by a successful ramming unpleasant.

The trireme, then, was less a ship than a weapon. Certainly it had no comfort, no cabins, no cover. It had to be beached, therefore, each night and in rough weather was very unstable. This explains, for example, why the Athenians in the Peloponnesian War took care to capture sites round the Peloponnese to establish ports of call for their fleets. With these ships Athens maintained her empire and her trade, and put down piracy. This last was no small advantage to her allies: piracy was very common at all times in the Mediterranean and, as Thucydides remarks, 'was considered quite honourable'. Trading ships were very vulnerable to swift piratical triremes (see fig 14.6), and so Athens' ability to protect merchant vessels was important.

14.8 Trade: a rarity, a vase from Sparta, shows King Arkesilaos II of Kyrene in North Africa supervising the weighing, packing and storing of wool. Notice the tame cheetah under his seat, the birds, the lizard and the monkey.

CHAPTER FIFTEEN

Education

The Traditional System

One Greek system of education has already been described in our earlier chapter on Sparta. The typical education provided for young Athenians was very different. The Athenians, although just as concerned that their sons should know how to behave correctly and to be good citizens, allowed the individual to develop much more freely than the Spartans.

In contrast to Sparta, with its state official in charge of education, Athens left the organization in private hands. Although there was probably no law compelling parents to educate their sons at school, it was certainly the strong tradition to do so. The state paid for the schooling of some children, whose fathers had died fighting for the city. There were some laws relating to education: parents had to make sure that journeys to and from school took place in daylight; unauthorized persons were banned from school property in school hours, so that pupils might be protected from bad influences. Otherwise the state did not much interfere.

Little will be said here about the education of girls, for, as far as we can tell, their upbringing took place almost entirely in their own homes. Some managed to learn to read and write, but they did not receive the same formal education as the boys. Their training was the responsibility of their mothers, by whom they were taught the skills necessary for running a home—weaving, spinning and so on—as well as correct behaviour. Whatever they learnt beyond that was picked up by their own efforts. There were certainly those who managed to become cultured and well-informed.

An Athenian boy first attended school at the age of about seven, and the primary stage of education lasted until he was about fourteen. He began by learning to read and to write, and to do simple arithmetic. His teacher in such subjects was called a *grammatistes*—*gramma* is the Greek word for a letter, with its obvious English derivations.

In many cases the school itself was simply a single room, perhaps hired, or even the corner of a courtyard in the open air. So the number of pupils in any one school would generally be small. Furniture was little more than stools or benches, and there were no desks (see fig 15.1).

The boy was constantly attended by a *paidagogos*, a slave whose duties were to supervise him at home and at school, where he generally sat in on the actual lessons, besides escorting him to and from school, and carrying his satchel. He was responsible for teaching the boy good manners and could cane him if he thought fit. In fact he was an ever-present representative of the boy's father, his owner. Of course the suitability of such slaves for their job varied widely, and many were not at all suitable. They were generally despised. Pericles, on seeing a slave fall from a tree and break his leg, is reported to have said 'There you are. He's only fit to be a *paidagogos* now.'

It is odd, when education was considered in theory so important by the Athenians, that they chose such people to supervise it. In a similar way the status, and often the ability, of the schoolmasters was very low. Anybody could set himself up as a teacher, without any qualifications. Their pay was poor, and they dared not offend the parents on whom they depended for their fees. An idea of their reputation is given by the orator Demosthenes, in a speech made in the fourth century B.C., when he taunted his political opponent, Aischines:

> 'Your childhood was spent in an atmosphere of great poverty. You had to help your father in his job as assistant teacher—preparing the ink, washing down the benches, sweeping out the class-room, and taking the rank of a slave rather than of a freeborn boy. . .'

(On the Crown 258)

And later, by way of an insult: 'You were a teacher. I went to school.'

Corporal punishment was accepted as normal. We are told that even before the boy reached school age he was, if disobedient, 'straightened up with threats and beatings, like a warped and twisted plank.' It must often have appeared the only way for a desperate schoolmaster, given little respect by anybody. The fact that pupils were allowed to bring their pets into class cannot have helped, nor the presence on occasion of bystanders with nothing better to do.

There were no school holidays of the modern type, but the schools were closed on the days on which the city celebrated its various festivals. The month roughly equivalent to our February was particularly full of such days and so became the nearest thing to a prolonged break from school.

15.1 Lessons in music and reading: a *paidagogos* sits to the right. The boy on the left is being taught the *kithara* (lyre).

162

The teaching of the *grammatistes* must have been extremely dull. He certainly made no deliberate effort to make it interesting. Learning by heart and continual reciting were stock methods. Reading was made more difficult by the fact that there was no punctuation, nor were there any spaces between written words. All reading was aloud, as the Greeks did not practise silent reading. For writing they used wooden tablets with wax surfaces, on which they would write with the sharp end of a stylus and rub out with the blunt end. There were also sheets made up of strips of papyrus reed, which could be written on in ink with a reed pen.

As soon as the boys were able to read well enough, they were made to study and learn by heart extracts of poetry, especially from the *Iliad* and the *Odyssey* of Homer. Some even learnt these entire poems by heart. All kinds of moral lessons were drawn from the poetry studied.

Greek poetry was intended to be sung to the accompaniment of the lyre, and it was partly because of this that the Athenian boy also received instruction at his school from the *kitharistes*, or music-teacher. He was taught to play the *kithara*, that is the lyre, and the *aulos*, which was rather like an oboe, and to sing. The Greeks regarded it as essential for a cultured man to be able to sing and to play an instrument, especially the lyre. Apart from its connection with poetry, musical education was considered very important because of the Greek belief that music—of the right sort—had a beneficial effect in the moulding of character.

All the education provided by the *grammatistes* and the *kitharistes* went under the general name of *mousiké*. The Greeks used the term in a much wider sense than our word 'music', to include all the classroom side of schooling. The name is derived from that of the Muses (*Mousai*), the goddesses of the arts.

During his elementary education in other subjects, the Athenian boy also attended the *palaistra*, or wrestling-school. This was a courtyard with changing and washing

15.2 A *paidagogos*.

facilities at the side. The *palaistra* was an educational establishment owned privately by the chief instructor, the *paidotribes*, recognizable by his purple cloak. Here the boys were given athletic training, mainly for the sports which made up the Greek *pentathlon* (see Chapter 8). They were also given instruction in general bodily care.

The physical side of education was emphasized because the Athenians thought that physical appearance and fitness were as important as, and a great help to, high moral and intellectual standards. A frequent description of the ideal man occurring in Greek literature is that he is *kalos k'agathos*, literally 'handsome and good'. Yet the training received at the *palaistra* was also useful as preparation for military service, for which every citizen was liable, if required, between the ages of eighteen and sixty.

A good summary of the traditional elementary education given at Athens, and of the theories behind it, is to be found in the writings of the Athenian philosopher, Plato:

'Parents send their boys to school and instruct the schoolteachers to pay much more attention to the good behaviour of their boys than to their letters and their music. The teachers take note accordingly, and as soon as the boys learn their letters and have reached the stage of understanding what they see written down as well as they have previously understood what they hear spoken, then they give them the works of the good poets to read at their benches and make them learn them by heart. In these works there are many moral lessons, and there is much description and praise of the good men of history, so that the boys may strive to imitate them and endeavour to become men such as they.

Then in a similar way the music-teachers take care over the correct behaviour of the boys and see that they do nothing wrong. Also, when they learn to play the *kithara*, they are taught the works of other good poets, the composers of the songs which are set to the music of the *kithara*. The music-teachers make sure that the boys' souls become familiar with rhythms and harmonies, so that they become more civilized, and, by becoming more rhythmic and harmonious in themselves, become effective in word and deed. For all human life requires rhythm and harmony.

Finally, besides all this, parents send their boys to the *paidotribes*, so that by improvement their bodies may be the servants of their minds, which are now in a healthy state, and so that the boys are not compelled to be cowardly in wars and their other duties, because of the weakness of their bodies.

The parents who do these things are the ones best able to do so, and those who are best able are the wealthiest. The sons of these people are the ones who begin to go to school at the earliest age and finish their schooling the latest.'

(*Protagoras* 325 Dff.)

The children of poorer parents had to find some form of employment once their elementary education had been completed. The wealthier, however, continued their education in a less formal secondary stage. They were now expected to attend the assembly, the market-place, the law courts and the theatre. Here, in the company of their fathers and others older than themselves, they learnt at first-hand about adult life in the city. They often now continued their physical education at the *gymnasion* (see p. 149), and those with a particular talent in any sport were given further training in it by specialists.

Sophists and a New Education

So far we have been looking at the education provided for an Athenian boy in the traditional manner. From about the middle of the fifth century B.C., however, the system began to take on a new look, principally in its secondary stage. This change was a reflection of new developments in society as a whole.

Athens had by now reached a state of complete democracy. Important decisions were reached by all of the citizens in the assembly, all the citizens had the right to take part in the debate, all citizens were eligible for public office. It followed that, to influence the assembled people to one's own way of thinking and to become politically powerful, it was more necessary than it had been in the past to be a good public speaker. The old educational system provided no training in rhetoric, the art of public speaking.

Furthermore, this was a time when all kinds of traditional beliefs, especially those about religion, were coming under attack. Philosophers and scientific thinkers were developing and spreading new ideas about the world, and about men and morality. The existing schools taught nothing of such subjects as philosophy, physics, astronomy, medicine or geometry.

These gaps were now filled by a new type of teacher called sophists, a name meaning 'experts'. They were lecturers who travelled from city to city, teaching rhetoric especially, and all the other important subjects not covered by the ordinary school curriculum, which were developing so quickly.

The sophists, especially in the early days, were likely to be non-Athenian. They charged for their teaching, and the sons of the more wealthy flocked to study under them. This they would do in the period after their elementary education when, as we have seen, they had few binding commitments on their time elsewhere.

One of the first to arrive in Athens, about 450 B.C., was Protagoras of Abdera, who was also one of the most distinguished of them all. In one of Plato's works, Socrates describes the first sight he had of Protagoras:

15.3 A statue base on which young men play an early form of hockey.

165

'When we entered the house, we found Protagoras walking about in the portico, and walking around with him in a line were on one side Kallias, son of Hipponikos and his half-brother Paralos, the son of Pericles, and Charmides, the son of Glaukon; on the other side were Pericles' other son, Xanthippos and Philippides, son of Philomelos, and Antimoiros of Mende, who has the highest reputation of Protagoras' disciples and is learning the art so as to become a sophist himself. Behind them followed people listening to what was being said, strangers for the most part, whom Protagoras draws after him from every one of the cities he passes through, charming them with his voice like Orpheus, and they follow spellbound. There were also some locals in the group. I was extremely delighted seeing this group and the way in which they took great care never to get in the way in front of Protagoras, but when he and those with him turned about, the listeners split up in formation on either side, and wheeling round in a circle they always took up position at the back, quite superbly.'

(*Protagoras* 314 Eff.)

The teaching of the sophists was mainly intended to produce men who would make successful statesmen. They taught how to speak and to argue in public, and it was often thought more important to win the argument than to reach the truth. Literature was studied not so much for its own sake as for its style, to improve the student's ability as a public speaker.

While virtually everybody would learn rhetoric, the other subjects which a young man studied would vary. Some of the sophists claimed to be able to teach any subject at all, and no doubt their skill as speakers often allowed them to sound impressive on subjects of which they really knew very little. Such behaviour on the part of some gave the whole group of sophists a bad name in the minds of many. The word 'sophist' came to mean, as it does in English, someone who argues cleverly, but dishonestly. Yet there is no question that the best were very good teachers indeed— men like Protagoras, Isokrates, Gorgias of Leontinoi and Hippias of Elis. Even youths who only studied rhetoric would learn from a good sophist a large amount of literature, logic and ethics, as part of the training necessary for the future orator and statesman. In the absence of universities, these men provided higher education.

Socrates

We have said that not everybody thought highly of the sophists. Those who jeered at them were the more conservative citizens, who naturally saw them as undermining the old social values and educational system. Many of them classed the philosopher Socrates as a sophist, as did the comic poet Aristophanes, particularly in his play *The Clouds*. Socrates in this play is supposed to run

'a logic factory for the extra-clever. There are men there who can convince you heaven's a sort of fire-extinguisher all around us, and we're like cinders—yes, and they teach you (if you pay enough) to win your arguments, whether you're right or wrong.'

(94ff.)

Socrates himself spends a good deal of time suspended in a basket in the sky, where he finds it easier to contemplate the sun and other heavenly matters. At other times he solves such vital problems as the distance a flea can jump, what makes a gnat buzz, and how to conjure up supper for himself and his students. The clouds of the title are, according to Socrates in the play,

> 'Great Goddesses of the empty-headed. They fill us with skill in logic and brain-waves and *savoir-faire*, and the art of duping fools, garbling the truth, talking beside the point, spell-binding, meaningless oratory, and brow-beating.'
>
> (316ff.)

It says much for Socrates' character that he and Aristophanes remained apparently on friendly terms. The play was presumably too ridiculously exaggerated to be taken personally, but it reveals behind the laughter the opinion some held of the sophists and Socrates. It is said that Socrates stood up from his seat at a performance of the play so that the rest of the audience could see for themselves whether he was really as extraordinary as Aristophanes made him seem. In fact he was a ready-made target, for he was a well-known figure in the streets of Athens, always arguing and easily recognizable by his rolling walk, snub nose, shaggy eyebrows and bulging eyes.

However, there were deep differences between Socrates and the majority of the sophists. He was not satisfied with their emphasis on what was practical and useful, at the expense of what he regarded as real morality. Moreover, while the sophists made extravagant claims for their knowledge and their teaching, perhaps the most basic of Socrates' beliefs was that men were extremely ignorant, and would never reach understanding of virtue, truth and so on without first realizing their ignorance. When the Delphic oracle said that he was the wisest of men, Socrates could not at first believe it. Eventually, after going round questioning all the so-called experts, he concluded that, after all, the oracle was right, because he alone was aware of his ignorance.

The fact that his methods of arguing were new, that he went around with a faithful band of followers, that he was always engaged in discussions, made it easy to class him as a sophist. However, those who did so failed to understand the special quality of his mind and character.

Misunderstanding of Socrates, and the hostility which his incessant questioning aroused, in the end led to his death. He was put on trial for his life, accused of undermining the official religion and corrupting the minds of the young. Plato in the *Apology* gives us a record of the speech Socrates made in his own defence. Convincing though his arguments were, he was condemned, and though he could

15.4 Portrait of Socrates on an engraved gem.

almost certainly have escaped into exile had he wished, he died in prison after drinking the hemlock administered to convicted men. The year was 399 B.C.

Isokrates

The greatest and most influential of the true sophists was Isokrates, an Athenian who lived from 436 until 338 B.C. By the end of the fifth century B.C. the sophists were firmly established as a part of Athenian education. At the beginning of the fourth century, permanent schools were begun, run by native Athenians who had been trained by the earlier wandering teachers coming from outside the city. Isokrates began his school in 393 B.C. in his house near the Lykeion. The main subject was, of course, rhetoric, with a good range of other subjects, like literature, as aids to rhetoric. His vision of what rhetoric should be used for was far wider than that of the earlier sophists. Greece was as disunited as ever, with the cities always weakening each other by their wars. Isokrates was convinced of the superior intelligence of Athenians. His idea was that Athens should lead a united Greece, with all Greeks sharing in the same culture and civilization. The men to bring about this ideal of 'panhellenism' were Athenians trained in rhetoric. The training must be of the highest standards. At the age of ninety-four he summarized his ideal:

'Whom do I consider educated? Those who manage well their daily lives, who possess sound judgement and seldom miss the appropriate course of action; those who are decent and honourable, good-natured, not quick to take offence, controlled in their pleasures, brave in misfortune, unspoiled by success. Those who have a character which conforms, not just to one of these things, but to all of them, these are the wise and complete men, possessed of all the qualities.'

(Panathenaikos 30)

At more or less the same time as Isokrates was setting up his school, another was being established, also in Athens, where philosophy was more important than rhetoric. Plato, the pupil of Socrates, founded his school in the Akademé, continuing and developing the philosophical theories started by Socrates. Later, in 335 B.C., Aristotle founded another school. These schools were well-attended and influential, but the more practical rhetorical training of Isokrates was the dominating force in education.

The sophist movement indirectly caused changes in the elementary stages of schooling, just as nowadays universities may affect the syllabuses studied in schools. In Athenian elementary schools the study of style and grammar became more important than studying the poets for moral lessons. Since it was now thought that a boy could be taught by words how to be wise and moral, music and sport were less highly thought of as methods of training character. Their importance in education declined, and they became more and more the concern of professional specialists.

CHAPTER SIXTEEN

Science, Mathematics and Philosophy

'Philosophers from Thales onwards,' Bertrand Russell once wrote, 'have tried to understand the world.' This was what the early thinkers in Ionia had done (see Chapter 4). They had been interested in the subjects we now call physics, astronomy, pre-history and meteorology. The curious thing is that, after that fascinating start, progress was one-sided: great advances were made in mathematics and philosophy, but far fewer in science, and virtually none in technology. In this chapter we shall look at developments down to Alexander (*c.* 330 B.C.), and at later developments in Chapter 19.

In the fifth century B.C. intelligent theorizing went on. Anaxagoras, the friend of Pericles, for example, believed that the moon, because 'it is made of earth and has plains and ravines on it, has no light of its own but takes it from the sun.' He thought that the rainbow is a 'reflection' of the sun—did he guess at refraction? He also said that 'eclipses of the moon occur because it is screened by the earth, and those of the sun because of screening by the moon.' More fundamentally, he held that 'nothing comes into being or perishes, but is made up from and is dissolved into things that exist'—what we call now the law of the conservation of matter. And Demokritos (430 B.C.), who came from Abdera in northern Greece, argued that matter consisted of an infinite number of indivisible and invisible atoms which 'become intertwined with each other according to the matching of their shape, size, position and arrangement and so create compound objects.'

But, acute though all this was, it was still theory. What the Greeks did not do was to advance, either to scientific laws, or to the practical application of these theories in technology. There seem to have been three reasons for this. First, they relied more on the mind than the senses, because the senses could be deceived. A stick in water *looks* bent; it is the mind that corrects what the eye sees. In any case, of course, they lacked instruments to support and improve the senses, telescopes, microscopes, test-tubes and so on. The best they could do was to use analogy, a *mental* process of comparison, regarding 'visible objects', in Anaxagoras's words, 'as a clue to invisible ones'. But that leads only to probability, not certainty; the analogy, the comparison may be wrong. So the evidence of the senses was unsatisfactory. But logic and mathematics were different; by these methods truth and certainty could be reached. You can *prove* that the angles at the base of an isosceles triangle are equal; that is true, and there is no doubt about it!

The second reason for the lack of development in science was the Greeks' preference for abstract theory rather than practical activity. Their aim was to know, not to do or change or control. As Aristotle later said, 'The act of observation is what is most pleasant and best.' This reluctance to be involved in practicalities may be due

16.1 Miletos: layout of fifth-century B.C. city.

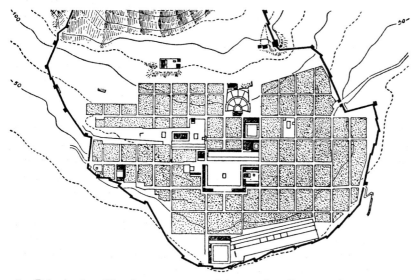

16.2 Priené: plan. The theatre, *agora*, *palaistra* and stadium are clear.

170

to the fact that most Greek philosophers came from the upper classes. They therefore reflect aristocratic values: trade and crafts were for the lower classes; gentlemen occupied themselves only with war, diplomacy, poetry and oratory. Certainly inventions were rare after 500 B.C.; and, despite the immense experience of craftsmen in bronze-casting and pottery, the philosophers did not apply their thinking to chemistry; so no theoretical chemistry was ever developed.

Thirdly, in the late fifth century B.C. Greek thinking moved decisively away from the natural world to human beings. 'The proper study of man is man', man both as an individual and as a member of society. So the sophists and particularly Socrates (see p. 166) were concerned about virtue, justice, piety, friendship and education, and not so much with science. Socrates blamed his fellow Athenians for 'caring a great deal about money and status and reputation and for trying to get as much of these as you can, while you neglect wisdom and truth and are not concerned about improving your souls.' (*Apology* 29E). He believed that what people had to do above all else was to discover what true goodness was. This was difficult because ignorance and prejudice abounded. Socrates himself was disliked for his deflation of people who were confident that they knew what words like 'good' and 'right' and 'just' meant. He urged people to continue the search: 'the unexamined life,' he said, 'is not worth living.' But, he believed, if you went on looking, you might in the end discover what true goodness was and, when you knew it, you would put it into practice, because 'virtue is knowledge'.

Plato

Socrates himself wrote no books. What we know of him comes from other writers, particularly two of his pupils, Xenophon and Plato. Xenophon's book about his master is sensible, factual, straightforward, rather like Xenophon himself, who was a soldier and a landowner. Plato, a mathematician and a philosopher, wrote books that are elegant, dramatic dialogues, full of charm—but which put into the mouth of Socrates, who is the main character in them, an elaborate and impressive philosophical system that owes more to Plato himself than to his teacher. So profound is his philosophy that one distinguished twentieth-century philosopher has said that 'the history of western philosophy is a series of footnotes on Plato'. This may be an exaggeration, but it gives some indication of the range and power of his thought.

In the course of his dialogues, he discussed politics, education, ethics, aesthetics, ontology, epistemology and logic. [Most of these words are Greek in origin; looking them up in a dictionary will tell you something about Greek and English.] Plato's main concern, however, was like Socrates': how do you produce good men and a good state? His most famous book, *The Republic*, is his answer. You do it by educating a few people properly and then making them rule the state. Proper education is a training primarily in mathematics and philosophy so that the pupil ultimately can understand what the ideal is. For Plato believed that there was a perfect world, of which our world and the things we see and know in it are merely imperfect copies. True education gives students the ability to discover and love these ideals. Then armed with this understanding, they can rule the state in such a way that everybody is benefited. This is perhaps unrealistic. Yet it is worth asking how many later schemes of education or of political organisation have been successful. And, as far as Plato's ideal world is concerned, how, in fact, do we know what a perfect triangle (or table or husband) is? After all, the ones we actually see are in varying degrees imperfect. A stronger objection to Plato's blueprint for the ideal state might be that it allows its citizens no freedom and is based on the principle that men are unequal.

Mathematics

'Mathematicians Only' was written up over the door to Plato's school. It shows the importance he placed on mathematics, as does his saying that 'God is always doing geometry'. In this he reflected the dominant position that the study of mathematics gradually reached—despite an awkward system of numbers which used letters for digits (see Appendix) and did not have the economical method of columns for tens, hundreds, thousands, and so on, which was invented by the Arabs a thousand years later. It is possible that this very difficulty may explain why the Greeks put such emphasis on geometry.

Pythagoras and his school (see Chapter 4) laid the basis for the subject. Indeed, it was they who took over the general word *mathemata* ('learning') for this particular branch of it. In addition to the hypotenuse theorem, they discovered—and regretted!—irrational numbers. The square root of 2 was the first, apparently because they were unable to define precisely the ratio between the side of a square and its diagonal. They developed the theory of numbers, and they did a good deal of algebra, especially simultaneous equations. In the fifth century B.C. progress continued; much ingenuity was spent on three problems of higher geometry, the squaring of the circle, the trisection of any angle, and the duplication of the cube. One dilemma was the relationship between the base of a cone and its next section: either this section is equal to the base, in which case the cone becomes a cylinder, or it is smaller, in which case the surface of the cone is jagged, like steps—which is absurd. And Eudoxos discovered the method of exhaustion for measuring curvilinear areas and solids. Meanwhile, in the allied subject of astronomy, one of Plato's pupils, Herakleides, stated that the earth rotates on its own axis once in twenty-four hours, and that Mercury and Venus revolve round the sun like satellites.

16.3 Greek mathematical notation, with Arabic equivalents.

Aristotle

Aristotle (384–322 B.C.) was in many ways the most remarkable of the Greek thinkers. The son of a doctor at the court of Philip of Macedonia, he was trained under Plato, became tutor to Philip's son, Alexander (later the Great), and then set up his own school (see p. 168). His range was enormous; he systematized the whole province of learning. He applied his rules—one, collect information; two, analyse it; three, classify—to poetry and politics. And his books on these subjects are still relevant and powerful. But he was primarily a scientist; and science down to the Renaissance was totally under his influence. It is not surprising that he was called 'the master of them that know'. Darwin's remarks in a letter of 1882 show the same sort of admiration: 'From quotations which I had seen, I had a high notion of Aristotle's merits, but I had not the most remote notion what a wonderful man he was. Linnaeus and Cuvier (two eighteenth-century biologists) have been my gods . . . but they were mere schoolboys to old Aristotle . . . I never realized . . . to what an enormous summation of labour we owe even our common knowledge.'

His early work in physics and astronomy shows—and suffers from—Plato's influence. Theory is more important than observation: the heavens *must* be a sphere because the sphere is the perfect figure; the planets *must* rotate in a circle because the circle is eternal. He even argued that there must be a special substance which he called quintessence. The earth was made up of the traditional four elements, earth, air, fire and water. The stars, on the other hand, were divine and perfect and therefore had to be composed of something totally different! However, he knew some of the true facts: 'the mass of the earth is infinitesimal compared with the vast universe which surrounds it.' Gradually he moved away from Plato's ideal world to the study of this real and actual one. 'People who indulge in long discussions fail to observe facts,' he says, 'and are too ready to theorize from few observations.' He himself made many observations: 'we must partly do research ourselves, partly accept the discoveries of other researchers. . . If there is conflicting evidence, we must follow the more accurate.'

He was especially interested in biology; about a third of his huge output deals with this subject. There had been some biology earlier. Empedokles (450 B.C.), for example, had argued that originally there had been more sorts of creature than there were now; but 'those creatures survived which accidentally developed a suitable form; the rest became extinct.' Was this a hint of Darwin's 'survival of the fittest'? Aristotle, however, made biology into a science—not without some difficulty. 'Even in the case of animals which are unattractive, Nature offers enormous pleasure to those who are able to recognize causes and who have a scientific outlook. . . We should approach the investigation into every kind of animal without distaste, because in all of them there is something scientific and beautiful.' This is admirable. But he goes on: 'For in the works of nature above all we see purpose and not chance operating. And the perfect form which determines the nature of everything made or born is part of beauty.' Here is the Platonic influence again. The 'perfect form', it is true, is for Aristotle no longer in some other world of ideal perfection; it is in this world, shaping everything we see towards its full nature. But it leads him to think that everything is as it is by design; and that is faith, not science. It makes him, for example, reject the sensible view of Anaxagoras 'that it is because he has hands that man is the most intelligent of the animals.' 'It is more probable,' Aristotle argues, 'that man got hands because he was the most intelligent.'

However, this bias should not hide the greatness of his work. His energy was phenomenal—he classified more than five hundred sorts of animal—and his attention to detail set the standard for future biologists. He describes every type of cuttle-fish, for example, their anatomy, habits, development. He does the same for very many fish and insects—the gnat's life-history, for example, from aquatic larva to chrysalis to insect is precisely explained.

His influence on science has deservedly been very great. Yet in the first book of his *Metaphysics* he shows quite clearly why Greek science made so little progress. He is talking about the emergence of philosophy and science which arose, he thinks, from mankind's sense of wonder and dislike of ignorance:

> 'It is clear that men pursued knowledge for its own sake, not for any practical use they might make of it. History itself confirms this: for it was only after almost all the necessities of life had been obtained that people began to look for this knowledge. They did so for pleasure and recreation.'
>
> (I, 2, 11)

This is an utterly amazing statement: did Aristotle really think that there was no need for further technological advance, that enough had been invented? The fact that even this degree of comfort, such as it was, was available only for the wealthy is not mentioned. But then Aristotle believed that many men were 'slaves by nature'.

Medicine

There is one area of Greek science, however, where real progress was made through careful, steady observation—medicine. Hippokrates was the most famous name in it. He had a medical school on the island of Kos in the south-eastern Aegean, and his hospital there can still be seen. Training was important, and other places, too, were well-known for producing doctors: Kyrene in north Africa, Knidos in Asia Minor, and Kroton in southern Italy. Herodotus has a story about one very successful doctor from Kroton, named Demokedes. The island of Aigina, south of Athens, paid him a talent a year as resident physician, that is, twenty times as much as the average skilled worker; Athens tempted him away by offering him more, and then Polykrates of Samos (see p. 42) employed him at two talents a year—enviable rates for state medicine! Later, captured by the Persians and forced to treat the Persian king, Darius, he cured both Darius and his wife and so 'stood very high with the king. He had a very large house in Sousa, ate at the Great King's table and had all he could wish for except one thing, the freedom to go back to Greece.' This he managed in the end to do, by escaping from an expedition on which he was sent by the king.

Many doctors moved like Demokedes from place to place: a medical book *Airs, Waters, Places*, written to help them, has survived. It shows how the climate, water supply and situations of different places affect the health of the inhabitants. But there was a lot of non-scientific medicine, too: one medical writer complains about 'witch-doctors, faith-healers, quacks and charlatans'. And, on a different level, the trainers at *gymnasia* developed a working knowledge of dislocations, surface anatomy, diets and exercise. Doctors, therefore, had to defend the status of their profession. There were no degrees, and so people judged them by result. Another writer, on *Prognosis*, says that

'if a doctor can discover and tell his patients their past and present symptoms and what is going to happen, people will trust his diagnosis and have the confidence to put themselves in his hands... It is impossible to cure all patients; but, if he recognizes and announces before the event which cases will turn out to be fatal and which not, he will avoid criticism.'

Treatment varied. Fractures and dislocations were often dealt with successfully. But diseases were different. The Greeks had no notion of micro-organisms, and so their understanding of the causes of disease was slight. Hence, although surgery, drugs, bleeding and purges were used, most treatment was cautious and concentrated on diet, exercise and keeping the patient as comfortable as possible. Experience was built up through careful observation and embodied in a series of *Aphorisms*:

'Life is short, the science of medicine long. Opportunity is brief, experiment dangerous, judgement difficult. The doctor must not only do what is necessary himself, but ensure that the patient and his attendants play their part. The circumstances, too, must be right.'
'In acute cases use drugs rarely and only at the onset of the disease. And do so only after a careful preliminary examination.'
'It is better to be full of drink than full of food.'
'In all illnesses a vigorous frame of mind and the enjoyment of food and drink are good signs; the opposites, bad.'
'The drinking of neat wine relieves hunger.'
'Very fat people are more liable to sudden death than those who are lean.'
'Those who contract tetanus either die within four days or, if they survive longer than this, recover.'

Many case-histories, too, have come down to us. They are carefully and regularly observed. Here is one that sounds like diphtheria:

'A woman living near Aristion's house suffered from a sore throat. The illness began with indistinctness of voice. The tongue was inflamed and parched.

16.4 Clinic about 470 B.C.: the view on this jar shows the doctor bleeding a patient.

First day:	shivering and high temperature.
Third day:	rigor, acute fever, a reddish, hard swelling on her throat, extending to her chest on both sides; extremities cold and livid, breathing superficial. Drink regurgitated, unable to swallow. Stools and urine ceased.
Fourth day:	All symptoms much worse.
Fifth day:	Died.'

Progress in medicine was, however, restricted because the Greeks disliked the idea of dissecting human corpses. And so it was not until Greek doctors had a chance to work in Egypt (see Chapter 19) that their knowledge of anatomy and physiology increased. Nevertheless, Greek medicine influenced future developments in two important ways: first, it set high standards of professional conduct; and, secondly, it was rigorously scientific. The Hippocratic Oath is well-known, and its demands for integrity and confidentiality have continued to characterize medicine:

'I will give treatment to help the sick to the best of my ability and judgement. . . I will not give lethal drugs to anyone if I am asked . . . nor will I give a woman means to procure an abortion. . .
Whatever I see or hear which should not be spoken to any person outside, I will never divulge. . .'

Then, medicine was a science, not philosophy:

'In medical practice one must pay attention to experience and logic rather than to plausible theorizing. . . I approve, however, of theorizing if it is based on actual cases and draws its conclusions from observed facts. . . But if it starts from some plausible fiction, it often causes patients discomfort and pain.'

(*Hippocratic Precepts* I)

A fifth-century B.C. writer on epilepsy supports this attitude:

'The so-called "Sacred Disease" (epilepsy) is not, in my opinion, any more divine or sacred than any other. It has specific characteristics and a definite cause. . . Quacks concealed their own ignorance and inability to give any useful treatment by claiming a divine element. To hide their lack of understanding they called the disease "sacred". . . The fact is that the cause of this disease, as of all other serious diseases, lies in the brain. . .'

And he goes on to explain how the functions of the brain can be damaged. Another writer in the next century wants to show how the human embryo develops:

'If you take twenty or more eggs and place them to hatch under two or more fowls, and on each day, starting from the second right up until the day on which the egg is hatched, you take one egg, break it open and examine it, you will find that everything is as I have described—making allowance, of course, for the degree to which one can compare the growth of a chicken with that of a human being. You will find, for instance, that there are membranes extending from the umbilicus. . .'

This is not proof, of course, as the writer realizes, but it is a sensible experimental use of analogy.

So in medicine, at least, Greek science displayed two of the essential characteristics of any science, observation and experiment.

176

CHAPTER SEVENTEEN

A Different Greece

The defeat of Athens in the Peloponnesian War left Sparta as the leading power in Greece. Yet her bullying attitude to the cities under her control—which now covered most of the mainland and the Aegean Sea—soon led to resistance against her. Her policy of setting up pro-Spartan oligarchies in the cities, together with Spartan governors and garrisons, was naturally unpopular.

Athens herself got over the catastrophe of defeat remarkably well and quickly. After the short reign of terror by a small oligarchic group, installed by the Spartans and known as the Thirty Tyrants, democracy was restored by 403 B.C. Although Athens never regained her previous strength, she remained one of the strongest Greek cities in the fourth century B.C.

By 395 B.C. Athens was taking part, with Argos, Corinth and Thebes, and supported by Persia, in a war attempting to throw off Spartan repression. The early years of this fourth century B.C. were years of continued and confused fighting among the Greek cities, mainly Athens, Sparta and Thebes, in various alliances. In the background Persia was still a significant factor, supporting one side or the other according to her own interests. In fact, in 386 B.C., peace was temporarily imposed on the Greeks in a humiliating way, by a decree from the King of Persia, 'The King's Peace', with terms favourable to Sparta, but also abandoning the Greek cities of Asia, and Cyprus, to Persian rule.

Sparta's arrogant treatment of others, however, continued to cause trouble. In the end, her downfall came in a way which had begun to seem impossible, for her army was defeated in a straight battle, against Thebes, on the Boiotian plain at Leuktra in 371 B.C. Thebes at this time happened to have two outstanding generals, Pelopidas and Epaminondas. At Leuktra they used a new tactic of massing troops at one end of the battle-line and so breaking through at one point by sheer force of numbers. The Spartan king, Kleombrotos, and four hundred out of seven hundred Spartiates were killed in a crippling defeat.

So, for a while, Thebes became the dominant city, campaigning especially in the Peloponnese in order to weaken Sparta further. Yet when Epaminondas was killed at the battle of Mantineia in 362 B.C., fighting against a combination of Spartans and Athenians, Thebes' brief period of power came to a close. For, although Thebes won that battle, there was nobody capable of leading Thebes in the same way, since Pelopidas was already dead.

Philip and Demosthenes

With the cities of Greece in a weak and disorganized condition, the way lay open for the rise to power of the king of a previously undistinguished state to the north, which was not even purely Greek. He brought virtually the whole of Greece under his control by the time of his death in 336 B.C. The king was Philip of Macedonia, whose capital was Pella.

The fact is that the Greek political system of separate city-states or *poleis* had reached its dying stages. During the fourth century B.C. the Greeks in general seem to have become increasingly less interested in their city as the focus of their lives and less prepared to become involved in its politics. They were no longer so proud of its achievements, or prepared to fight and make sacrifices for it. They had become more concerned for themselves, their private problems and interests. Also there was much greater specialization—trade was more complicated, so demanding more time, military tactics developed in a way which required professional soldiers to operate them, rather than the old amateur citizen-armies. This also accounts for the growing use of mercenary troops. So, as time went by, it became much harder for the individual citizen to combine various rôles. In earlier times a man could have been a

17.1 Hermes holding the god Dionysos as a baby: an original work (about 340 B.C.) by Praxiteles.

178

farmer, politician and soldier, but now the circumstances were different. The involvement of the individual in the affairs of the *polis*, which had been the strength of the old system, weakened, and change was inevitable.

Nevertheless, the fourth century B.C. was certainly not an undistinguished one for the Greeks: to it belong the great sculptors Praxiteles, Skopas and, later, Lysippos. It was also, as we have seen in Chapter 16, the century of the philosophers Plato and Aristotle. It was the period in which the art of rhetoric or public-speaking was developed to its peak under the direction of such men as Isokrates (see Chapter 15). It certainly produced one of the greatest orators in history—and Philip's implacable enemy—Demosthenes, the Athenian.

According to tradition, Demosthenes suffered from speech defects which he overcame by reciting on the sea-shore, against the noise of the waves, with pebbles in his mouth. At first he was a professional speech-writer for people involved in private law-cases, but he moved on to public prosecutions and in 351 B.C. he entered political life with the first of his speeches called *Philippics*. For Demosthenes saw more clearly than anyone else the danger which the growing power of Philip presented to the liberty of the Greeks and he devoted himself from now on to trying, often desperately, alone and in vain, to get the Athenians to organize themselves against Philip before it was too late.

Philip was a formidable opponent. An outstanding soldier, statesman and diplomat, he could be charming, cunning or ruthless as the occasion demanded. In his youth he had been for a while a hostage at Thebes in the time of Epaminondas, where he doubtless learnt much about that general's new developments in military tactics. As king, from 359 B.C., he trained the Macedonian army to a high degree of professionalism and loyalty. In particular he developed the 'phalanx' formation of his infantry, which was the basis of both his own triumphs and those of his son, Alexander the Great.

17.2 Demosthenes.

The infantrymen were extremely tough and well-disciplined. They were armed with a frightening pike, or *sarissa*, up to more than five metres long, used for thrusting rather than throwing at the enemy. Despite their densely packed ranks, their perfect drill enabled them swiftly and precisely to adopt whatever formation their officers ordered. In battle their function was to stand firm and immovable against the enemy's front-line, while the cavalry attacked in wedge-shaped formations on the flanks. Once the cavalry had broken the enemy ranks, the phalanx moved forward, terrifying and irresistible, to complete the victory.

Step by step, by any method which worked, either military, diplomatic, or just deceitful, Philip extended his influence over the rest of Greece, steadily southward and nearer to Athens. Demosthenes continually struggled to waken the Athenians to the danger:

> 'When, men of Athens, when are you going to act as you should? What has got to happen? "When there is a need," you say. But what are we to call what is happening now? For in my opinion the greatest need which can face free men is to avoid shame at their own state of affairs. Or do you intend, tell me, to go around asking each other, "Any news?" Could there be anything more newsworthy than the fact that already there is a Macedonian fellow fighting against the Athenians and managing the affairs of Greece? "Philip is dead," the rumour spreads. "No he isn't, but he is ill." What difference does it make to you? If anything did happen to him, you would soon create another Philip, the way you manage your affairs.'
>
> (*Philippic I*, 10f.)

Eventually Demosthenes began to get his way, and Athens took more positive steps. When, in 338 B.C. Philip appeared at Elateia not far to the north of Thebes, with his army, there was great consternation in Athens, as Demosthenes later described:

17.3 A silver coin issued by Philip. *Left*: head of Zeus. *Right*: horse and jockey commemorate a victory for Philip in the Olympic Games.

'It was evening, and someone came to the councillors on duty with the news that Elateia had been captured. Immediately after that, although they were in the middle of their meal, some got up and drove the people out of the stalls in the market place and set fire to the wickerwork stalls as an alarm, while others sent for the generals and summoned the trumpeter. The city was filled with panic. On the next day at dawn the councillors on duty called together the council to the council-chamber, but you citizens went to the assembly, and before the council had even proceeded to business and passed a vote, the entire people was seated on the hillside. After that, when the council came and the councillors reported the news and brought forward the messenger and he had spoken, then the herald asked who was prepared to open the debate. No one came forward. Then, although the herald asked many times, still nobody stood up, despite the fact that all the generals were there and all the politicians, at a time when the united voice of our country was crying out for someone to speak out to save it.'

(On the Crown 169)

In the end, on Demosthenes' proposal, the Athenians made an alliance with Thebes, and the Athenians, Thebans and their allies marched bravely against Philip. They were defeated decisively at Chaironeia by the Macedonian phalanx and the cavalry, led by Alexander.

Philip treated Athens kindly—indeed he had always declared his admiration of Athens and wish for her friendship. Greece was now his, and in 337 B.C. at a conference in Corinth he was elected general and leader of a confederacy of the Greeks, the League of Corinth, the purpose of which was to invade Persia. Officially this was in revenge for the great invasion of Greece by Xerxes in 480 B.C. and to free the Greek cities of Asia. But it was also very necessary because Philip was in debt and he could not maintain his army without fresh wealth, for which Persia seemed an obvious source of supply.

17.4 This lion was set up in memory of the Thebans killed by Philip's army in the battle of Chaironeia.

The March of the Ten Thousand

That the prospects were good for such an invasion of Persia had already been shown at the turn of the century by an episode described by Xenophon, the pupil of Socrates, in one of the best adventure stories of history.

A Persian prince, Cyrus, in an attempt to overthrow the king, his brother Artaxerxes, enrolled ten thousand Greek mercenary infantrymen in the army with which he set out from Sardis in 401 B.C. The Athenian Xenophon, against the advice of Socrates, joined in on the invitation of his friend Proxenos, one of the Greek generals hired by Cyrus. We have the account, the *Anabasis* or *March Inland*, which he later wrote of the expedition.

After a long march Cyrus' army met that of Artaxerxes at Kounaxa, near Babylon. The Greeks themselves were victorious, but the others were not, and Cyrus himself was killed. To make matters worse, their generals were lured into a trap and captured. Xenophon describes their desperate situation:

> 'When their generals had been arrested, and the officers and soldiers who had gone with them had been killed, the Greeks were in great despair. They realized that they were at the King's doorstep and that encircling them on every side were many hostile peoples and cities, No longer would anybody allow them to buy supplies. They were a vast distance from Greece and they had no guide for the route. Impassable rivers blocked their path home. The Persians who had marched inland with Cyrus had also betrayed them, and they were completely abandoned. . . Thinking of these things, and in a state of despondency, few of them bothered with food that evening and few lit fires. Many did not go to their proper quarters that night, but lay down where they happened to be, unable to sleep from grief and longing for their countries, their parents, wives and children, whom they expected never to see again.'
>
> (*Anabasis* III, i)

Yet they did not give in. Xenophon persuaded them to elect new generals, of whom he himself was one, and he in effect took command. They set off northwards along the valley of the River Tigris, then through the wild mountains of Armenia, maintaining their courage and discipline in the face of countless dangers presented both by nature and by hostile tribes. At last, dramatically, the Ten Thousand reached the Greek-inhabited coast of the Black Sea and safety. As they reached the top of the last mountain,

> 'a great shout went up. When Xenophon and the rest of the rearguard heard, they thought that other enemies were attacking at the front; for men were pursuing them behind (from countryside which the Greeks had set fire to) of whom the rearguard had killed some and captured others by setting a trap. . . But as the shouts got ever louder, and new arrivals in their turn kept breaking into a run towards those already there, who kept up their shouting, and the more there were, so the shouting was much louder, then Xenophon realized that something unusual was happening. So he mounted a horse and took Lykios and the cavalry to go and give assistance. Soon they heard the soldiers shouting, 'The sea, the sea,' and passing the word back. Then all the rearguard also started to run, and the pack-animals and horses were driven on. And when all had reached the top they all, generals and captains as well, wept and embraced each other.'
>
> (*Anabasis* IV, vii)

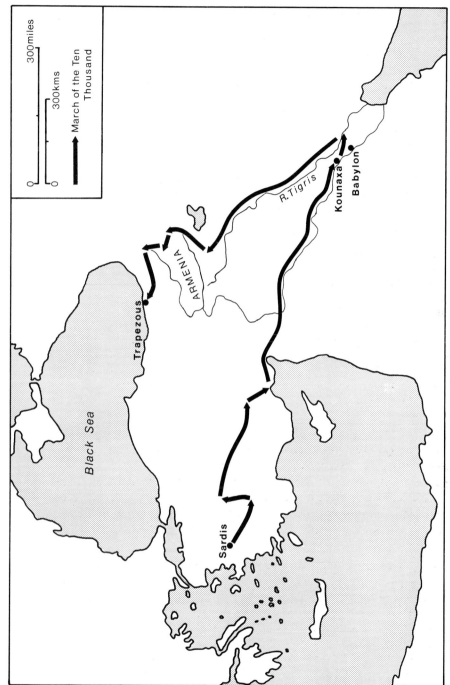

300miles

300kms

→ March of the Ten
Thousand

Black Sea

Trapezous

ARMENIA

R.Tigris

Kounaxa

Babylon

Sardis

17.5 The march of the Ten Thousand.

The historical significance of the *Anabasis* had been to show that a relatively small force of Greek soldiers could march deep into the Persian Empire, defeat a much larger Persian army and then get home safely. All this seemed to indicate the weakness of the Persians and the superiority of Greeks, and to show that a much more powerful expedition, such as that planned by Philip after his victory at Chaironeia, had every prospect of success. That success, however, as we shall see in the next chapter, was to be achieved not by Philip, but by his son.

17.6 Mountains near the Black Sea through which the Ten Thousand fought their way to safety.

CHAPTER EIGHTEEN

Alexander

The Early Years

Alexander the Great came to the throne of Macedonia in 336 B.C. at the age of twenty. He died a little under thirteen years later. In this short time his successful campaigns over an area from Greece to India established him as probably the finest general of the ancient world. His early death occurred before it was seen how successful he would be in controlling the empire he had acquired.

As is often the case with exceptional men, the name of Alexander attracted countless stories to it, many too extraordinary and unlikely to be believed. Legends grew up after his death in places as far distant as Britain and Malaya, and it is said that there are more than eighty versions of his story in twenty-four languages. Amongst other things, various stories made him a Christian, conquer Rome, Carthage and China, reach the 'Well of Life' at the world's end, and, in an ancient version of a submarine, descend to the floor of the sea. Yet the truth is amazing enough.

It was said that on the same day as Alexander was born, the great temple at Ephesos of Artemis, the goddess of childbirth, was burnt down:

> 'In connection with this, Hegesias of Magnesia made a comment capable of putting out the blaze with its coolness; for he said that it was not surprising that the temple of Artemis was burnt down when she was occupied with the birth of Alexander.'
>
> (Plutarch, *Alexander* iii)

Others at Ephesos took the fire as an omen of certain disaster, crying that a great calamity for Asia had been born on that day.

Philip received three messages at the same time: one announced that his general Parmenio had won a fine victory over the Illyrians, another that his horse had won at the Olympic games, and the third that Alexander had been born. Philip made a prayer to Fortune for a small piece of bad luck to balance against all this overwhelming good luck.

Alexander was evidently serious and ambitious from an early age. An early indication of his personality is given by Plutarch's story of the way in which he obtained his horse Boukephalas, which stayed with him until its death in India in 326 and had a town named after it there.

> 'When Philoneikos the Thessalian brought Boukephalas and tried to sell him to Philip for thirteen talents, they went down to the plain to try out the horse. He appeared to be difficult and completely unmanageable, not letting anybody mount him and not obeying the voice of any of those with Philip, but resisting everybody.

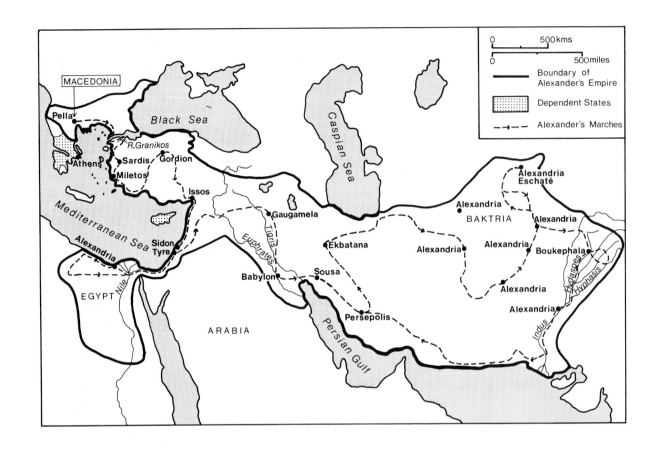

18.1 Alexander's empire.

18.2 An illustration from the mediaeval 'Romance of Alexander', showing Alexander's descent to the floor of the ocean.

Philip was angry and gave orders for the horse to be taken away as being totally wild and unbroken, but Alexander, who was present, said, "What a horse they are throwing away, not able to do anything with it because of their clumsiness and feebleness." At first Philip made no comment, but when Alexander murmured this often and showed his indignation, he said, "Are you criticizing your elders, thinking that you know better or can handle a horse better?" "I could handle this horse better at any rate," replied Alexander. "If you don't manage, what penalty will you pay for your failure?" "Of course I shall lose the price of the horse," was the reply. People laughed, and they agreed about the money to be forfeited. Alexander immediately ran to the horse and taking hold of the bridle, turned him to face the sun. He had evidently noticed that the horse was being agitated by his shadow falling in front of him and jumping about. After running beside the horse for a little while and stroking him, when he saw that the animal was full of confidence, he quietly threw off his cloak and, leaping up, safely mounted him. He pulled on the bit lightly with the reins and held it under control, without hitting or tugging it; then, when he saw the horse had lost his timidity and was eager to gallop, he gave him his head and urged him on with stronger voice, digging his heels into him. Philip and those with him were at first anxious and silent, but when Alexander wheeled the horse and brought him round neatly, proud and happy, everybody applauded, and Alexander's father is even said to have cried from joy, and to have kissed him and said, "My son, look for a kingdom big enough for yourself. Macedonia is too small for you."'

(*Alexander* vi)

Alexander is also said to have complained to his companions, when news came of great victories by his father, that Philip would leave nothing great for Alexander to achieve.

Among Alexander's tutors was the great philosopher Aristotle, who taught him for three years. The subjects included philosophy, rhetoric, geography, geometry, astronomy, biology and medicine. The last two were favourite subjects for Alexander, who always kept up his interest in learning. A large number of scientists and scholars accompanied him on the great expedition into Asia.

Relationships between Philip on the one hand and Alexander and his mother Olympias on the other were very stormy. All three of them had such strong personalities that they could not exist together peacefully. Olympias was an especially proud and emotional woman, and there was a lot of her personality in Alexander, who was always immensely attached to her. Later on, when his general Antipater complained about her, Alexander said that Antipater could never understand that one tear from Olympias was more important to him than all that Antipater could ever say. While Philip was still alive, the tension reached its highest point at a banquet, after Philip had decided to rid himself of Olympias and re-marry. The new bride's father proposed a health to the newly-married couple and prayed to the gods that they might have a legitimate heir to the throne of Macedonia. Alexander, enraged, threw a cup at the speaker, asking whether his words meant that he thought Alexander was illegitimate. Philip came at him with drawn sword, but was so drunk that he fell flat on his face. 'Look,' said Alexander, 'this is the man who was preparing to cross from Europe to Asia, and he topples over crossing from one couch to another.' Alexander and his mother went off into exile. Eventually the row was patched up sufficiently for Alexander, but not Olympias, to return.

By the time of Philip's assassination in 336 B.C., Alexander had already at sixteen acted as regent in Macedonia in his father's absence, and at eighteen played a vital rôle as commander of part of the army at the battle of Chaironeia. The reasons for Philip's murder are uncertain. The assassin was a young man with a personal grudge, but perhaps the plot was engineered by the Persians, whom he was planning to attack, or possibly Olympias had something to do with it.

Confusion followed the murder, but Alexander by prompt and confident actions took over in Macedonia and established himself in the rest of Greece as Philip's successor as general of the League of Corinth (see p. 181). He then dealt with hostile tribes on his northern frontiers. While he was occupied in this, a rumour spread that he had been killed in action, and Thebes rebelled, supported by others. After he had razed the city to the ground, apart from the temples and the house of the poet Pindar, the rest of the Greek cities immediately gave in. Alexander was said later to have regretted his harshness to Thebes, for in addition many Thebans were sold as slaves.

The Conquest of Persia

He was now ready to invade Persia, taking over from his father as leader of a united Greece in a war of revenge for the Persian invasions of Greece at the beginning of the fifth century B.C. This was the official version. There is no doubt that Alexander's personal ambition and a need to refill his treasury were more pressing reasons.

The expeditionary force was some thirty-five thousand men, of whom about five thousand were cavalry. The core of the army was the Macedonian infantry, whose phalanx formation had been developed to such a degree of efficiency by Philip (see

18.3 Alexander.

p. 180). On entering Asia, in 334 B.C., Alexander, by going to the ancient site of Troy and sacrificing to Athena, imitated the Homeric warrior Achilles, who, together with Herakles, was Alexander's personal hero. Throughout the Asian expedition he kept a copy of the *Iliad* with him.

Moving south, he won, between 334 and 332 B.C., decisive victories at the river Granikos and at Issos, captured Miletos and Tyre after bitter sieges, and occupied Phoenicia, Palestine and Egypt. He added to his reputation and authority by his own fearless courage. He was wounded at Granikos and Issos, and during the capture of Gaza. At another point he nearly died from a severe fever.

Alexander paid great attention to religious matters and to heavenly signs. At Gordion there was an ancient waggon, the pole of which was fastened to the yoke by an extremely complicated knot, which had no ends visible. The story was that the person who undid this knot would be the Lord of Asia. Alexander loosed the knot, apparently by slashing through it with his sword, so desperate was he to have this prophecy in his favour.

After the battle of Issos in 333 B.C., Darius fled, leaving behind his mother, wife and two daughters, who were taken prisoner. As he sat down to supper after the battle, Alexander heard their crying; he sent a message assuring them of good treatment. This promise he kept, and indeed eventually married one of the daughters. However, when Darius asked for their return, offering friendship and alliance with Alexander, the latter replied in strong terms, as we read in the historian Arrian. This is the end of the dispatch:

'Come then to me as the Lord of all Asia. If you are afraid that, if you come, you will suffer something unpleasant at my hands, then send some of your friends to receive my guarantees. When you come, ask for and receive your mother and wife

18.4 Alexander in battle, on Boukephalas. Part of a mosaic from Pompeii.

and children and anything else you wish, for whatever you persuade me will be yours. And in future, when you communicate with me, communicate with me as King of Asia, and do not instruct me as though on equal terms, but speak to me as master of all your possessions, if you have need of anything. Otherwise I shall take measures concerning you as though you are a criminal. And if you dispute the throne, stand and fight for it, and do not run away, for I shall march after you wherever you may be.'

(Arrian, Anabasis II, 14)

The winter of 332–1 B.C. was spent in Egypt, where two events of particular importance occurred. On the coast by the mouth of the Nile Delta he established the city of Alexandria. Although he founded many cities of this name, this became *the* Alexandria, one of the finest cities of the ancient world. Inland, Alexander made a trip across the desert to the great oracle of Ammon, where he was greeted by the priest as 'Son of Ammon', the standard address for the Pharaoh of Egypt.

In 331 B.C., at Gaugamela, came Alexander's greatest victory where he brilliantly defeated and routed Darius, who fled to Ekbatana. Darius was in an increasingly desperate position and had before this battle made a further attempt to come to terms with Alexander, offering all the land west of the Euphrates, a huge ransom for his captured family, one daughter as bride for Alexander, and a son as hostage. When Alexander discussed these terms in his Council of War, the general Parmenio said that he would accept them, if he were Alexander. 'So should I,' said Alexander, 'if I were Parmenio.'

Alexander marched on through Babylon, Sousa and Persepolis to Ekbatana, amassing enormous wealth as he did so. At Persepolis, the royal city, he set on fire the palace of Xerxes in a symbolic act of revenge for that king's invasion of Greece so many years earlier. Darius by now only had troops from the eastern part of his empire, led by Bessos, satrap of Baktria. When Alexander pursued them from Ekbatana, Bessos and his confederates arrested and then murdered Darius. Alexander gave him a royal burial.

18.5 The ram's horn on this coin-portrait of Alexander identified him with the Egyptian god Ammon, whose symbol it was.

Reproduced by Courtesy of the Trustees of the British Museum.

190

Now, although Bessos claimed the title for himself, Alexander was the Great King. The next three years were spent in subduing the eastern part of the Persian empire, wild country with large areas of mountain and desert. When Bessos was captured, his ears and nose were cut off before his execution, not so much for his murder of Darius as for his audacity in setting himself up as Great King. There were dramatic attacks on mountain forts, involving the climbing of precipitous rocks by the use of iron pegs and ropes in ice and snow. By 327 B.C. opposition was crushed, and Alexander was ready for his next venture, the invasion of India. He also married Roxané, the daughter of a conquered chieftain.

Despite his spectacular successes, Alexander's relations with his Macedonian officers and troops during this period became increasingly uneasy. For one thing, many had had enough of perpetual fighting and marching for so long and so far from home. Also Alexander was behaving more and more like a Persian, wearing Persian dress, appointing many Persians to positions of high authority, and allowing Persians to prostrate themselves on the ground when they greeted him. Greeks only prostrated themselves before gods, so that when Alexander wanted them to do so before him there was trouble; some refused and some just laughed. The idea was dropped.

Behaviour of this kind on the part of Alexander led to ugly events. In 330 B.C. Philotas, commander of the Companions, who were the élite cavalry, failed to report a conspiracy and was put to death. Philotas' father was the great and loyal general Parmenio; Alexander had him murdered, too, as a precaution. Later Kleitos, another officer, who had on one occasion saved Alexander's life in battle, became drunk at a banquet and taunted Alexander with his behaviour until Alexander lost his temper, snatched a spear and killed Kleitos. He was immediately filled with bitter remorse, shutting himself away in his tent without food for three days.

18.6 Remains of the royal palace at Persepolis.

Into India

Part of India had formerly been in the Persian empire, and its conquest therefore seemed necessary to Alexander. He was probably also genuinely anxious to see and discover for himself the country of which he had heard such stories. His notion of its actual size and geography was very hazy and inaccurate. In 326 B.C. he pushed across the river Indus. The main resistance then came from the king Poros at the river Hydaspes. A tense battle raged in which Poros' two hundred fighting elephants caused the Macedonians severe problems. Arrian describes the meeting of Alexander and Poros after the battle:

'Alexander, as he halted his horse, admired the size of Poros, more than two metres tall, and his good looks and the way in which he did not seem humiliated in spirit, but came as a brave man would approach a brave man after a noble struggle with another king for his kingdom.

Then Alexander, speaking first, asked him to say what he wanted to happen to him. Poros is said to have replied, "Treat me as a king, Alexander." Alexander was pleased and said, "As far as I am concerned that will be done; for your part ask what you want." Poros said that everything was included in this one request.'

18.7 River gorge in Afghanistan: an area in which Alexander's army fought some of its toughest campaigns.

Alexander, even more delighted by this reply, gave him rule over his own Indians and he granted other territory besides, in addition to his former land and greater in size. So he had treated a fine man as king and from then on he found him loyal in every respect.'

(Arrian, *Anabasis* V, 19)

Near the site of the battle at the Hydaspes Alexander founded two cities. One of these he called Boukephala, after his horse who died here of old age and fatigue.

On they pushed, although it was the monsoon season, over two more rivers. At the third, however, the river Hyphasis, the troops, after marching vast distances from Greece, refused to go further. Although Alexander tried all his art of persuasion, they would not give in. He shut himself away in his tent, refusing to see anyone, still with no effect. Eventually he gave way, to the great relief of his men. Their hardship, even so, was far from finished.

First the army went down the Hydaspes and the Indus to the sea, encountering fierce resistance on the way. Alexander himself was again wounded, very nearly fatally. At the sea he divided his forces into three. The majority of his troops he sent by a direct route back to Persia. Another batch was sent by sea, under the command of Nearchos, to explore the sea route along the coast to the head of the Persian Gulf. He himself marched with the third force along the coast, with the object of supporting the fleet, supplying provisions and digging wells.

They set out towards the end of summer in 325 B.C. It was a terrible journey for the forces led by Alexander. They suffered in the desert from heat, hunger and thirst; at one time they lost their way; they were driven to eating baggage animals and to leaving stragglers to die; more death and destruction was caused by the sudden flooding at night of a stream by which they had camped. Alexander himself went on foot rather than horse, and also refused to take any special privileges in the distribution of drinking water. The loss of life was heavy, especially among the women and children accompanying the force. At last they got through after sixty days and rejoined Nearchos, who had also had an arduous journey. In the spring of 324 B.C. Alexander was back in Sousa.

It was not before time, for in his absence many of the satraps and generals whom he had left behind in positions of authority had got out of hand. They were now punished severely. At Sousa took place the 'Marriage of Sousa'—a great feast at which Alexander married married Darius' daughter, and many of his officers and ten thousand of his troops married Asian women. This was another example of his policy of attempting to unite the races which he ruled. Some five years previously he had also arranged for thirty thousand young Persian subjects to receive military training. These were now ready; Alexander was delighted with them, even calling them his

18.8 Alexander in an elephant headdress, symbolizing his eastern conquests. The coin's reverse shows the goddess Athena in battle.

Reproduced by Courtesy of the Trustees of the British Museum.

'Successors'. Once again there was discontent among his own Macedonians who felt that he was further favouring Persians and Persian ways at their expense. When he proposed to send home those of his Macedonians who were old or disabled, there was a revolt: those to be discharged felt insulted, while the others felt unfairly treated by not getting their discharge. The revolt was quelled by the force of the king's personality, and the execution of the ringleaders. Nevertheless, a considerable number of troops were discharged, with generous bonuses.

It was at this stage, too, that he demanded that the cities of the League of Corinth should honour him as a god, provoking the reply of a Spartan, 'If Alexander wants to be a god, let him be a god.'

Premature Death

Alexander's next project was a naval expedition to explore from the mouth of the river Euphrates round the coast of Arabia to extend yet further his realm. Preparations were well advanced, but destined to come to nothing, for in Babylon Alexander fell ill with a fever after another of his very heavy drinking sessions. After a few days, according to Arrian, his soldiers insisted on seeing him:

> 'Some wanted to see him so that they might see him while he was still alive; others because it had been announced that he was already dead, and it was suspected that the death was being concealed by the bodyguards, as I think. Yet the majority insisted on seeing Alexander from their grief and longing for the king. They say that he could not speak as the army filed past, but greeted each one by raising his head with difficulty and signing to them with his eyes.'

> (Arrian, *Anabasis* VII, 26)

A few days later, in June 323 B.C., he died at the age of thirty-two. The illness may have been malaria, although some said it was poisoning. At any rate, his resistance to disease was weakened, despite his youth, by the wounds and sicknesses he had suffered on his campaigns. In addition, the sheer physical effort of his life, and probably excessive drinking, had taken their toll. He was asked on his death-bed whom he wished to succeed him: his answer was 'the strongest'.

His brilliance as a soldier is undisputed. He was a master at maintaining his troops' morale and adapting his tactics to the many different circumstances which he encountered, and he carried out his campaigns at incredible speed. He also made an enormous contribution to existing scientific knowledge by his journeys. Judgement of him as a statesman cannot fairly be made, for his early death prevents us from knowing how he would have administered the empire which he had won. So far, he had generally continued existing systems, and there was still much confusion and poor government by those whom he had appointed. Once his dominating influence had gone, the empire immediately became divided, and his dream of uniting east and west never reached the degree of fulfilment for which he had hoped.

In one respect, however, the dream was spectacularly successful. The many cities which he founded, including sixteen Alexandrias, were organized on Greek lines and contained a number of Greek settlers. Thus Greek culture was spread over a very wide area, and the so-called Hellenistic civilization was created.

CHAPTER NINETEEN

After Alexander

So Alexander changed the world. What that changed world was like, how different its Greekness was from fifth-century B.C. culture, how it affected the Romans (to say nothing of the Indians and the Chinese)—all this is a whole new subject. Hellenistic history, which runs roughly from 300 to 31 B.C., when the battle of Actium made Octavian the first Roman emperor and the ruler of the world, is often regarded as a last, watered-down chapter of classical Greece. It is not. It is the story of how Greek ideas permeated the whole of the eastern Mediterranean and the Near East, thus defining its character for the next thousand years. All this chapter can do is to give some indication of what is most interesting in that process.

The Hellenistic Kingdoms

The enormous expansion that Alexander caused in the Greek world had three major effects. The first was change in the *polis*. Although Alexander's vast empire was divided after his death among his successors, their quarrels ended in the emergence of three large and powerful kingdoms (see fig 19.2): the Ptolemies in Egypt (Cleopatra was the last of the dynasty), the Seleukids in Syria and Persia, ruling over thirty million people in four million square miles, and the Antigonids in Greece. These kingdoms were Greek: the governing class, as well as the royal families, was Greek: and Greek was the official language. But they had established themselves in lands where powerful monarchs were normal, and they, too, became absolute rulers, governing through official bureaucracies. There was no room here for independent *poleis*. Cities, of course, continued, and, following Alexander's example, these kings founded many more. Some existing ones, too, were renamed in Greek fashion, Baalbek in Syria changing to Heliopolis, Arsuf to Apollonia. Some of these cities grew large and rich, like Alexandria, Seleukeia on the Tigris, Antioch in Syria. They all, great and small alike, maintained a vigorous life of their own: councils, assemblies, magistrates went on; festivals, education, art flourished; and theatres, temples, *gymnasia*, colonnades were built. But the scope was limited. An independent military or foreign policy was no longer possible. So the important officials were no longer the *strategoi*, but the *gymnasiarchos*, who was in charge of education and was often the senior magistrate, and the *agoranomos*, responsible for the economic side of city life. Still, these cities kept alive the idea of effective local government independent of distant kings, and thus were a not unimportant link in the development of urban life from Greek *polis* to Roman *municipium* (town).

19.1 Baalbek in the Lebanon: the temple of Bacchus. It was built in the first century A.D. and is bigger than the Parthenon.

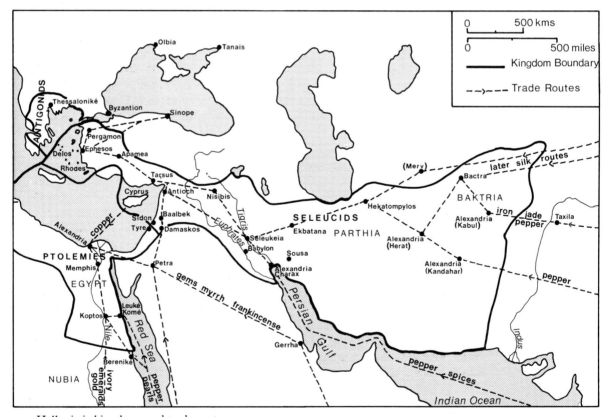

19.2 Hellenistic kingdoms and trade routes.

Trade

The second result of wider horizons was that trade grew. Men knew more about the world, and trade routes therefore expanded. Alexander had ruled from the Aegean to India and from southern Russia to Ethiopia; and travellers added to what the surveyors and scientists he had taken with him had discovered. Megasthenes, for example, went to India as Seleukos' ambassador to the court of Chandragupta at Patna on the Ganges. He sent back reports about that country, including elephant-hunting, the absence of slaves, and

'the wise men who go naked and who in winter live out in the open in the sun, but in summer, when the sun is fierce, under huge trees, which cast a shadow, Nearchos (Alexander's admiral) says, of 150 metres in circumference.'

(Arrian, *Indika* XI, 7)

There was Pytheas of Marseilles, too, who sailed from Cadiz, up to Brittany, across to Cornwall, all round Britain to Kent and then across to the Baltic. Another man, Eudoxos from Kyzikos on the Black Sea, while sailing 'south of Ethiopia', found the bow of a wrecked ship from Cadiz and so went to Cadiz and sailed south until his crew refused to go further. Perhaps he was trying to check Herodotus' story of the Phoenicians who set sail from the Red Sea and in three years (because they spent the winters ashore) returned to Egypt after doubling round the Pillars of Hercules (Gibraltar) and who claimed—but Herodotus doubted it—that 'as they sailed round Libya (that is, Africa), they had the sun on their right.' (IV, 42)

But the discovery that was most significant for Hellenistic trade was made by Hippalos, probably about 100 B.C. This was the south-west monsoon which enabled traders to sail from the southern end of the Red Sea straight across the Indian Ocean to near Bombay. It reduced the length of the journey greatly, because previously ships had been forced to hug the Arabian coast; for the compass was not invented until the twelfth century A.D. Thus trade with India—ivory, gold, sugar (but used only as a medicine), ebony, pearls, cotton, spices, especially pepper—increased. This was by sea; overland trade with India and China came through what is now Afghanistan and Iran to Seleukeia and thence to Antioch and so to the Mediterranean. From the far East came furs and high-grade iron, perhaps silk and jade, too.

As well as the essential corn and wood, all sorts of other trade was carried on. The wine of northern Syria and Chios was particularly admired and so exported all over the Mediterranean to discriminating, and wealthy, buyers. Frankincense from southern Arabia was in enormous demand for thousands upon thousands of altars. Alexandria supplied papyrus, linen and glass, Athens still exported the best olive-oil, Babylonian dates were in great demand, as were prunes from Damaskos. Silver came almost entirely from Spain, copper from Cyprus, tin from Cornwall and Brittany. And gold came from India and Ethiopia: Agatharchides, a writer of about 120 B.C., has a horrendous account of these Ethiopian gold-mines, worked by slaves and criminals, and even Greek prisoners of war, for the Ptolemies:

'The strongest prisoners, with lamps tied to their foreheads, quarry the quartz,

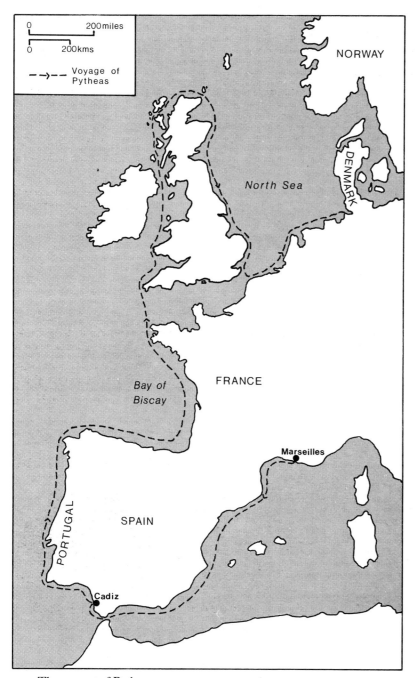

19.3 The voyage of Pytheas.

cutting tunnels as they follow the veins of gleaming rock. An overseer watches, cursing and flogging them as they work. Young boys laboriously collect the rock lump by lump as it is thrown out and carry it outside; there, older men smash it with iron hammers in stone pestles until it is in pieces the size of beans. Then almost naked women take these pieces and grind them in mills, pushing them round, three to a beam. To all those who undergo this savage slavery death is more welcome than life.'

(The Red Sea 25 and 26)

One other point about trade is important: people as well as goods moved about the world—or were moved (for slavery increased throughout the period). So populations became much more mixed. Alexandria was known for its riots between Jews and Greeks; and most cities had inhabitants of different races. The process was made easier by the rapid spread of an easy, colloquial Greek. *Koiné* or 'the common tongue', as it was called (see Appendix), was spoken everywhere—and so, in due course, the books of the New Testament were written in it. Thus the eastern Mediterranean world became increasingly cosmopolitan.

Individualism

The third effect of the opening up of a bigger world was a change in people's outlook. The small, tight-knit community of the fiercely independent *polis* had disappeared. In its place people found themselves in huge empires, whose populations were counted in hundreds of thousands. How could any one person matter in these vast numbers? So there developed an interest in individuals, their psychology, their variety, their importance, which can be seen in many spheres—in religion, in art, in philosophy, in literature, in social life.

Individualism in religion

The 'mystery religions' gained more and more adherents for the reasons mentioned

a   *b*   *c*

19.4 Hellenistic coins are noteworthy for realistic portraits. Here (a) a gold coin commemorates Ptolemy II and Arsinoé II of Egypt, in whose reign (276–246 B.C.) the Pharos, the Mouseion and the Library were built at Alexandria; (b) a silver 4-drachma piece issued about 200 B.C. honours the founder of the Attalid dynasty in Pergamon, Philetairos; (c) a silver 4-drachma coin of the Seleukid king Antiochos III (241–187 B.C.), who expanded his kingdom eastwards into Armenia and Parthia but was thrown out of Greece by the Romans.

in Chapter 7. People chose to join, and the blessings were given to them as individuals. One new cult especially, originating in Egypt, in honour of Serapis and his consort Isis, swept all over the eastern Mediterranean and reached as far as India. It promised its followers immortality and, in Isis, had the greatest deity of the Hellenistic world. Isis of the Myriad Names, Lady of All, Queen of the Inhabited World, Star of the Sea, Diadem of Life, All-seeing and All-powerful—her titles show her popularity, a popularity that was later taken over by Christianity: for many Isis statues were re-dedicated as images of the Madonna. The Olympian gods were in retreat, except for Dionysos. But his worship had always been something like a mystery religion: his female devotees, the Bacchantes, fiercely guarded the secrets of the cult, as Euripides' play *The Bacchae* makes horrifyingly clear when they tear to pieces a man who spies on their rites.

Other people believed in Fortune, which was elevated into a goddess. Menander, the playwright, has a character saying,

'All we decide, all we say, all we do
is Fortune; we simply add our signatures. . .
Fortune pilots the universe. She is the goddess
solely entitled to the names intelligence and forethought. . .'

And Pausanias the traveller (see p. 83) describes many sanctuaries to Fortune, which contained large statues of her. In the same sort of way, astrology and magic flourished: the stars could perhaps guide and help you, even if nothing else did.

Individualism in philosophy
Philosophy, too, was affected. The three most influential teachers were Diogenes,

19.5 A mid-fourth century B.C. head in bronze, perhaps of Aphrodite. It is more than life-size.

Reproduced by Courtesy of the Trustees of the British Museum.

Epicurus and Zeno. Diogenes and his followers, who were known as Cynics, were the original 'drop-outs': they protested against their society by living in total destitution, without homes, without possessions, defying all conventions. Diogenes himself lived in a huge clay pot (not 'a tub')—rather as his modern successors use concrete pipes. He inured himself to hardship by rolling on hot sand in summer and embracing snow-covered statues in winter, and dismissed mathematics, astronomy, music and all intellectual studies as a waste of time. Athletes were 'creatures of pork and beef', politicians 'the lackeys of the mob', and the theatre 'a peep-show for fools'. This was an extreme way of becoming independent, perhaps, but it caught people's attention.

'Live in secret', was Epicurus' advice to mankind. He himself in 306 B.C. bought a house with a large garden in Athens, and there lived simply and off vegetables with his friends of both sexes. Public life brings ambition, anxiety, fear with it; Epicurus therefore wanted none of it. 'Friendship,' on the other hand, 'dances round the world, calling us all to awaken to the joys of a happy life.' His philosophy had two great aims, freedom from pain and freedom from anxiety. The first, of course, cannot be total; but 'pain, if it is long, is light; if it is sharp, is short.' So the wise man, he said, will be happy even on the rack. Freedom from anxiety depends on knowledge: if you know how the universe works, you will not be afraid of unforeseen catastrophes. Epicurus took over the atomic theories of Demokritos. They explained the universe—and got rid of the gods. So you need not fear their interference with you in this life or punishment from them after death. Finally, he taught that the most important thing in life is pleasure. But excessive indulgence in pleasure (*too* much rich cake) can in the end bring more pain than pleasure; and so the wise man contents himself with little. Our word 'Epicurean'—a man who pursues pleasure at any price—is therefore unfair to Epicurus.

Epicureanism is escapist but attractive; and it continued to appeal for many centuries. Stoicism, however, was the philosophy that had the greatest effect on the Hellenistic and Roman worlds. Zeno, its founder, began to teach in Athens a little later than Epicurus, and his doctrines were still inspiring people, including the Roman emperor Marcus Aurelius, in the middle of the second century A.D. Stoics involved themselves in public life, and so it appealed to the Romans particularly. Conscience and duty were stressed. The wise man ignores his circumstances, bad or good. The soul is the only important thing, because it is 'a spark of the divine fire'. So the condition of the body is insignificant, and the wise man accepts whatever fate allots him—hence our word 'stoical'. This self-sufficiency is achieved by virtue, by leading a good and honourable life. It was an impressive philosophy; and it had another interesting feature. If all men have in them this divine spark, then all men to that degree are equal. Thus a later Roman Stoic said: 'They are slaves, you say. Yes, but they are men, they are people who live with us, they are humble friends.' The tone is patronising, of course, and class-conscious; but stoicism shows some of the few doubts in the classical world about the whole institution of slavery.

Individualism in social life

The stress on the individual led to all sorts of clubs, societies and associations. Fifth-century B.C. Athens had had political clubs. In Hellenistic times that was impossible, but the variety of other sorts of club was enormous: 'The Artists of Dionysos' (actors), 'Doctors trained at Kos', 'Veterans of Egyptian Garrisons', 'Old Boys of the *Gymnasion*'; and there were hundreds more. The members were often of mixed nationality, sometimes even slaves, and usually small in number (clubs with a hundred members were rare). There was a club shrine and a subscription. All this is familiar to us; but it was a marked change from *polis* life, where the *polis* itself was the first and greatest association.

Individualism in art
Sculpture in the same way showed individuals rather than ideal types. Its subjects were often complicated and exotic, and it had lost the strict classical perfection of fifth-century B.C. work. One good example of Hellenistic art is the range of coins minted by the Greek kings of Baktria and India. They, like all Hellenistic monarchs, put their own heads on coins, which is itself a significant change from Athenian tetradrachms (see fig 20.1). It is an impressive series of Greek coins, and yet comes from the very edge of the Hellenistic world.

Individualism in literature
It is difficult to say that literature became more personal, because most literature is inevitably personal, anyway. Nevertheless Aristophanes' comedies (see p. 138), for example, had a good deal to say about fifth-century B.C. history and society; whereas in 'New Comedy' (from 320 B.C. onwards) the political content disappeared, and the plots were concerned with people in complicated and amusing situations. Menander was its greatest exponent. His characters may be stock characters, but they are typical of ordinary men and women in all societies—hence his lasting popularity. A Greek critic wrote of him 'Menander! Life! I wonder which has copied which.' And a modern one 'Witty, elegant, more at home with men's mistresses than their wives, he set a mark on literature which lasted until Shakespeare and Molière.' Apollonios of Rhodes wrote an epic about 250 B.C. on the story of Jason and Medea, which is like the *Iliad* and *Odyssey* only in its length and metre; for it is romantic, psychological and learned. A lot of short poems, too, were written. One of the most exquisite, a love poem written by a girl, has been preserved in a surprising place. Part of it runs:

'Sustain me with raisins, refresh me with apples;
For I am sick with love.
O that his left hand were under my head,
And that his right hand embraced me!'

(*The Song of Solomon* 2, 5 and 6)

Much of this writing went on in Alexandria, which rapidly became the intellectual centre of the world. The university there with its library—perhaps 700 000 books by Roman times—attracted men of culture and learning—and the Ptolemies paid their salaries! It stimulated both arts and sciences and, by establishing a tradition of scholarship, enabled Greek learning to reach its peak. This was particularly true of mathematics and science, in which Alexandria saw the culmination of the earlier work discussed in Chapter 16.

Mathematics and Science

The great mathematicians were Euclid, whose thirteen books of geometry, written *c.* 300 B.C., were in use until this century; Apollonios, who in his book on Conics (200 B.C.) gave us the words 'parabola', 'hyperbola' and 'ellipse': and, greatest of them all, Archimedes, killed when the Romans captured Syracuse in 212 B.C.. On his tomb, which Cicero later boasted he had given back to Syracuse after finding it overgrown and neglected, there was engraved a cylinder circumscribing a sphere, and the figures 3:2. Did he regard the discovery of this ratio as his outstanding contribution to mathematics? He also invented hydrostatics, the science of solids in liquids (the story of his relevation in the bath is well known), and produced fundamental proofs in mechanics, especially for the principles of the lever and the pulley. In practical application of these, he invented the so-called Archimedes screw, and constructed enough clever devices to keep the Romans out of Syracuse for two years.

Other Alexandrians also invented machinery: Ktesibios is famous for his ingenious water-clocks and water-organ, while Heron, in the first century B.C., combined work in physics and mechanics with the construction of various toys worked by steam or compressed air, including a model 'steam-engine'. It seems strange that no real application was made of all these discoveries.

Astronomy, too, made great strides. Aristarchos (250 B.C.) not only made an attempt at estimating the relative masses of earth, moon and sun, but stated that 'the fixed stars and the sun remain unmoved, while the earth revolves about the sun in the circumference of a circle, the sun lying in the middle of the orbit.' This heliocentric (sun-in-the-middle) view was not only condemned as impious, but could not be proved without better instruments than the Greeks possessed. Its next discoverer was, of course, Copernicus in the sixteenth century. Eratosthenes (230 B.C.), another polymath in the Aristotle mould, is especially famous for his calculation of the earth's circumference (see fig 19.9); it was only eighty kilometres out. But his geographical work, too, was valuable; among other things, he realized you could sail westwards from Spain and reach India.

Despite Ptolemy II's zoo at Alexandria, whose exhibits included leopards, buffaloes, a giraffe, a polar bear, parrots and peacocks, zoology and botany made little progress. But medicine did. Herophilos identified the brain as the centre of the nervous system and traced the sensory nerves. His younger contemporary, Erasistratos, plotted the subdivisions of the heart and, more impressively, realized that the action of the heart caused the pulse. Thus he almost discovered the circulation of the blood; but that had to wait another two thousand years for Harvey.

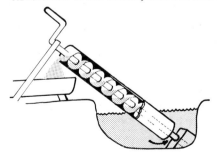

19.6 The Archimedes screw is a means of raising water from one level to another. It is still used extensively in underdeveloped countries.

19.7 Automatic doors: Heron's machinery for opening the temple doors depended on the expansion of heated air and careful counter-balancing. How did it work? (See p. 206.)

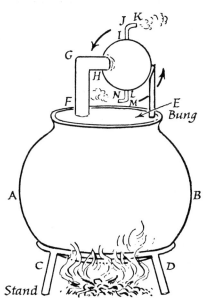

19.8 The first jet engine: in modern reconstructions, the ball revolves at 1500 r.p.m., but it has proved difficult to make the joint of the pipe H and the ball efficient. (See p. 206.)

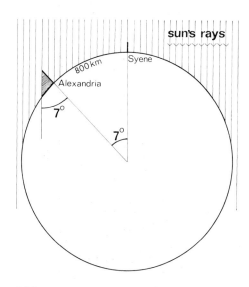

19.9 Diagram of earth's circumference. Eratosthenes knew that at Syené, to the south of Egypt, the sun cast no shadow at midday on midsummer's day, whereas at Alexandria it cast one of 7°. (The diagram is exaggerated.) He also knew that the distance between the two places was about 800 km. He therefore calculated that the earth's circumference was roughly 41 000 km. The true figure (over the poles) is 40 008 km.

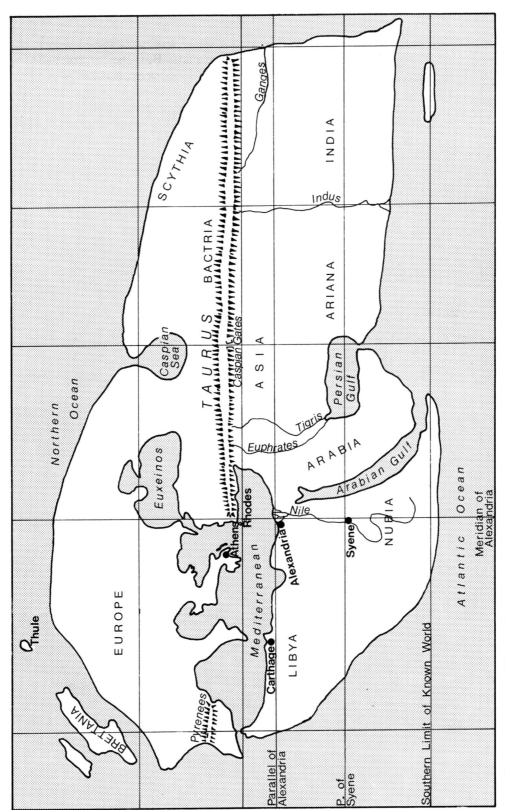

19.10 Eratosthenes map of the world.

Greece to Rome

So the cultural and intellectual life of the Hellenistic world was rich, varied and productive. This chapter has said nothing of the historians. But one of them, Polybios (140 B.C.), a Greek from Megalopolis in the Peloponnese, realized the enormous change coming over his world. He described the rise of Rome to being a world power; and, although his book ends with the Roman annexation of Greece in 146 B.C., he predicted that the world would be divided between Rome and Parthia. This more or less happened, with Rome, of course, controlling Europe, North Africa and the Near East. But it is important to realize that, although politically Rome was supreme, in most other respects she was herself in debt to Greece. In the famous words of Horace, the Roman poet of the end of the first century B.C., 'Greece, although overcome, overcame her uncivilized conqueror.' Rome, of course, made her own unique contribution to history—in law, in military efficiency, and in the skills of governing a huge empire with remarkable fairness. But the European tradition is rich precisely because it is both Greek and Roman.

Notes on the working of figs 19.7 and 19.8 (p. 204)

19.7 (i) a fire is lit on the altar; (ii) the air inside expands and travels down pipe FG; (iii) water from the full container H is forced through pipe L into container M; (iv) this causes it to drop and so turn the posts, on which the doors are mounted; (v) when the fire dies down, the air will cool and contract, and the process will be reversed.

19.8 (i) water in the container AB is heated by the fire below; (ii) the steam produced goes up the pipe FGH; (iii) it passes through the ball and out of the bent pipes IJK and LNM, thus making the ball spin.

19.11 An Ethiopian acrobat on the back of a tame crocodile; made of Parian marble, 75 cm high.

CHAPTER TWENTY

Epilogue

Thus by 100 B.C. the Mediterranean world was both Greek and Roman, and it continued so to the fall of the Roman Empire. Thereafter, too, for another thousand years the Byzantine empire carried on the tradition, and Greek remained the official language. One of the many things we owe to the Romans is the passing on of what they received from the Greeks. We should know very much less about the Greek achievement if the Romans had not preserved and copied their masterpieces. Some Romans, of course, disliked the Greeks: 'I cannot bear a Greek Rome,' the satirist Juvenal wrote about A.D. 100.

> 'Here they come from Sikyon, from Andros, from Samos—and they're going to run our great houses and soon be the masters, quick-witted, talkative dare-devils that they are. The Greek will do whatever you want: teacher, orator, mathematician, painter, trainer, prophet, acrobat, doctor, astrologer—he knows the lot. Tell him to fly, and the miserable Greek, if he's hungry, will take off for heaven.'
>
> (III, 60–78)

But many Romans admired them. Cicero, for example, according to Quintilian, the Roman writer on oratory, 'devoted himself heart and soul to the imitation of the Greeks and so reproduced the vigour of Demosthenes, the richness of Plato, and the charm of Isokrates.' Other Roman writers, too, paid them the same compliment: poets like Catullus, Vergil and Horace, dramatists like Plautus and Seneca, all began from Greek originals. And Roman houses were full of Greek statuary, both originals and direct copies.

The Greek influence on Europe through Rome is, however, well known. The lasting impact of Greek ideas can also be seen in a very different place. One of the eastern provinces of Alexander's empire, Baktria (northern Afghanistan), broke away from his successors. It became an independent Greek kingdom about 250 B.C., and by 180 B.C. had extended Greek rule over much of Pakistan and north-west India. Inscriptions written in Greek have been found in Afghanistan, and coins with Greek legends were issued not only by the Greek kings who ruled in the Punjab but by their barbarian successors up to A.D. 150. All this is surprising enough. But Greek influence persisted in the Indian sub-continent: the Zoroastrian temple, for example, at Taxila, not far from Islamabad, built about 100 B.C., is utterly uneastern; its traditional Greek plan and Ionic pillars would not have looked at all out of place in Attica (see fig 20.2). Gandharan sculpture, too, (A.D. 200–500), which established the tradition of Buddhist statuary and sent its products as far as Indo-China, is as much Greek as Indian (see fig 20.3).

Why have the Greeks had such an influence? There are probably many reasons; but three are important. First, they invented so many things: tragedy, lyric poetry, history, comedy, philosophy, mathematical theory, coinage, and perhaps organized sport. Secondly, they did all this to a degree of excellence that still compels admiration; and that excellence is seen, too, in their handling of what others had started before them, architecture, sculpture, painting. But the third reason is perhaps the most significant, their belief in freedom. Freedom is, of course, dangerous; but it seems to have been part of the Greek character to prefer risky adventure to playing safe. The achievements of Egypt and Babylon earlier had been impressive. But the rigid conformism of those societies had not led to the enormous diversity that the Greeks produced. Freedom marked Greek thought and action alike, freedom to experiment, to differ, to contradict. One of the more notable products of it was democracy. And it was the rediscovery at the Renaissance of this intellectual vigour and excellence which has so profoundly moulded western Europe.

Reproduced by Courtesy of the Trustees of the British Museum.

Reproduced by Courtesy of the Trustees of the British Museum.

20.1 Baktrian four-drachma coins: (a) of Antimachos (about 180 B.C.), the king wearing a *kausia*, a typical Macedonian cap, on the obverse, Poseidon on the reverse; (b) of Eukratides (about 160 B.C.), the king's head on the obverse, Castor and Pollux on the reverse; (c) of Menander (about 150 B.C.), who extended Greek rule into central India and perhaps became a Buddhist; (d) this coin of Menander has Greek on the obverse, Kharoshthi, an Indian dialect, on the reverse, showing the mixture of people in his kingdom.

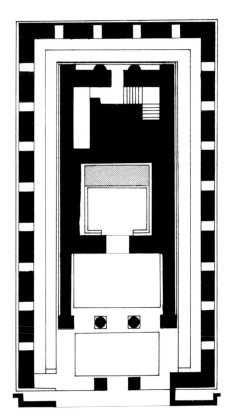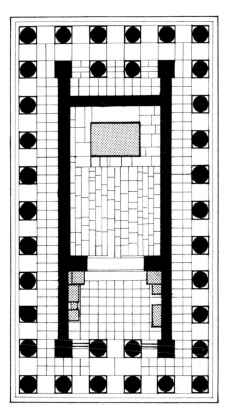

20.2 The Jandial temple (left) and the temple of Athena at Priené. Notice the similarity of these two plans.

20.3 Sculpture from Gandhara (north-west Pakistan): the Greek sea-god Triton in an Indian setting.

Appendix: The Greek Alphabet and Language

The Alphabet

The Greek alphabet, which is still in use, was taken over from the Phoenicians, the sea-faring people who inhabited what is now the coast of Syria. This probably happened at a date near 750 B.C. The alphabet was modified to suit the requirements of Greek. The names of letters are Phoenician words (aleph or alpha=ox-head, beth or beta=house, and so on), but have no meaning in Greek. One way in which the Greeks referred to the letters was as *Phoinikeia* or 'Phoenician things'.

Letter		Name	Pronunciation
A	α	alpha	a (either as in 'that', or as in 'father')
B	β	beta	b
Γ	γ	gamma	g
Δ	δ	delta	d
E	ε	epsilon	e (as in 'tent')
Z	ζ	zeta	zd
H	η	eta	e (as in '*ae*roplane')
Θ	θ	theta	th
I	ι	iota	i (either as in 'hit' or as in 'mach*ine*')
K	κ	kappa	k
Λ	λ	lambda	l
M	μ	mu	m
N	ν	nu	n
Ξ	ξ	xi	x or ks
O	ο	omicron	o (as in 'hot')
Π	π	pi	p
P	ρ,ῥ	rho	r (ῥ used when first letter of word)
Σ	σ,ς	sigma	s (ς only used for last letter of word)
T	τ	tau	t
Y	υ	upsilon	u (also=y)
Φ	φ	phi	ph
X	χ	chi	ch
Ψ	ψ	psi	ps
Ω	ω	omega	o (as in 'p*o*rter')

NOTES

a. There was no letter 'h'; this sound was indicated at the beginning of a word by ῾, e.g. ῾Ελλας =Hellas (Greece). Its opposite sign, ᾿ showed that no 'h' was to be sounded, e.g. ἀλφα=alpha, not halpha.

b. The letters, with additional symbols, were also used as numerals, e.g. $\beta' = 2$, $\iota' = 10$, $\iota\alpha' = 11$.

c. On a page of printed Greek, accents similar to those used in French will be seen. These were invented, as an aid to pronunciation for foreigners, by a scholar in about 200 B.C. and were not used before that.

The Language

Greek is one of the Indo-European family of languages, which includes Persian, German, Russian and Italian. Greek is especially similar in many ways to Latin, another of the same family.

During the period of time covered by most of this book, Greek was spoken in differing dialects in various regions. The most important were the Aiolic, Doric, Ionic and Attic dialects. The latter was spoken in Athens during the time of her greatness, and the plays of Aeschylus, Sophocles, Euripides and Aristophanes, the histories of Thucydides and Xenophon, and the philosophical works of Plato are written in it. Literature written in other dialects does survive, however.

Gradually the dialect differences disappeared, and from the third century B.C. a common dialect (Koiné) was used. This was the dialect in which the New Testament was written.

Modern Greek, especially in its written form, is descended directly from classical Greek. Despite some differences, it is essentially the same language. Thus it has been in use with its present alphabet for more than two and a half thousand years.

It is hoped that this book will have given the reader a clearer idea of the Greeks and their influence over other peoples. This influence comes as strongly as anywhere from the Greek language. It can be seen in the vast number of words in English which derive, either directly or indirectly, often by way of Latin, from classical Greek. This is particularly the case, for instance, in the sciences, mathematics and the arts. Often when a new word has been needed to describe some new discovery or invention, it has been made up from Greek words, as will be seen in the case of some of the words below.

The following lists contain examples of Greek words which have passed into English, and also some words which have been invented for English from Greek, written here as Greek words. With the aid of the alphabet set out on page 210 it should not be difficult, even without any other knowledge of Greek, to work out their English equivalents. A good dictionary will give further explanations and examples. Some words in the list of numbers will also be recognized as similar to Latin numerals, and as forming parts of English words.

Note : a   There is no 'c' or 'y' in Greek, but the letters kappa ($\varkappa$) and upsilon (υ) have often become 'c' or 'y' respectively in English derivations.

  b.   In some cases the typical endings of Greek nouns will be seen to be slightly different from the final letters of their English counterparts.

The School Timetable
βιολογια
γεωγραφια
μαθηματικη
φυσικη
μουσικη
ἱστορια

People
Πηνελοπη
Περικλης
Σοφοκλης
Σωκρατης
Ὁμηρος
Ἡροδοτος
Φιλιππος
Χριστος
Ἑλενη
Ὀδυσσευς

Places
Ἑλλας
Κρητη
Μακεδονια
Μαραθων
Σαλαμις
Ἀθηναι
Κορινθος
Μυκηναι

A Horse
Βουκεφαλας

Nature
ὀκταπους
ἱπποποταμος
κροκοδειλος
ναρκισσος
ῥοδοδενδρον
ὑακινθος
κροκος
ἀνεμωνη

Science
(including medical terms)
ἀτομα
ἠλεκτρον
συνθεσις
φωτογραφια
πρωτον
πρωτοτυπος
μικροφωνη
τηλεγραμμα
κωμα
παραλυσις
πνευμονια
ἀναιμια
ὀφθαλμια
διαβητης
διαγνωσις
ἀναισθησια
σκελετος
συμβιωσις
μηχανικος
τεχνικος
ἀσβεστος
ἑλικοπτερον
ἀστροναυτης
τηλεφωνη

Mathematics
παραλληλος
θεωρημα
ἑξαγων
ἰσοσκελης
παραβολη
γεωμετρια
τριγωνομετρια
διαγραμμα
ἀριθμητικη
συμμετρια
ὑποτεινουσα

Politics
δημοκρατια
μοναρχια
ὀλιγαρχια
ἀναρχια
ἀριστοκρατια
πολιτικη

The Arts
δραμα
ὀρχηστρα
σκηνη
προγραμμα
θεατρον
τραγωδια
κωμωδια
χορος
κινημα
Ὠδειον
χαρακτηρ
συμφωνια
βιογραφια
ποιημα
ἁρμονια
κριτικος
μουσειον
φιλοσοφια

Miscellaneous
καταστροφη
ἀθλητης
συμπαθεια
πανοραμα
ἀπολογια
ὑποκριτης
ἀτλας
βασις
κρισις
ἰδεα
ὑγιεινη
ἀγωνια
βουτυρον
ἀκαδημια

Numbers
1 εἱς
2 δυο
3 τρεις
4 τετταρες
5 πεντε
6 ἑξ
7 ἑπτα
8 ὀκτω
9 ἐννεα
10 δεκα

As a further exercise, take some of the many Greek words and names, which are printed in italics in the chapters of this book, and re-write them in the Greek alphabet (e.g. *polis*= πολις).

Further Work

Teachers may find among the following questions suitable ideas for further work by their pupils, either individually or in groups. The questions vary greatly in their nature and difficulty: in many cases it is hoped to encourage private research in libraries, museums, or elsewhere.

Chapter 1 *People and Land*
1. Using information from weather reports in a daily newspaper, compare the daily temperatures in Athens with those given for the city nearest to which you live.
2. Find out, by comparing an atlas of the modern world with the map on page 41, how many modern countries contained Greek settlements in classical times.
3. What influence can geographical factors (e.g. mountains, plains, sea, climate) be said to have had on the Greeks?
4. Take an example of a country very different from Greece (e.g. Britain), and try to assess the importance of geographical factors in the development of its people and way of life.
5. Study closely the map and illustrations in this chapter and see how much information could be extracted *from these alone* about the nature of Greece.
6. Find and copy a map of modern Greece, marking in the main roads and railway lines, and the Corinth Canal. How much easier does it seem to be to get from one place to another in Greece nowadays?

Chapter 2 Part 1 *The Minoans*
1. What links can you see between legends concerning King Minos and the discoveries of archaeologists?
2. What, on the evidence available to you, do you find most impressive about the Minoans, bearing in mind the early date of their civilization?
3. How much more information could we expect to have about the Minoans if any Minoan literature had survived?
4. Design your own fresco in the Minoan style, or make a copy of an actual one from an illustration.
5. Imagine that you are a foreign visitor who has just arrived at Knossos during its finest period. Describe your impressions of it in a letter home to your family.

Chapter 2 Part 2 *The Mycenaeans*
1. What seem to have been the main similarities and differences between the Mycenaeans and the Minoans?
2. What is meant by Linear B? How important to our knowledge of the Minoans and the Mycenaeans has been its decipherment?
3. How important a part do palaces seem to have played in the Mycenaean world?
4. Find out, by using your school and public library, as much as you can about the life and achievements of Heinrich Schliemann.
5. What evidence can you find, from illustrations here and elsewhere, that the Minoans and the Mycenaeans were outstanding artists and craftsmen?

Chapter 3 *Homer*

1. Consider why the poems of Homer have retained their appeal for nearly three thousand years.
2. Are the poems of Homer of any value as historical evidence?
3. The *Iliad* and the *Odyssey* can be described as 'oral', 'epic' or 'heroic' poetry. What is meant by these terms?
4. Do you think that the *Iliad* and the *Odyssey* would make good films or television series?
5. If you were writing a story about a present-day counterpart of Odysseus, what sort of a man would you make him, and what sort of adventures would he have?
6. How are the *Iliad* and *Odyssey* different from each other in the sort of stories which they deal with?

Chapter 4 *City States*

1. Do you think the Greeks were right in regarding the *polis* as the best form of state? Draw up a balance-sheet of the advantages and disadvantages of these small communities.
2. Draw two Greek vases, a Geometric one and a fifth-century red-figure one (see Chapter 11 and other illustrations for this kind). Is the later vase more beautiful than the earlier? Or merely different?
3. There were three main periods when Greeks settled far outside Greece. Using Chapters 3 and 18 as well, discover when these were, where the Greeks went each time, and why.
4. Why did the Greeks have 'tyrants'? How do you think the word came to have its English meaning?
5. Draw a hoplite, based on figure 4.4 and others in the book, and list his armour and weapons.
6. Discover—or remind yourself of—Pythagoras' theorem of the square on the hypotenuse. Write it out and add a diagram.
7. Which of the three men, Solon, Peisistratos, Kleisthenes, in your opinion did most for the ordinary citizen in Athens?

Chapter 5 *Sparta*

1. Explain in your own words the terms 'Spartiates', 'helots' and '*perioikoi*', and the relationship between these groups.
2. Why did Sparta develop as she did? The historian Herodotus (I, 65), in describing Sparta, uses the Greek word *eunomia*—'good order'. Is this an appropriate description?
3. Would you have liked to be brought up in Sparta? Give reasons for your answer.
4. Try to think of parallels with the Spartan system, or aspects of it, from elsewhere in history.
5. Do you feel that there are dangers or weaknesses built into a state organized like Sparta?

Chapter 6   *Wars against Persia*

1. Who were the Ionians? (See also Chapter 3.) How did there come to be an 'Ionian revolt' against Persia?
2. Who were (a) Herodotus (b) Darius (c) Themistokles (d) Pausanias? Try to find out more about them from library books.
3. How great an achievement do you think it was for the Greeks to defeat the Persians?
4. Does it seem to you that Athens or Sparta did more to defeat Persia?
5. Had the Persians won, would it have made a great deal of difference to the course of European history?
6. Do you think that the Persians could justifiably blame bad luck and poor leadership for their defeat?
7. Choose one of the main battles between the Greeks and the Persians, and use reference books (e.g. an encyclopaedia) to discover more about the details of the battle, and make your own diagram.

Chapter 7   *Religion*

1. You are present at the annual festival of your 'deme'. Describe the events at it and your feelings about them.
2. Try to find out why the calendar in most countries is linked with religion.
3. Are there any advantages in not having weeks?
4. List the Olympian gods in their order of importance to you.
5. Write down the main differences between Christianity and Greek religion. Was religion to the Greeks a public or a private affair? Were they religious in our sense of the word?
6. Do you believe in omens? If you do, explain why. If you do not, explain why black cats and walking under ladders have come to be regarded as ominous.
7. What sort of questions would you yourself ask the Pythian priestess?
8. Find out why the Greeks called Delphi 'the navel of the earth'.

Chapter 8   *The Games*

1. List the main differences between the Greek Olympic Games and the modern ones. Why are some of the Greek events no longer seen? Ought there to be a limit to the number of events in the Olympic programme?
2. Do you agree with silver and bronze medals? (See page 87.)
3. Why do you think the Olympic games were regarded as the greatest?
4. Draw a Greek athlete, using illustrations in this chapter.
5. Is professionalism in sport a bad thing?

Chapter 9   *Imperial Athens*

1. Do you agree that the achievements of the Greeks between 480 and 430 B.C. were 'unparalleled' (page 93)?
2. Compare the Athenian empire of the fifth century B.C. with the British empire of the nineteenth century A.D. Think about how they came into being, their size, the peoples involved, and the organization.
3. How did Athens impose her will on the members of her empire?

4. Find out more about the Peloponnesian War and make a date-chart of the main events in it.
5. Can you think of foreign campaigns in later history that had a disastrous effect on the side conducting them?

Chapter 10   *Democracy and Law*
1. List what you consider to be the most important differences between Athenian and British democracy.
2. Imagine you are at that meeting of the *ekklesia* mentioned on page 106. If possible, look at Thucydides' report of the debate (VI, 8 onwards). Describe your feelings as you listen to the views expressed by the main speakers and when the result of the vote is announced.
3. Do you think it is a good idea for all the citizens of a country to be able to decide on every major issue? Is a 'referendum' the modern equivalent?
4. Is there anything to be said for electing people by lot rather than by vote?
5. Do you think it is right that some people should be given state help? Find out what sort of people receive public assistance in modern Britain.
6. Summarize the main features of the Athenian legal system. How fair was it?
7. Should everybody be allowed to vote (see page 115). If not, how do you decide who should and who should not? In some countries today, people are compelled to vote. Is that a good idea?
8. How many countries do you know of which are not democratic?

Chapter 11   *Architecture, Sculpture and Pottery*
1. Do you think, from the photographs in this book and elsewhere, that the Parthenon and its sculptures deserve their great reputation?
2. *Either* make a drawing or painting of the Acropolis with Pericles' building programme in progress *or*, as a foreign correspondent in Athens at the time, write a newspaper report describing it.
3. Was the Parthenon like a cathedral either in appearance or the way in which it was used?
4. Look carefully at buildings in your neighbourhood to find as many examples as you can of architectural features which show the influence of classical Greek architecture (e.g. columns, pediments and carvings).
5. Make as accurate a model as you can of a Greek temple.
6. How much historical evidence is provided by Greek art, especially pottery? What sort of information does it give which is unlikely to be found elsewhere, e.g. in literature?
7. Do you think that the use of paint and other decorations on Greek sculpture and architecture must have spoilt their effect?
8. Is sculpture as important a branch of art to us as it was to the Greeks (and Romans)? If not, why do you think this is so?
9. Would broken pieces of our pottery be able to tell men of the future as much about us as those of the Greeks have told us about them?
10. If a modern statesman wanted to undertake a building programme, what sort of buildings would he be likely to choose? How would he find the money for it?

Chapter 12 *The Theatre*

1. Write a description of an imaginary day spent at the Great Dionysia, as though writing to someone of the time who has never been to the theatre.
2. From what you have read, what seem to you to be the main differences between the Greek and the modern theatre?
3. Make your own plan (or model) of a Greek theatre, marking in as many features as you can.
4. How restricted do you feel that the Greek playwright was by the theatres of the time and the accepted ways in which the plays were presented?
5. Give, with an explanation, the answer to the riddle set to the Thebans by the Sphinx (page 134).
6. What do you think were the advantages and disadvantages of the fact that Greek plays were part of religious festivals, officially organized by the city?
7. On the basis of what you have read, try to suggest a theme which a modern writer might choose if trying to compose a tragedy in the Greek style, but relevant to the present-day.
8. What sort of people, fashions and ideas in our own society do you think that Aristophanes might make fun of? Outline a possible plot of such a play, with suggestions for characters and a suitable chorus.
9. If a modern actor were transported in time to the fifth century B.C., what difficulties would he find in acting in a Greek play and in a Greek theatre?

Note for teachers: many translations of Greek plays are available, e.g. in the *Penguin Classics* series, which could be used for private or class reading, or for acting.

Chapter 13 *Every Day*

1. Copy the plan of the house in figure 13.1. Find and draw the plan of a Roman town-house (many have been excavated at Pompeii). Are there any significant differences?
2. Using the illustrations in this book (and others, if you wish), draw a typical Greek room.
3. Why was Greek jewellery more elaborate than their fashions in clothes?
4. If you were transported back to Greece in the fifth century B.C., what parts of your normal diet would you miss most?
5. Try to find out why classical wine was sweet rather than dry.
6. Make a list of what women and girls can do nowadays which they could not do in classical Greece. Do you think the Greeks were unfair to women? If so, why do you think this was so?
7. List the good and bad points of the grid-pattern for cities.
8. Are department stores the modern equivalents of the *agora*?
9. What means of rest and recreation were available to the Greeks outside their own houses?

Chapter 14   *Work and Trade*
1. Do you agree with the Spartan attitude described in the Plutarch story on page 151?
2. List the jobs mentioned in this chapter and elsewhere in the book. Do they all have modern equivalents? If not, why not?
3. What are the advantages of big industry over the small workshops of the Greeks? Are there drawbacks, too?
4. Find out about the conditions of serfs in mediaeval Europe and of slaves in the southern states of America in the eighteenth century. What differences were there between those slaves and Greek ones? Why do we now consider it wrong to have slaves? Has slavery in fact been abolished?
5. Write the diary of an educated prisoner of war forced to work in the slave-mines.
6. Why did the Greeks not develop paper money?
7. Draw the plans for a trireme. Can you think of any improvements, using only materials known to the Greeks?

Chapter 15   *Education*
1. Do you find it surprising that schoolmasters had a low status in Athens?
2. Do you agree with the Athenian view that musical and physical education were of extreme importance and improved the character?
3. Who were the sophists? What rôle did they play in Athenian education?
4. What were the real reasons leading to the trial of Socrates? Could the same thing happen nowadays? Would Socrates be popular in our society?
5. How might the Spartans (see Chapter 5) have criticized the educational system in Athens?
6. Were the Athenians (and later the Romans) right to consider the art of public speaking an important part of education? Should we do the same?

Chapter 16   *Science, Mathematics, Philosophy*
1. Why did the Greeks make more progress in mathematics than in physics or biology? Does this have anything to do with the nature of the subjects?
2. Find out how atomic theories have developed in modern science.
3. Say what you think Socrates meant by 'virtue is knowledge' (page 171). Was he right? You might compare St Paul's view in the Epistle to the Romans, Chapter 8.
4. Do you agree with Socrates that examining one's life is important? Do you think he would have approved of psychiatrists?
5. Do rulers need to be educated people? If so, what should they be educated in?
6. Look at the same numbers in Greek, Roman and Arabic (modern) notation (see note (b) on page 211 and fig 16.3). What are the advantages of our system?
7. Find out what sort of things are dealt with in a university course in philosophy.

Chapter 17   *A Changed Greece*
1. Why did the *polis* system decline in Greece during the fourth century B.C.?
2. What was the phalanx? What military advantages did it have?

3. Explain how Demosthenes came to be such a dedicated opponent of Philip of Macedonia. Did he have good reasons?

4. Do you think it was inevitable that Athens in the fourth century B.C. would not be able to keep up her achievements of the fifth century?

5. What was the *Anabasis*? Work out from a modern atlas the approximate distance which the ten thousand Greeks covered between setting out from Sardis and reaching the Black Sea.

Chapter 18 *Alexander*

1. Did Alexander deserve the title of 'the Great'?

2. Using the map on page 186 and an atlas, work out which modern countries were wholly or partly within the area of Alexander's empire. About how far did he travel in his marches through Asia (and Egypt)?

3. Is the story of Alexander material for a successful film? As a film director, how would you treat it?

4. Can you find other soldiers in history who have matched, or come near to matching, Alexander's achievements in a similar length of time?

5. Do you think that Alexander would have been able, if he had lived longer, to keep his empire intact?

6. Why do you think that Alexander founded so many cities, planned on Greek lines, in the lands which he conquered?

7. Why did Alexander so much catch the imagination of men both in his own time and later?

Chapter 19 *After Alexander*

1. What is the derivation of the word 'Hellenistic'?

2. The Indian king Ashoka about 250 B.C. set up inscriptions written in both Kharoshthi (an Indian dialect) and Greek. Find out from an encyclopaedia why he did this and why he was described by Kipling as 'a lone star outshining all the myriads of other monarchs'.

3. Two religious words in English derived from Greek are 'liturgy' and 'ecclesiastical'. Can you discover any more and explain their derivations?

4. List the most important differences between the Greek world of the fifth century B.C. and the Hellenistic one of two hundred years later.

5. Which of the two philosophies, Epicureanism or Stoicism, appeals to you more? Why?

6. Look up other poems in the Song of Solomon (the whole book is of Hellenistic date). How do they compare with other love poetry you know? (Many pop lyrics are a sort of love poetry.)

7. Make a model of Heron's steam-toy. Would it have been difficult to make it into an engine?

8. The Pharos at Alexandria was one of the seven wonders of the classical world. What was it and when was it built? Make a drawing of it. Find out the other six, and draw a map with them all shown on it.

Date Chart

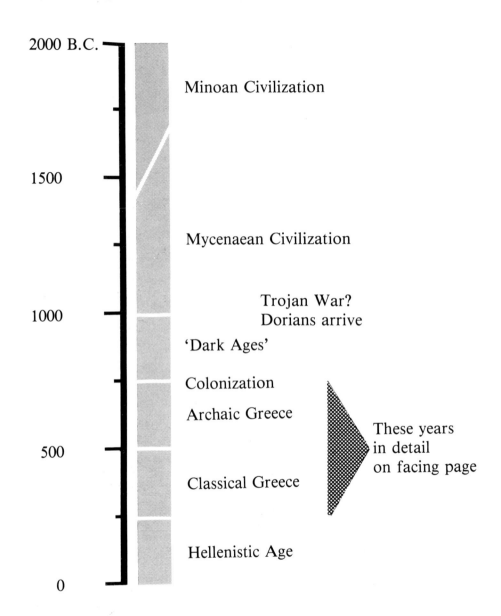

2000 B.C.

Minoan Civilization

1500

Mycenaean Civilization

Trojan War?
Dorians arrive

1000

'Dark Ages'

Colonization

Archaic Greece

These years
in detail
on facing page

500

Classical Greece

Hellenistic Age

0

The Greek World   Elsewhere

	Events	People	Writers	Elsewhere
			Homer?	Rome founded?
700			Hesiod	End of Israel
	Byzantium founded	Lykourgos?		
	Coins start			
600	Marseilles founded	Solon	Sappho Thales	Nebuchadnezzar (Babylon) Captivity of the Jews
		Peisistratos	Xenophanes	Persia conquers Medes and Croesus Buddha Confucius
		Kleisthenes	Herakleitos	Expulsion of Tarquin from Rome
500	Persian Wars		Pindar Aeschylus Sophocles Herodotus	
	Parthenon built	Pericles	Anaxagoras Thucydides	
	Peloponnesian War	Socrates	Aristophanes	
400			Plato	Gauls capture Rome
	King's Peace			
	Theban supremacy		Aristotle Demosthenes	
	Alexandria founded	Philip Alexander		
		Pytheas		Chinese discover tea
300			Euclid Epicurus Zeno Menander Eratosthenes	Rome controls Italy Asoka rules India First Punic War

Further Reading

Two sorts of books are not listed here: (a) those which give a good but elementary introduction to the Greeks; (b) the many good translations of Greek authors there are in the *Penguin Classics* series and elsewhere. There remain:

1. MORE DETAILED GENERAL BOOKS
   A. Andrewes, *Greek Society*. Penguin
   P. D. Arnott, *An Introduction to the Greek World*. Macmillan
   C. M. Bowra, *Periclean Athens*. Weidenfeld and Nicolson
   A. R. Burn, *Pelican History of Greece*. Penguin
   M. I. Finley, *The Ancient Greeks*. Penguin
   Sir Paul Harvey (ed.), *Oxford Companion to Classical Literature*. Oxford University Press
   H. D. F. Kitto, *The Greeks*. Penguin
   ★C. and S. McEvedy, *Atlas of World History, Vol. I*. Hart-Davis
   P. McKendrick, *The Greek Stones Speak*. Methuen
   B. K. Workman, *They Saw it Happen: in Classical Times*. Blackwell

2. BOOKS ON SPECIFIC TOPICS
   Crete:
   ★L. Cottrell, *The Bull of Minos*. Evans/Pan
   R. Higgins, *The Archaeology of Minoan Crete*. Bodley Head
   R. Higgins, *Minoan and Mycenaean Art*. Thames and Hudson
   Mycenae:
   J. Chadwick, *The Decipherment of Linear B*. Cambridge University Press
   J. V. Luce, *The End of Atlantis*. Paladin
   Lord William Taylour, *The Mycenaeans*. Thames and Hudson
   Homer:
   C. M. Bowra, *Homer*. Duckworth
   M. I. Finley, *The World of Odysseus*. Penguin
   ★M. Thorpe, *Homer*. Macmillan
   Sparta:
   ★R. Barrow, *Sparta*. Macmillan
   W. G. Forrest, *A History of Sparta 950–192 B.C.* Hutchinson
   Persian Wars:
   A. R. Burn, *Persia and the Greeks*. E. J. Arnold
   Religion:
   ★J. Pinsent, *Myths and Legends of Ancient Greece*. Hamlyn
   R. Graves, *The Greek Myths (2 volumes)*. Penguin
   C. Kerényi, *The Gods of the Greeks*. Penguin
   H. W. Parke, *Greek Oracles*. Hutchinson
   ★Rex Warner, *Men and Gods*. Heinemann
   Games:
   M. I. Finley and H. W. Pleket, *The Olympic Games*. Chatto and Windus
   H. A. Harris, *Sport in Greece and Rome*. Thames and Hudson

Democracy:

*R. Barrow, *Athenian Democracy*. Macmillan

A. R. Burn, *Pericles and Athens*. English Universities Press

Art and Archaeology:

J. Barron, *Greek Sculpture*. Studio Vista

J. Boardman, *Greek Art*. Thames and Hudson

R. V. Shoder, *Ancient Greece from the Air*. Thames and Hudson

Theatre:

P. D. Arnott, *An Introduction to the Greek Theatre*. Macmillan

*H. C. Baldry, *The Greek Tragic Theatre*. Chatto and Windus

C. M. Bowra, *The Greek Experience* (literature generally). Penguin

A. Lesky, *Greek Tragedy*. Benn

Daily Life:

R. Flacelière, *Daily Life in Greece*. Weidenfeld and Nicolson

T. B. L. Webster, *Life in Classical Athens*. Batsford

Trade and Slaves:

L. Casson, *The Ancient Mariners*. Gollancz

*C. Mossé, *The Ancient World at Work*. Chatto and Windus

Education:

*R. Barrow, *Greek and Roman Education*. Macmillan

E. B. Castle, *Ancient Education and Today*. Penguin

Science and Philosophy:

F. M. Cornford, *Before and After Socrates*. Cambridge University Press

B. Farrington, *Greek Science*. Penguin

Alexander:

A. R. Burn, *Alexander the Great*. Penguin

R. Lane Fox, *Alexander the Great*. Allen Lane

Hellenistic Times:

M. Cary, *The Greek World 323–146*. Methuen

J. Ferguson, *The Heritage of Hellenism*. Thames and Hudson

*The asterisked books are relatively easy and short.

3. NOVELS

H. Baumann, *Alexander's Great March*. Oxford University Press

P. Green, *Achilles His Armour*. Murray

P. Green, *The Laughter of Aphrodite*. Murray

N. Mitchison, *Cloud Cuckoo Land*. Cape

N. Mitchison, *Corn King and Spring Queen*. Cape

S. Plowman, *The Road to Sardis*. Bodley Head

M. Renault, *The Bull from the Sea*. Longmans/Four Square

M. Renault, *The King Must Die*. Longmans/Four Square

M. Renault, *The Last of the Wine*. Longmans/Four Square

M. Renault, *The Lion in the Gateway*. Longmans/Four Square

M. Renault, *The Mask of Apollo*. Longmans/Four Square

G. Trease, *The Crown of Violet*. Macmillan

H. Treece, *Electra*. Bodley Head

R. Warner, *Pericles the Athenian*. Collins

Index

This index makes no pretence of being exhaustive. Nor does it include references which clearly belong to particular chapters: information on sacrifices, for example, will be found in the chapter on Religion, and on the Athenian *boulē* in the chapter on Democracy and Law.